Pursuing Moral Warfare

Also from Georgetown University Press

Ethics Beyond War's End
Eric Patterson, Editor

The Ethics of War and Peace Revisited: Moral Challenges in an Era of Contested and Fragmented Sovereignty
Daniel R. Brunstetter and Jean-Vincent Holeindre, Editors

Just War: Authority, Tradition, and Practice
Anthony F. Lang Jr., Cian O'Driscoll, and John Williams, Editors

War's Ends: Human Rights, International Order, and the Ethics of Peace
James G. Murphy

PURSUING MORAL WARFARE

Ethics in American, British, and Israeli Counterinsurgency

MARCUS SCHULZKE

Georgetown University Press / Washington, DC

Library of Congress Cataloging-in-Publication Data
Names: Schulzke, Marcus, author.
Title: Pursuing moral warfare : ethics in American, British, and Israeli counterinsurgency / Marcus Schulzke.
Description: Washington, DC : Georgetown University Press, 2019. | Includes bibliographical references and index.
Identifiers: LCCN 2018019379 (print) | LCCN 2018029495 (ebook) | ISBN 9781626166592 (ebook) | ISBN 9781626166585 (pbk. : alk. paper) | ISBN 9781626166578 (hardcover : alk. paper)
Subjects: LCSH: Military ethics. | Counterinsurgency—Moral and ethical aspects. | War—Moral and ethical aspects.
Classification: LCC U22 (ebook) | LCC U22 .S385 2019 (print) | DDC 172/.42—dc23
LC record available at https://lccn.loc.gov/2018019379

♾ This book is printed on acid-free paper meeting the requirements of the American National Standard for Permanence in Paper for Printed Library Materials.

20 19 9 8 7 6 5 4 3 2 First printing

Printed in the United States of America.
Cover design by Jeremy John Parker.

To PB.

Contents

Acknowledgments

I am indebted to my wife and collaborator, Amanda Cortney Carroll. She offered feedback on many drafts of the book and, more importantly, kept me motivated to write it. I could not have done it without her. I am thankful for the love and support I received from Amanda, Ember, and Panda. My parents, Rein and Pam Schulzke, helped more than I can explain, most of all by facilitating my education in every way they could. Victor Asal, David Rousseau, Rey Koslowski, and Bryan Early helped me through many administrative barriers, provided invaluable feedback on drafts, and helped me find a publisher. The American Philosophical Society generously funded the interviews with British military personnel through a Franklin Research Grant. I am indebted to Henrik Syse and Martin Cook for helping me secure that grant and offering assistance along the way. I would like to thank the editorial team at Georgetown University Press, especially Donald Jacobs and the two anonymous reviewers who provided exceptionally constructive feedback. Finally, I am grateful for the many American, British, and Israeli military personnel who shared their experiences with me. Those soldiers and marines were extremely generous with their time and their willingness to revisit painful events.

Introduction

Soldiers are symbols of how states and their armed forces behave; they represent their countries in contested areas and are entrusted with the profound responsibility of enacting foreign policy on the ground. A soldier patrolling the streets of Baghdad, Basra, or Gaza City holds the power of life and death over others. A single misdirected bullet could kill a child, compromise efforts to build trust with the local citizens, and escalate cycles of violence. A lost opportunity to shoot first could result in an ambush or a suicide attack. Conversely, providing financial assistance to a struggling family or protecting a village threatened by insurgents may advance efforts to rehabilitate areas ravaged by war and deprive enemy fighters of vital resources. During conflicts, soldiers make critical decisions dozens of times a day—ranging from immediate dilemmas about whether to shoot a suspected insurgent to deeper quandaries about whether they should even participate in the war effort. Ethical decisions are especially important in counterinsurgency contexts because they directly advance or undermine the broader strategic and political objectives of gaining legitimacy within the contested area and building effective governing institutions.

The prominence enlisted soldiers and junior officers take on at critical junctures led US Marine Corps General Charles Krulak to proclaim that "we live in the era of the 'strategic corporal'" and to call for a new strategic framework acknowledging individual soldiers' importance in the complex landscape of post–Cold War operations.[1] It has caused armed forces to place greater emphasis on promoting ethical compliance throughout the ranks in an attempt to harness the strategic corporal phenomenon as an asset, rather than a liability.[2] My goal in this book is to investigate how armed forces have pursued this goal and how renewed attention to military ethics actually shapes soldiers' conduct. I focus on counterinsurgency operations because these have been central to building the narrative of the strategic corporal and prompting armed forces to devote more attention to ethics training. As I will show, it is often experience with decentralized and politically sensitive counterinsurgency missions that compels state military forces to intensify their commitment to moral warfare and explore new ethics doctrines.

The ethical challenges that arise during wars are difficult to resolve even for professional philosophers who have the luxury of time and extensive training to help them carefully consider possible solutions. Soldiers must make choices quickly and under intense pressure. At times they have only seconds to resolve issues of life and death. The immediacy of ethical problems arising in combat and the myriad background conditions that interfere with soldiers' cognitive abilities—stress, uncertainty, and lack of sleep—conspire to defy clear answers while making decisive action imperative. In his classic work *The Warriors*, World War II veteran Glenn Gray explains that dilemmas are ubiquitous in war and far more complex than observers might imagine:

> Modern wars are full of border situations where a soldier is forced to choose between evils and where every choice is like leaping into the dark because its consequences are unforeseeable. Rarely will he find a situation as clearly wrong as the shooting of hostages or the strafing of fleeing civilians. On the contrary, he will often have to choose between helping a wounded comrade to safety or remaining at his post to protect others whom he does not know. Sometimes he will have to choose the welfare of his unit at the expense of other units or the civilian population.[3]

These decisions become even more significant when we recognize that soldiers are political actors. They are entrusted with enacting their countries' foreign policy objectives and representing their countries in contested areas. They help to shape international opinion of conflicts, assist in building government institutions, work as cultural emissaries, and fight alongside foreign security forces. It is essential for political scientists, military professionals, policymakers, and concerned citizens to have some sense of what it means for soldiers to bear this burden.

Soldiers' experiences can give us insight into how wars are fought, why soldiers act well or badly, what influences their behavior, and how armed forces attempt to direct their members' actions. This requires a careful look at how soldiers are socialized, how they are influenced by their institutional contexts, and what they endure in combat. It also demands a more general understanding of what it is like to make ethical decisions during war—an understanding of what goes through a soldier's mind when facing the kinds of dilemmas that could potentially have strategic importance. It is with these goals in mind that this book examines the theory and implementation of military ethics. The analysis begins with the theory of military ethics and then devotes two chapters to each of the three case studies: one covering the institutional context and formal ethics doctrine and a second discussing the experiences of soldiers from each country. This way of framing the research question is essential for capturing the interplay between the institutional context and individuals' ethical decisions.

I use the term *military ethics* to refer specifically to codes of conduct that are meant to apply to all members of the military, regardless of rank. This distinguishes military ethics from moral precepts that are primarily meant for elites, such as chivalry and Bushido. I focus on junior officers, noncommissioned officers, and enlisted soldiers rather than on the high-ranking commanders and civilian policymakers who are usually featured in studies of morality and war, especially work coming from the just war tradition. I show that personnel in the lower and middle ranks of contemporary armed forces make critical decisions that can have an enormous impact on the lives of civilians in contested areas and on the course of the conflicts in which they participate. Moreover, I explore the psychological, cultural, and institutional factors that produce dilemmas and shape the reasoning strategies soldiers employ to resolve them.

The military ethics I describe encompass and are partially constituted by the law of armed conflict (LOAC) or international humanitarian law (IHL). These terms refer to international legal provisions governing the use of military force. Military ethics goes beyond legal requirements to include formal guidelines and informal norms that are particular to each military and that can therefore vary considerably cross-nationally. Throughout the book I reflect on the relationship between LOAC and less formalized ethical guidelines that arise to fill in gaps in the law and to guide legal interpretation. I also discuss the rules of engagement (ROE) that are meant to guide soldiers through quotidian ethical challenges. These rules attempt to distill LOAC, military ethics, and strategic considerations into a brief series of directives guiding the use of force. One of my central arguments is that armed forces should pursue greater formalization of norms by codifying them in international law. This would promote greater consistency in systems of military ethics and a more seamless integration of these various sources of guidance.

I address the subject of military ethics at various levels of abstraction, from the theory of applied ethics, to its operationalization in training, to individual soldiers' struggles to make the right choices when they are at war. Working across these different levels of analysis makes it possible to cover a range of topics in security studies and applied ethics, including, What kinds of ethical systems do militaries adopt? What kinds of challenges do soldiers contend with? How do they overcome these? Do styles of military ethics vary cross-nationally? How do strategic and political considerations influence military ethics?

I address these questions by comparing the US Army, the British Army and Royal Marines Commandos, and the Israel Defense Forces (IDF). The focus is on conflicts from 2000 to 2012, although I borrow some insights from historical sources and from soldiers' comments about earlier campaigns, and I explore how the legacy of incidents like the My Lai Massacre and Bloody Sunday continue to shape military ethics. These countries are among the world's most active belligerents and provide a model for other states that are attempting to improve their security forces. The American and British militaries routinely train foreign combatants and influence their NATO allies.[4] Most importantly, a comparative look at three countries highlights the different approaches states may take to military ethics education. Drawing comparisons between the US and UK is made easier by their involvement in the same wars, albeit in different regions. The IDF's recent fights have been shorter and less intense, which adds another dimension to the comparative view by showing the broad range of experiences soldiers may have in counterinsurgency operations.

I focus on counterinsurgency operations for three reasons. First, the armed forces I discuss have become preoccupied with fighting wars against unconventional adversaries. Understanding their recent histories would be impossible without looking at their counterinsurgency operations. Second, counterinsurgency exacerbates the moral challenges of war insofar as soldiers must contend with police work, social work, and development assistance alongside the usual challenges of combat. As the US field manual *Insurgencies and Countering Insurgencies* notes, "The environments where counterinsurgency operations exist can be much more ethically complex than those associated with conventional conflicts. Many leadership and ethical imperatives are prominent and, in some cases, unique to counterinsurgency."[5] Soldiers endeavor to distinguish between civilians and nonuniformed combatants, maintain good civil-military relations, and work alongside foreign security personnel. They even grapple with their own identities as military professionals when they are trained as conventional war fighters and then assigned roles that seem to have more in common with police work. Finally, counterinsurgency has produced an ethical crisis for each of the militaries I cover. They dominate conventional battlefields but struggle when adjusting to emerging problems. Looking at counterinsurgencies provides an opportunity to see not only how military ethics is framed but also how it is reframed (or not) when armed forces try to adapt.

I use the term *counterinsurgency* in the same sense as the US *Insurgencies and Countering Insurgencies* field manual to refer to "comprehensive civilian and military efforts designed to simultaneously defeat and contain insurgency and address its root causes."[6] This combination of civilian and military effort is essential to conceptualizing counterinsurgency as a distinctive ethical context apart from conventional warfare, with special challenges linked to unifying civilian and military operations and interacting with foreign civilian populations. Attention to the root causes of insurgency likewise entails a more thorough investment in foreign societies than is characteristic of operations that aim at achieving narrower and more purely military goals. Across the three militaries investigated, there is a shared belief that counterinsurgency signals a commitment to prioritizing political objectives over military objectives, which helps to construct the unique moral environment by forcing soldiers to show greater restraint and more nuanced reasoning when making use of force decisions.[7]

At times I also use the term *small war*, especially when referring to operations prior to the 1990s. This is in keeping with the preference for this term in American and British strategic discourse during this era and has a slightly different emphasis than *counterinsurgency*. I use the label *small war* to refer to operations that "vary in degrees from simple demonstrative operations to military intervention in the fullest sense, short of war," meaning that these operations are distinct from conventional war, but do not necessarily encompass the political and social goals that help to define counterinsurgency.[8]

The US Army's ethics is virtue based. Rules are employed to set absolute boundaries on what soldiers may do, but they are broad and few in number. They are also largely concerned with use of force decisions, which only encompass some of the myriad problems soldiers face during counterinsurgencies. Guidance is supposed to come primarily from values soldiers internalize—values that empower them to intuitively make good decisions. This encourages soldiers to act on initiative, entrusts them with making independent decisions, and downplays the role of explicit ethical decision procedures. The US Army's ethics is designed for conventional wars and can be difficult to reconcile with counterinsurgency operations because of the emphasis on inculcating a warrior ethos, embedding values in traditional military roles, and drawing a sharp distinction between soldiers and civilians. Many of the US Army's problems throughout the wars in Afghanistan and Iraq can be traced to the tension between its identity and values based around conventional warfare and the unconventional mission the soldiers were given.

The British military borrows some insights from virtue ethics and uses rules to set boundaries on soldiers' conduct, yet it relies primarily on a pragmatic ethic. Decisions are not informed by a clear reasoning procedure or by some conception of good character / good judgment. Rather, soldiers are taught to make decisions with an eye to what will be most effective in achieving political objectives. They also rely heavily on an assemblage of practices extrapolated from past conflicts. Most notably, the British military attempts to employ minimal force, pursue relatively modest political goals, cooperate with local militaries, and cultivate cultural respect. In principle, these norms seem ideally suited for counterinsurgency, and there is a tendency in the literature to romanticize the British approach. However, I take a critical perspective on it to show that the imagined supremacy of British counterinsurgency is illusory because many of its core values are difficult to operationalize. The British military's small size, challenges adjusting to foreign cultures, and overconfidence in its repertoire of counterinsurgency practices hindered the enactment of its norms in Iraq and Afghanistan. Worse still, because the pragmatic approach depends on slowly building norms over time and resists formalization, it can hinder quick adaptation.

The IDF's ethics is more thoroughly rule based. The primary source of guidance comes from an elaborate set of general rules called the Spirit of the IDF, which is supplemented by dozens of specific guidelines governing soldiers' actions in various contexts. Moreover, the rules are framed as being able to relieve soldiers of the burden of using their own judgment. This reflects the demand of bringing a diverse mixture of conscripts together for relatively brief terms of service as well as Israel's need to avoid being seen as an oppressive occupier. The rule-based ethic is supplemented by consequentialism, which urges soldiers to do what is in Israel's best interest. This is in tension with the rules, providing grounds for deviating from them whenever there seems to be a strategic rationale for doing so. The IDF's ethical system holds the advantage of being clearly defined and well suited for conscripts, yet it disempowers soldiers from objecting to immoral and illegal orders. The permission to do what is best for Israel is also too broad, as it can excuse the kinds of actions that ethics should help to prevent.

It is vital to remember that the institutions I discuss are heterogeneous and marked by different modes of thinking, so any points I make about tendencies do not preclude alternative strands of thought. To say that a particular ethical style predominates does not mean it is uncontested or will consistently remain the primary guide. Indeed, one of my central arguments is that military ethics is an ongoing project and that specific ethical traditions continually change in response to new challenges and new ways of thinking that upset orthodoxies.

None of these ethical systems is inherently superior to the others. Each comes with its own set of costs and benefits. Moral perfection is illusory within any system of military ethics, leaving each armed force to strive for improvement within the framework it creates while accounting for strategic and political demands. This does not mean that all systems of military ethics are equal but rather that moral considerations related to war are far too complex to make any sweeping claims about one approach consistently exceeding the others in terms of efficacy. Such claims would be misplaced anyway, as ethical systems are so contextually embedded that it is doubtful any armed force could consistently take another as its model. Each military pursues moral improvement within the context of its own system of ethics and may advance or regress to the extent that it is able to recognize and correct the most urgent ethical demands within that system and in a way that coheres with the political, strategic, cultural, and historical conditions that constrain institutional change.

Despite the differences between the three countries I investigate, there are some important basic similarities between their ethics doctrines and in how soldiers make decisions in practice. Each military sees itself as a profession that must operate within the boundaries of international law. Their ethical systems reflect this, with classes in international law and efforts to ground laws in the ROE. Soldiers across the three countries generally agree on the necessity of legal compliance, especially when it comes to the treatment of civilians and prisoners. The cross-national variations in ethics are generally over issues that are not explicitly covered in international law or that are open to divergent interpretations. As David Whetham points out, "The law itself can rarely provide the actual answers. Judgment is always required in order to answer questions relating to not just whether a particular action (or even inaction) is lawful, but also if it is actually the right thing to do in that particular situation."[9] Thus, law is helpful for establishing boundaries but falls short of being a comprehensive guide.

When soldiers described dilemmas that occurred in combat, such as deciding whether to shoot at an insurgent hiding behind a human shield, those from each military typically prioritized self-defense and defense of their comrades over civilian welfare. When they were relatively safe from insurgents' gunfire, soldiers generally agreed that it was best to avoid attacking insurgents if there was a high likelihood of harming innocent bystanders. The most challenging dilemmas for personnel from each country were escalation of force decisions about when to initiate combat. One typical scenario that soldiers of each military struggled with was whether to attack unidentified vehicles approaching checkpoints. The soldiers would shout warnings and fire warning shots, but if a vehicle failed to stop, they had to choose whether to attack it. A misdirected attack could kill an innocent person who was frightened by the warning shots and panicking, while not shooting could allow a suicide bomber to reach the checkpoint. Making this kind of decision demanded a leap into the unknown, guided by military ethics and luck.

Studying Soldiers

My research for this book is based on four sources: interviews with American, Israeli, and British soldiers; textual analysis of military publications; veterans' published narratives; and previous studies of military ethics. My findings are drawn primarily from interviews with thirty-four soldiers from the US Army, twenty-five from the IDF, seventeen from the British Army, and eight from the Royal Marines Commandos. All had been deployed to a conflict between 2000 and 2012. The US Army soldiers had been sent to Iraq and Afghanistan, with several having prior experience in Bosnia and the Gulf War. The British soldiers were veterans of the wars in Iraq and Afghanistan, though two had also been deployed to Northern Ireland and Bosnia. The IDF veterans were involved in security operations in the Palestinian territories and along the borders with Lebanon and Syria. Thirteen of the participants were women (six from the United States, four from Israel, and three from the United Kingdom). Although women were formally excluded from combat roles in each of the countries during the time period being studied, the women I interviewed were involved in field operations, usually as members of military police units. The participants also came from a range of different ethnic groups, religious backgrounds, and occupational specialties that will be discussed where these are relevant. The American and Israeli soldiers were interviewed between 2010 and 2012. I interviewed twelve of the British Army soldiers during this time. The additional interviews with British soldiers and Royal Marines Commandos took place in 2014. Most of the interviews were conducted in person, although nine members of the IDF were interviewed via email.

In addition to the veterans of recent counterinsurgency operations, I also talked to dozens of other military personnel who either provided ethics training or who served in previous conflicts. I exclude these interviews from my assessment of how soldiers from each country tend to engage in ethical reasoning in counterinsurgency operations specifically, but they do inform some of my more general comments on training and the experience of resolving ethical challenges in combat. These other interviewees were particularly important for providing insight into how ethics training is conducted and how it has changed over time.

The interviews show patterns in ethical reasoning among soldiers of different countries that, while not generalizable in themselves, coincide with patterns that are evident in training materials, official doctrine, and soldiers' published narratives. Because these patterns appear in various sources and can be linked to underlying causal mechanisms, it is possible to draw generalizations about how armed forces conduct ethics training and how their personnel resolve dilemmas. I also borrow from previous research on military ethics for additional insight into how ethics training is framed and to substantiate generalizations from individual interviews.

There is some risk of bias in veterans' self-reports. Soldiers may want to avoid discussing instances in which they or others acted wrongly. They may shape their responses to give a positive impression of the military and the operations they participated in. Conversely, those who have become antiwar advocates could overstate the incidence of atrocities. Bias is unavoidable when attempting to uncover how soldiers make ethical decisions, as we must have some insight into their subjective experiences. I guard against it by only using the interviews to draw conclusions about soldiers' reasoning strategies. I do not attempt to reach any inferences about which military is the most responsible or which attacks civilians more often. Those kinds of questions are better approached with a systematic review of after-action reports, casualty figures, and investigations by nongovernmental organizations. Moreover, any effort interviewees make to censor their comments or to give a particular impression are guided by their moral attitudes and may further clarify what those attitudes are.

To reach a diverse range of soldiers, I used three methods of recruitment: contacting representatives of the militaries for assistance, contacting nonpartisan veterans groups, and snowball sampling. The US Army was the only military that directly assisted by inviting me to attend an internal ethics and professionalism review involving members of the 82nd Airborne Division. Around one-third of the US soldiers interviewed were approached during this study. Most interviewees from each military were contacted through nonpartisan veterans' organizations at universities and veterans' health organizations. Roughly one-fifth of the interviewees were contacted when soldiers to whom I talked referred me to acquaintances.

The textual analysis portions of the book focus on training manuals, ethics education materials, and doctrinal statements. Most of the texts I analyzed were available publicly, as each of the militaries included in this study strives to make its ethics easily accessible to soldiers and visible to outside observers. This information is usually treated either as not being dangerous to make public or as being advantageous to publicize because it is evidence of armed forces' efforts to improve themselves. The exception to this are the ROE, which are generally classified. My comments on the ROE are based on those that have been released and soldiers' descriptions of them.[10]

Existing collections of interviews and personal accounts from veterans of recent wars offer additional insight into the subjective experience of participating in counterinsurgencies. Many American and British veterans have written narratives of their time in Iraq and Afghanistan.[11] Few of these discuss ethics explicitly, but many of the descriptions of events include explanations of how soldiers made ethical decisions. Soldiers' narratives also provide more background information on counterinsurgency operations and military culture, which is important for putting ethical practices into context.

Over the past decade a number of books have been written about military ethics education or as educational materials to assist in training.[12] Most of this work has come from practitioners who work for military educational institutions or who are directly involved in training. The rapid growth of this literature shows the importance that armed forces around the world are placing on ethics education, and especially the efforts to contend with emerging challenges related to counterinsurgency, new technologies, and the transformation of the profession. I am indebted to this work, especially when it comes to insights about how ethics training is conducted and how educators approach the subject. Whereas most of this work takes an applied focus in the sense that it is directed at improving ethics education directly, my analysis is a comparative examination of military ethics with the goal of understanding why armed forces select certain ethical guides, what influence ethics training has on soldiers, and what lessons can be drawn from looking at the strengths and limitations of different approaches to promoting moral warfare.

Theoretically, I draw on the moral philosophies I discuss in chapter 2 and insights from the just war tradition. Over the past two decades, research on just war theory has been divided by orthodox or traditionalist and revisionist perspectives.[13] The former derive moral evaluations from the conventions of war and with a preference to ensure that norms are applicable in practice, while the latter tend to prioritize philosophical consistency, even when it conflicts with established practices of fighting. What is particularly important for my analysis is that orthodox just war theorists see a close relationship between the morality of war and laws of war, with laws developing from shared moral norms and emerging norms being a potential source of future legal agreements, while revisionists think that morality and law may diverge because the former makes demands that may be difficult or dangerous to apply in practice.[14] Because my goal is to produce a kind of phenomenology of war from the perspective of soldiers and to explain moral norms as they are developed by armed forces, it fits much closer into the orthodox understanding of the just war tradition. When talking about the morality of war, I mean the norms that develop out of the practice of war in the orthodox sense. I avoid making claims based on the revisionist conception of a morality of war that may be more abstract and not always applicable in practice because of my interest in the implementation of military ethics.

Overview of the Book

The first part of the book discusses the political and strategic factors that influence systems of military ethics as well as the types of challenges that emerge on the battlefield and during counterinsurgencies in particular.

Chapter 1 presents a brief history of military ethics. During the late nineteenth century, when militaries began employing soldiers in dispersed formations and devolved decision-making to lower levels, it became necessary to provide general ethics training and to create professional codes of conduct that encompass all members of armed forces. Systems of military ethics are heavily shaped by larger social forces, which explains the historical contingency of codified military ethics and cross-national variations in normative systems.

The second chapter introduces the four moral philosophies that I employ to identify the salient characteristics of systems of military ethics. These are virtue ethics, deontology, consequentialism, and pragmatism. The theories are sometimes explicitly appropriated by armed forces and figure heavily in commentaries from military ethics educators. Systems of military ethics may also approximate these philosophies without any clear intent to do so simply by reflecting the same overall orientation and reasoning strategies. In either case, moral philosophies make a useful heuristic for explaining the American, Israeli, and British codes of conduct. The strengths and limitations of each of the theories also show up when they are applied in military contexts.

In the third chapter I turn to the impediments that interfere with ethical decision-making during war. Soldiers must contend with an array of situational and cognitive constraints when they encounter ethical challenges on the battlefield, including uncertainty, fear, chronic stress, and sleep deprivation. These constraints alter the range of actions that soldiers can take and affect their abilities to make decisions. The task for military ethics is bridging the divide between theory and practice to ensure that norms can realistically inform soldiers' actions. I argue that in some cases the situational and cognitive constraints become so profound that they preclude effective ethical judgment and that these cases can be identified based on their structural characteristics—above all, the level of uncertainty. However, in most situations, the constraints impairing soldiers' reasoning abilities make good decisions more difficult without making them impossible.

Chapter 4 considers the different types of ethical challenges that soldiers face in counterinsurgency operations. Although some of these occur during combat, most are decisions about the escalation of force, such as determining when an unknown vehicle might be hostile or how to respond to nonlethal threats. I draw on my interviews to show that these challenges, rather than those that occurred during combat, were often the most arduous. These types of dilemmas are also the ones that produced the most pronounced cross-national differences in ethical thinking.

The second part of the book is structured around the three case studies, with a pair of chapters for each country. The first chapter about each country sets out the formal ethics training and doctrine; the second discusses soldiers' experiences of applying these in practice. Thus, as the book considers each case, it moves from the institutional level to the individual level. This is essential for capturing the interaction between institutions and individual choices when it comes to accounting for how soldiers, acting both as representatives of their armed forces and as moral agents in their own right, make decisions during counterinsurgency operations.

The US Army, which is the focus of chapters 5 and 6, encourages soldiers to embody a warrior ethos and to make decisions based on a reflexive ethical sense that is ingrained in the character of US soldiers. This is supported by the US Army's emphasis on professionalism, voluntary service, and long-term membership, which establish the basis for the extensive socialization that virtue ethics requires. I argue that virtue ethics provides a useful foundation for military ethics because of its practicality but that it is also potentially dangerous because soldiers are trained in virtues that are designed for conventional wars.

In chapter 6 I argue that US soldiers tend to be skilled at finding their own solutions to unexpected dilemmas but that their responses are informed by a shared warrior ethos that was developed for conventional war. Relying on virtues suited for high-intensity combat leads many soldiers to struggle when they are involved in counterinsurgency operations that force them to work with local authorities and to act with restraint to avoid harming civilians. The combination of an ethical system based on quick, decisive action and a warrior ethos based on conventional fighting can lead soldiers to overreact to potential threats during escalation of force decisions or when interacting with civilians. The US Army case shows that while virtue ethics can be an effective model for military ethics, it must be operationalized in different ways depending on the type of conflict.

In chapter 7 I explain how the British military, drawing on a long experience of colonial military operations and recent counterinsurgency operations, takes a pragmatic approach to military ethics. Its norms arise from the enactment of the British counterinsurgency doctrine. This doctrine takes on an ethical character because it provides instructions for how soldiers should interact with foreign populations and when they should use violence. Soldiers are taught to take a minimalist attitude in their military and political missions, which means using the least amount of force necessary to achieve objectives and leaving local institutions intact. They also learn to see foreign civilians as an audience that is always watching and that must be won over through good deeds and acts of restraint that can establish legitimacy.

Chapter 8 discusses the experiences of British soldiers and marines in Afghanistan and Iraq as they endeavor to adapt their counterinsurgency doctrine and its corresponding ethic in places for which it was poorly suited. Because of the British military's small size, it attempts to cooperate with local military and police forces, taking an integrated approach to security and institutional reconstruction. With few supporters in Afghanistan and Iraq, the British military had to cooperate with unreliable security forces that at times acted against British strategic interests. By relying on local militias for support, British soldiers were able to outsource some sensitive operations, but this came at the cost of empowering militias. Worse still, some interviewees and soldiers' narratives of the wars describe feeling pressure to use force more liberally as they became overstretched and were unable to contend with all threats simultaneously.

In chapter 9, I discuss the IDF's hybrid ethic, which merges deontological and consequentialist thinking. Israeli soldiers are trained to follow complex rules that are meant to cover all situations, but these are supplemented with an authorization to act in the interests of Israeli national security. This system coheres with the IDF's use of conscription and its close relationship with the civilian population. However, combining different forms of ethical thinking creates a tension between absolute rules that are framed with reference to claims about universal human dignity and the defensive imperative that privileges national security.

Finally, chapter 10 analyzes the operationalization of the IDF's hybrid ethics. My interviews and other firsthand accounts reveal that Israeli soldiers are highly cognizant of the ethical challenges associated with counterinsurgency and are aware of the intense international scrutiny of their actions. Nevertheless, soldiers struggle when applying the IDF's extensive rules to real-world situations and find it especially difficult to decide how to act in situations that were not covered by their rules. Paradoxically, despite their ethical awareness and commitment to restraint, the IDF soldiers are also prepared to abandon restraints whenever they must do so for reasons of national security. This creates some permissiveness in the deontological framework that must be addressed more directly for this system to preserve its coherence.

1

The Emergence of Military Ethics

"In all wars throughout history, general orders have been given or personal decisions have been taken about who should be killed or spared, raped or respected, rendered destitute or protected, enslaved or freed."[1] Historically, "it is religious authorities and political power which have defined who can be killed or hurt."[2] This is why the just war tradition that is one of the dominant normative frameworks for evaluating wars arose from theological roots and was subsequently shaped by the early modern state formation process, during which time the morality of war was remapped onto more secular sources of authority.[3] Changes in the conduct of war during the nineteenth and twentieth centuries prompted a radical normative shift. Religious and political authorities continued to shape the overall structure of norms related to war, but the audience changed. Individual soldiers at the lower and middle rungs of the military hierarchy took on greater importance as moral agents who could think and act with more autonomy. It became necessary to adjust ethical guidelines that previously spoke primarily to elites so they could apply broadly to everyone in uniform.

Military ethics, understood as a code of conduct that applies to all members of a military, emerged during the nineteenth century via efforts to delineate a military profession and to codify its rules; it only became widespread during the twentieth century.[4] It is possible to find informal precedents for military ethics earlier than this, such as in chivalry and Bushido, but the decision to codify norms marks a turning point by signaling a commitment to apply more consistent and transparent standards. The demand for systematizing military ethics came from changes in how wars were fought, especially the increased complexity, mobility, and dispersion of armed forces. These changes required the devolution of authority to lower-ranking personnel and increased the extent to which soldiers acted without direct supervision.

The gradual formalization of military ethics over time and in response to a constellation of structural conditions that vary by country generated inconsistencies in the form and content of ethical systems cross-nationally—inconsistencies that I highlight throughout the book. The highest level of formalization came from the codification of some ethical precepts in the law of armed conflict (LOAC), and this is the basis for cross-national agreement in ethical systems. The LOAC forms the core of military ethics, but only covers some of the myriad dilemmas that soldiers may encounter, and even the meaning of the LOAC may vary slightly cross-nationally depending on what interpretations are privileged. The relationship between military ethics and the LOAC is, like the history of military ethics more broadly, constantly evolving as military institutions and the style of warfare change.

It is important to establish the historical origins of military ethics for several reasons. First, this shows that for much of modern history ordinary soldiers have been treated more as instruments obeying their commanders' wishes than as moral actors in their own right. This explains why strategic corporals have come as such a shock in recent conflicts. Second, the historical development of military ethics helps to account for why many countries continue to show little interest in military ethics and why even countries that have pursued it (including the US, UK, and Israeli militaries) tend to give much less attention to the education of enlisted soldiers than to ethics education for officers. Finally, the history of military ethics demonstrates that normative constraints on war change in response to structural and cultural shifts.

The Historical Origins of Military Ethics

Before the nineteenth century, pitched battles were usually fought by armies that were relatively small and organizationally simple by modern standards, which permitted unified control by a single commander or a small group of them.[5] Armies were rarely divided because this might upset centralized control and interfere with coordination—serious concerns in the time before telecommunications. When they were split, independent units were put under the supervision of trusted and loyal companions who could maintain control. Thus, commanders and their closest associates were ultimately responsible for conducting their armies according to the prevailing norms, and they exercised authority in ways that left little room for those in lower positions to make independent judgments.

The centralization of command and the use of mass formations limited soldiers' opportunities for making independent moral decisions. They made choices, of course, and informal ethical guidelines were imposed along with associated punishments. Soldiers were autonomous and could decide to disobey their orders or to leave the ranks and act alone. There were also cases in which soldiers could venture beyond an officer's reach, especially when raiding or foraging.[6] Nevertheless, the scope of moral decision-making was circumscribed and the punishments for misconduct were harsh.[7] In practice, this meant there was little need for armies to develop ethical systems that would apply to low- and mid-level soldiers. A general military ethics could even be threatening to the commanders whose authority might be undermined by subordinates' independent actions.

The limited autonomy of ordinary soldiers was further constrained by early efforts at military professionalization during the seventeenth and eighteenth centuries. Professionalization was guided by reforms from military strategists like Maurice of Nassau and Gustavus Adolphus, for whom success in war was contingent on training masses of soldiers to perform routinized tactical maneuvers.[8] Early professional soldiers underwent continual drill, with the goal of transforming them into integrated units that could operate as parts of a machine. Training was designed to condition soldiers to follow orders without stopping to consider the ethical implications.[9] The unwavering discipline of militaries in the age of muskets allowed soldiers to execute precise maneuvers and to stand at attention while receiving volleys of enemy fire, but it depended on curtailing autonomy, which threatened soldiers' status as ethical actors.

The rigid hierarchical control that characterized early professional armies began to break down during the nineteenth century. To some extent, this was a product of changing political sentiments. Members of popular armies with egalitarian ideologies like those of Revolutionary France or the US Army during the American Civil War loosened restrictions and removed some of the harsh penalties that soldiers of previous generations had endured.[10] The most significant event in nineteenth-century military ethics was the introduction of the Lieber Code by the US Army in 1863. The Lieber Code formalized norms that had previously been maintained customarily and applied them consistently across the ranks.[11] Although it was largely addressed to those in command positions, it showed a growing awareness that smaller units were acting independently or semi-independently when raiding, foraging, performing guard duty, skirmishing, or marching over rough terrain. By taking up subjects such as the treatment of prisoners, spies, deserters, and civilians as well as forbidding torture and uncivilized weapons, the Lieber Code provided a clearer account of soldiers' individual rights and responsibilities as combatants.

The rise of military ethics was closely linked to the devolution of command authority—a process instigated by changes in military technology and organization. War in the late nineteenth and early twentieth centuries was characterized by rapid increases in "complexity, mobility, and dispersion"—factors that contributed enormously to the difficulties of controlling militaries.[12] The complexity of war increased, with armed forces growing in size and with greater specialization of military occupations. As armies grew throughout the nineteenth century and into the early twentieth century and as the diversity of weapons in use required ever more elaborate logistical networks, militaries became more bureaucratized and compartmentalized. The result was that armies could no longer be controlled by a single leader, or even by a small team of trusted associates. Command itself had to undergo bureaucratization, leading to the proliferation of officers and subdivision of responsibility.[13] These processes simultaneously elevated more soldiers to leadership positions, where they would have to make ethically significant policy decisions, and increased the opportunities for those outside of leadership positions to overcome ethical challenges independently.

During the early twentieth century, the means of maintaining control of subordinates led to still more complexity and further bureaucratization. Direct communication was superseded by more advanced communications technologies, from radios and telephones to computers and satellite imagery. Each new means of communication required its own technicians to maintain and operate, and each tended to increase the number of levels messages had to pass through, thereby ensuring that even as communications technologies facilitated command and control they did so while increasing organizational complexity.

In addition to disrupting commanders' abilities to directly control their soldiers, the growing complexity of militaries generated a need for ethics to serve a unifying function. In large militaries, it is impossible for most combatants to know each other personally. This anonymity is a consequence of bureaucratization and is potentially disastrous for armed forces that may be ineffective and have low morale if soldiers lack confidence in their comrades and in their collective abilities. There must be trust between people whose lives depend on each other but who are not acquainted. Jonathan Shay perfectly captures how this challenge distances modern soldiers from those in ancient armies:

> Compared to the modern soldier, the Homeric soldier hardly depended on others at all, and when he did it was upon comrades he knew personally and called on by name without technology to assist his own voice. He depended upon himself for his weapons and armor; his eyes and ears provided most of the tactical intelligence he required. He did not need to rely on the competence, mental clarity, and sense of responsibility of a chain of people he would never meet to assure that artillery or air strikes meant to protect him did not kill him by mistake.[14]

A unifying system of ethics is one way of countering the complexity of modern warfare and the anonymity that tends to go along with bureaucratization. Soldiers need an organizational ethos that can replace personal connections and build trust among those whose lives depend on each other. Formalized codes of conduct provide this by creating a single culture and a shared sense of purpose.

The second structural change responsible for the formalization of military ethics was the increased mobility of armed forces. It is hard to overstate how profoundly new technologies of mobility have altered warfare. Throughout the twentieth century, advances in weaponry and logistics made it possible to move resources farther and faster than ever before. Trains revolutionized movement in the Franco-Prussian War and American Civil War and then became vital logistical tools in the First World War and the Russian Civil War.[15] During the Second World War, tanks, the use of motorized vehicles to move troops and supplies, more advanced ships, and aircraft dramatically increased the tempo of fighting, serving first as the centerpieces in Germany's devastating blitzkrieg and then as the tools with which the Allies were able to overwhelm the Axis powers.

Combined arms tactics involving quick maneuvers by different types of units in the air, on land, and in the sea depend on careful coordination. And this in turn requires decentralized command and control as well as strong mutual trust between the military personnel acting in concert. The hierarchical model of military organization that prevailed in the past is giving way to more adaptable networked structures. This is a continuing process that is evident in ongoing conflicts as state armed forces decentralize in response to dynamic and evasive threats by nonstate actors.[16] As with the growing complexity of war, increased mobility generates a need for decentralization. This places a greater burden on lower-level personnel to act independently and gives corporals strategic value.

Finally, the dispersion of militaries has been influenced by new technologies and the increasing scale of battlefields. In the late nineteenth century, the dense formations of the past were abandoned as machine guns, high explosives, and more powerful artillery wrought unprecedented destruction. French and German military theorists developed new tactical models based on dispersion, which others were quick to emulate after coming into contact with the instruments of modern warfare.[17] The disruption was especially profound for the ground combat personnel who are my focus in this book. As Gwynne Dyer notes, "For the infantry, who fought shoulder to shoulder all through history, the world has been turned upside down . . . the battlefield has become a desperately lonely place, deceptively empty in appearance but bristling with menace, where he can expect neither direct supervision by his officer or NCO in combat, nor the comforting presence of a group of other men beside him."[18]

Tactical innovations took a decisive turn toward dispersion near the end of the First World War. The German military's use of small assault groups almost succeeded in breaking the stalemate on the Western Front, demonstrating the efficacy of this style of fighting and setting the tone for the aggressive, decentralized operations that characterized the blitzkriegs of the Second World War.[19] With the dispersion and growing size of armed forces came the extension of military operations over massive geographical areas. Commanders became unable to directly oversee their subordinates, as they had done in earlier times, and had to delegate responsibilities down to the junior officers and noncommissioned officers who still participated in front-line combat.

As with the other structural changes during this period, dispersion gave soldiers greater autonomy. They had to internalize norms that could guide them even when they were not under close supervision from disciplinarians, and these norms had to be formalized to ensure consistency. The need for soldiers to think and act independently has grown as tactics have developed beyond the massed formations and well-ordered lines of the past to tactics of dispersion that empower units down to the squad level to fight without constant supervision. Training has correspondingly focused more on transforming soldiers' character or teaching them rules of conduct that facilitate independent action, including independent moral reasoning.

Professionalism and Ethics

Military professionalism is closely linked to the structural changes in the conduct of war, as professionalization was required to produce the right kind of soldier for modern warfare. A central part of professionalism is the internalization of norms, which is meant to guarantee that individuals act according to collective interests. Asa Kasher reports that based on his experience as an educator, "the best way to introduce military ethics to officers in military environments is by embedding it in some project of professional development."[20] Professionalism distinguishes regular armed forces from the ad hoc assemblages of fighters brought together for short campaigns that typified many premodern armies, and from the mercenaries and conscript armies that dominated European warfare during the Renaissance and early modern period.[21] Professionalism is a quality exemplified by disciplined militaries built around institutions and a culture that persist over time.

Professionalism gives unity to military organizations, yet it is also a contested concept that militaries define differently according to the characteristics that join their members. A theory of military ethics must start with some idea of who should be considered part of the profession. Any system of applied ethics needs a sense of its audience, but this is particularly important when it comes to military ethics because of the exceptional roles that military personnel perform. Soldiers are exceptions to many of the norms that others are expected to follow. They are among the few people for whom killing is a sanctioned activity. Killing is not just excusable but is considered a professional obligation, for which soldiers are praised and rewarded.

As a sociological concept, the idea of the military as a profession is fairly new, having been popularized by Samuel Huntington and Morris Janowitz in the 1960s.[22] Despite their disagreements over how the profession should be defined and how its members should be subordinated to civilian governments, Huntington and Janowitz—as well as most of those who have contributed to their respective schools of civil-military relations research—describe professionalism as being a distinctly modern phenomenon. Huntington finds that Prussia, France, and England formed the first professional militaries in the nineteenth century and that professionalism remained rare even in the early twentieth century. He describes military professionalism as something that developed quickly, over the span of less than a century. "Prior to 1800 there was no such thing as a professional officer corps. In 1900 such bodies existed in virtually all major countries."[23] Janowitz provides a similar history, concurring with Huntington's judgment that military professionalism is a novel phenomenon and that there were only a few hints of it prior to the twentieth century.[24]

These conceptions of professionalism emerged around the same time armed forces began to adopt more decentralized organizational structures and as collective ethics shared by all soldiers were being formalized. These processes complemented each other, each serving as cause and effect for the other and each playing an essential role in ensuring that militaries could be regulated even as they underwent dramatic changes in their composition and operations. The importance of the concept of professionalism is reflected in the ethics doctrines of the American, British, and Israeli armed forces. Each explicitly links their systems to the concept of a military profession, using this to delimit membership in a community that shares norms. And many of their internal ethical debates are related to the struggle of distinguishing members of the military profession who are bound to follow shared ethical codes from outsiders who are not.

Private military contractors are among the most controversial combatants in recent conflicts because they test the limits of inclusion in the profession and threaten to disrupt its norms. In recent decades they have come to play a central role in training and supplying military personnel as well as in combat.[25] They perform many of the same roles as regular soldiers but have greater independence from regulations. They often follow distinctive rules that are far more permissive than those given to soldiers.[26] This is evidence of contractors' ambiguous membership in the military profession, which aggravates relations between contractors and military personnel.

Concern over the threat contractors pose to military professionalism was evident throughout my conversations with soldiers from each of the armed forces I investigated. Aside from three former Royal Marines Commandos and one former US Army infantryman who were working as contractors at the time of the interviews, those I spoke with had a negative outlook on the privatization of military force. The foremost complaints were that contractors threaten the selfless patriotism that characterizes participation in state military forces and that they undermine the civil-military distinction that is fundamental to military professionalism. These complaints were reinforced by resentment about contractors being paid more money to perform the same jobs as the soldiers themselves—and with fewer restrictions. One American infantryman said the label "contractor" was "Orwellian language used to avoid calling them mercenaries, but a nice name doesn't change the fact that they're fighting for money."[27] An officer in the Judge Advocate General's Corps reported being frustrated when dealing with the contractors during his time in Bosnia and Iraq because they could easily slip beyond the military's system of justice. He claimed that on several occasions he was even prevented from helping soldiers and civilians who were victims of sexual abuse and other crimes because the perpetrators were contractors. "They get away with terrible things," he said "and they make the rest of us look bad. The people over there don't distinguish between contractors and soldiers. They think we're all part of the same team."[28]

Similar comments come up in many soldiers' narratives. Reflecting on the Blackwater contractors who were killed in Fallujah, Tyler Boudreau says, "They weren't one of us, one of the troops. They were mercenaries—soldiers of fortune. They were doing it for the dough. . . . It was unsettling to hear a man talk about money as he packed off to war. It kind of took the nobility out of it."[29] This antipathy often extends beyond military contractors who fight to the thousands of contractors who provide support services. Graham Lee, an officer in a British Air Assault Brigade, describes one firm he saw in action as "a dark and sinister conglomerate whose tentacles wrapped around every tender spot the army presented to it, and sucked its service supply budgets while offering the meagrest possible service in return."[30]

The threat to the military's sense of professionalism is borne out in research on contractors. George Lucas points out that "professional ethics in a military context remains vexed, contested, and not well understood by the public. If we take the problem of uncertainty and disagreement over professional ethics and military virtues out of its public context and place it instead in the private sector, we generate even more difficulties."[31] Here he rightly calls attention to the profound uncertainty about what contractors mean for the entire profession and notes that this could compound the kinds of ethical challenges I discuss later in the book, which are hard enough when they are contained within a clearly defined professional context. Even some contractors tacitly acknowledge that they pose this problem. Although Erik Prince, the founder of Blackwater, is an ex-Navy SEAL, he describes himself and other contractors as "civilian warriors" and acknowledges wearing civilian clothes, using civilian vehicles, and concealing weapons when operating in conflict zones.[32] Such behavior is deeply problematic from a moral standpoint since it eschews the clear identification of combatant status required by the Geneva Conventions and risks tarnishing the reputation of soldiers operating in the same areas as contractors.

As the debate over the moral and legal implications of private military contractors shows, the concept of military professionalism remains contested. From an ethical standpoint, this debate is essentially a disagreement about who should be granted the exceptional rights soldiers have to kill others, and who should be required to follow the codes of conduct that are meant to regulate that killing. This, like the effort to define the military profession, is likely an intractable debate that cannot be definitively settled. Continual changes in the military's composition and the substantial cross-national differences in military institutions preclude the discovery of any unobjectionable demarcation criteria. Conceptions of professionalism are, like the norms governing war, historical products that change over time. We can gain insight into how military ethics works and why it takes particular forms by looking at how issues of membership in the profession are resolved. This will become evident when comparing the volunteer militaries of the United States and United Kingdom with Israel's conscript military, as the former countries rely on a sense of professionalism that is at odds with the latter's.

Conclusion

During the nineteenth century, structural transformations in the character of war and corresponding efforts to professionalize military service generated a demand for formalized norms that could unify vast organizations and guide soldiers even when they were operating independently. A professional identity and an ethical code to govern members of that profession are mutually constitutive, with professionalism defining the scope of military ethics and the traits that define the profession becoming central components of ethical systems. The interplay between ethics and professional identity means these concepts continue to be difficult to disaggregate.

As this brief history shows, military ethics changes alongside shifts in the conduct of war and the composition of armed forces. Military ethics is therefore an unfinished and unfinishable project. Militaries must continually struggle for improvement in an environment where normative perfection will always be an elusive goal. This is especially clear from recent counterinsurgency operations, as militaries strive to adapt to unfamiliar political and military conditions. Counterinsurgency operations exacerbate the decentralization of militaries that I discussed in this chapter and in doing so generate a corresponding need for greater attention to systems of military ethics to direct increasingly autonomous soldiers. They have also brought new violent actors into combat, such as nonuniformed fighters, private military contractors, and intelligence operatives, exacerbating efforts to clearly define professional identities.

2

Moral Theory and Ethics at War

This chapter explores the moral concepts that I apply in the three case studies, and the theoretical significance of divergent approaches to military ethics. I discuss the cases in terms of four types of moral theories: virtue-based (aretaic), rule-based (deontological), consequentialist, and pragmatist. I present these as "pure" moral theories—ideal types that can be combined in various ways to create the hybrid ethical systems that armed forces use in practice. They are ideal in the sense that they are theoretical creations that are rarely, if ever, fully enacted, especially by entire institutions. However, each approach is useful for exemplifying a particular type of moral thinking that privileges certain considerations above others and may lead to divergent outcomes in practice.

These theories frame much of the literature on moral theory and applied ethics, including previous work on military ethics.[1] The history of moral philosophy is frequently described as a contest between deontological, consequentialist, and aretaic theories, with pragmatism sometimes making an appearance alongside them. By using these theories to describe the norms of the American, Israeli, and British armed forces I do not mean to imply that military ethics is intentionally formulated based on the model of a particular moral philosophy. My point is only that, whether by design or by coincidence, these theories highlight salient characteristics of the systems of military ethics I describe throughout the book. At times those civilian and military officials who construct systems of military ethics or who provide classroom training explicitly invoke these theories. Militaries also develop normative systems without clearly articulating the source of their norms but while still relying on identifiable styles of thinking.

Each of the pure theories comes with an assortment of costs and benefits. Virtue ethics is adaptable and promotes exceptional conduct, yet it also deepens the division between soldiers and civilians and places a heavy burden on individuals' moral reasoning skills. Deontological ethics provides transparent guidelines that are consistent and amenable to oversight, but can be inflexible and discourage soldiers from taking the initiative. Consequentialism holds intuitive appeal, especially when applied in military contexts in which difficult decisions must be made using cost-benefit calculations. Its greatest challenge is that it often takes a self-interested form that I characterize as "partisan consequentialism," which weighs outcomes disproportionately in favor of particular groups. Pragmatic norms are constituted informally through a practice or way of life and are only loosely codified. This links practices and the norms that are meant to govern them, though it also hinders efforts to apply external criteria to evaluate norms. Hybrid systems circumvent some of the problems associated with pure moral theories, combining multiple influences to offset their weaknesses. However, implementing two or more distinct and irreconcilable styles of moral thinking can raise new challenges if these create competing demands. The result is that some hybrid systems may avoid the problems associated with pure versions of moral theories while also creating internal conflicts between competing imperatives.

I start by discussing virtue ethics, which emphasizes the importance of cultivating good character. Virtue ethics is flexible and does not require complex rules or decision procedures. It affords individuals a great deal of freedom to use their own judgment, though this comes at the expense of uniformity and transparency. Next, I describe deontological ethics, according to which the moral character of actions is determined by actors' intentions. Deontological theories emphasize the use of universal moral obligations or decision procedures that should be applied in all situations. The third section discusses consequentialism—a broad category of ethical theories that are unified insofar as they judge the morality of actions based on their effects. Utilitarianism is one of the most well-known types of consequentialism, but I will focus on what I will call "partisan consequentialism," which is partisan in the sense that it determines the worth of actions in ways that disproportionately weight their consequences for a particular state or group. The fourth section introduces pragmatic ethical theories, which are derived from existing practices—in this case, counterinsurgency doctrines. Finally, I close the chapter with a comment on hybrid systems and discuss some of the advantages and disadvantages of drawing on multiple sources of ethical guidance. Each of the armed forces I analyze relies on a hybrid system, but they differ in the relative weight given to their various moral influences.

Virtue Ethics

Most moral theories are designed to judge *actions* and their consequences. Such theories are usually agent-neutral, labeling certain actions good or evil regardless of who performs them. That is, most theories assume that for any moral dilemma there is a right and a wrong course of action (or maybe several) that remain constant regardless of who is facing it. By contrast, virtue ethics is primarily interested in judging the character of *actors*. Character matters, according to proponents of virtue ethics, because it directs actions. A good person will act well, and a bad person will misbehave. Rather than assessing actions as right and wrong, virtue ethics uses aretaic predicates, calling people good and bad or admirable and deplorable.[2] Labeling a particular action good or bad is usually a shorthand way of saying that it is the kind of action that a person with good or bad character would perform. Thus, while an action may be described in moral terms, the person involved is the focus of moral valuation.

Aristotle is virtue ethics' most influential proponent, making him the best source for outlining this theory's core attributes.[3] Aristotle famously defines each of his virtues as the mean between two extremes—as the middle ground between the vices of excess and deficiency. His list of virtues is important to the theory of virtue ethics, but I will avoid discussing these here. The militaries that employ virtue ethics rarely follow any of Aristotle's virtues, aside from courage, nor do they define their virtues as being the mean between extremes. Instead, they rely heavily on conceptions of good conduct and processes of character education that are influenced by Aristotle.

Aristotle characterizes virtues as being actor relative and context relative. Actor relativity means that what counts as virtue for one person may not be virtue for another because of different abilities and resources. A poor person who donates a dollar to charity is generous because this is a major expenditure, while the same donation from a rich person is stingy.[4] Likewise, courage for a soldier differs from courage for a civilian because the former is expected to march calmly into battle, while the latter would be foolish to do so.[5]

Virtues are context relative because a given virtue may require radically different types of actions depending on the context, even if the actor is the same. Courage on the battlefield may consist in standing alongside one's comrades, while the moral courage a soldier must display in a war crimes trial may require defecting against those same people. Because virtues are actor relative and context relative, it is impossible to determine when a particular action is good or bad without taking the character of the actor and the context into account. The My Lai Massacre illustrates this. Hugh Thompson, Glenn Andreotta, and Lawrence Colburn showed moral courage because they refused to follow their comrades in committing an atrocity and rescued at least ten civilians.[6] Their noncompliance was good under the circumstances, yet it is easy to imagine other settings in which a similar refusal to follow the group could have been condemnable. This relativity gives ethical reasoning a practical orientation; it is best understood when it is instantiated in specific situations rather than being described in abstractions.

Aristotle argues that knowledge of the virtues is insufficient to ensure moral conduct. The problem he finds is that choosing the middle course can be extremely difficult unless one has a well-developed sense of what counts as virtuous action in various contexts. An intention to do what is virtuous is likewise necessary but insufficient. In addition to knowledge of the virtues and a desire to be virtuous, one also needs to have the ability to translate knowledge of virtue into action. This requires *phronesis*: the practical wisdom to recognize what is virtuous for oneself in particular contexts. As Aristotle says, ethical systems must be oriented toward producing real ethical conduct. "The most important thing is not to know what it is, but how it arises; we do not wish to know what courage is, we wish to be courageous."[7] *Phronesis* allows theory to become the basis for practice, shifting a person seamlessly from knowledge of a virtue to its enactment.

The practical orientation of virtue ethics shapes the framing of ethics education. Aristotle thinks that the way a person becomes virtuous is through imitation and habituation.[8] One must observe the way virtuous people behave and emulate them until good character becomes ingrained. Virtue ethics education therefore depends heavily on identifying exemplars who can reliably guide ethical development. The ultimate goal of ethics education, and the source of good conduct itself, is having good character. Aristotle argues that a person with good character will naturally choose the right course of action in a given situation simply by trusting their own judgment. Consequently, virtue ethics education begins with emulation and then permits greater autonomy when it comes to determining how to act virtuously.

Developing Good Soldiers

Virtue ethics' greatest advantage in a military context is its practicality. It does not require soldiers to process rules or decision procedures, nor do they need to weigh the potential costs of different courses of action. It also gives them the freedom to make quick, independent judgments when they cannot look to their superiors for direction. The promise of soldiers reliably making good decisions with minimal oversight is extremely attractive for armed forces, as this suggests that soldiers may comply with moral norms without the need for strict rules or accountability mechanisms that could hinder their effectiveness in combat.

Virtue ethics is a more comprehensive system than the others I discuss, in the sense that it is not simply a set of restrictions. It also provides motives for action and structures the group life of communities governed by common values. Because virtues are context and actor relative, groups of people in similar roles have shared conceptions of virtue that build solidarity. This is especially true for soldiers. Their contexts of action are unlike those of civilian life and mark soldiers as fundamentally different from civilians when it comes to their status and obligations. Thus, virtue ethics can simultaneously provide guidance and a sense of professional identity.

Virtue ethics helps to rationalize the harsh conditions of military life. Aristotle thinks the goal of virtue is *eudaimonia*, which can be translated as flourishing or happiness.[9] Happiness is a subjective judgment, whereas *eudaimonia* is something a person has or lacks regardless of their subjective feelings. Military life is short on pleasure and may not be conducive to happiness, as soldiers undergo intense training regimes, long periods of boredom, high stress, a lack of privacy, and myriad other challenges.[10] Yet it is because military life is demanding that it can promote *eudaimonia*. Hardships push soldiers to reach higher levels of excellence (*arete*), which is one of the central goals of virtue ethics. Virtue ethics is therefore capable of explaining why the hardships of military life are central to the ethical experience of being a soldier.

Finally, virtue ethics promotes supererogatory actions—actions that go beyond what is morally required. A praiseworthy warrior is not one who does the bare minimum but one who single-handedly defeats scores of opponents or risks his life to save his comrades. The pursuit of virtuousness urges soldiers to aspire to the highest levels of excellence, while ethical systems that only distinguish moral from immoral conduct struggle to provide a rationale for exceptional conduct.

Despite its compelling advantages, virtue ethics suffers from some serious limitations. First, and most importantly, allowing soldiers to rely on their own judgment when making moral decisions is a limitation just as much as it is a strength. This freedom means soldiers endure an extremely heavy ethical burden. Commanders may instruct subordinates to exercise their own judgment when encountering dilemmas rather than following standardized rules or procedures. This raises the risk of commanders displacing their own responsibilities onto their subordinates by giving those subordinates few guidelines while still holding them responsible for misconduct. Commanders not wishing to overtly order unethical or illegal actions may instead encourage their subordinates to perform those actions by allowing them to exercise their own judgment without supervision.[11]

Second, as I show in the case study of the US Army, virtue ethics education is extremely demanding for those who must learn to be virtuous as well as for the institutions that train them. Whereas other normative systems may only require soldiers to follow certain rules or decision procedures without undergoing any substantive personal transformation, training recruits to be virtuous entails the reconstruction of their character. Soldiers must endure the destruction of their civilian selves and be rebuilt according to the military's model of virtue. From an institutional standpoint, affecting a substantive transformation in the character of recruits requires a great deal of time and resources. There is also a high risk that anyone who fails to undergo this change will remain an outsider.

Third, there is a tendency for military leaders to think that calling a characteristic a "virtue" or a "value" is sufficient to establish that it promotes good conduct. Timothy Challans criticizes this tendency, correctly pointing out that many proclaimed virtues are vacuous and some can even be harmful.[12] Especially concerning are the virtues that seem to be good when formally defined but are prone to misinterpretation, thereby giving the appearance of high moral standards without adequate restraint.

Finally, because virtues are context and actor relative, virtue ethics establishes few clear prohibitions or requirements. This makes it difficult to determine when a person has acted well or badly, thereby interfering with efforts to employ standards for judging soldiers' conduct. Virtue ethics even suggests that outsiders with different conceptions of virtue may be incapable of passing judgment on soldiers because of the deep rift between their values. This risks promoting exceptionalist thinking and discouraging respect for outside authorities, including the civilian administrators who are supposed to oversee the use of armed force.

Deontology

Deontological theories formulate rules of conduct that specify which actions are forbidden, permitted, or required. They may either determine an action's moral status based on whether it conforms with a rule or they may determine its status based on the actor's intentions to comply with a rule. Immanuel Kant's is probably the most well-known deontological theory and is often the one used to exemplify this style of thinking, but the deontology evident in systems of military ethics is usually not Kantian in form.[13] Whereas Kant argues that good actions require good will—the intentional performance of good actions—deontological ethics in a military context is primarily concerned with promoting obedience to specific guidelines that more clearly dictate what actions should be performed than virtues are able to. Intentions still matter, but generally only insofar as promoting the right intentions can ensure adherence to the rules.

What distinguishes deontological moral theories from alternatives is that deontological theories treat rules as being good and worthy of respect in themselves. An action is good or bad simply based on whether it conforms to moral rules. The action's consequences matter, but these are of secondary importance. Following the rules may therefore be considered good, even if doing so produces harmful effects, while violating them is bad even if doing so produces better results in some instances. The rationale for prioritizing rules over consequences is that rules are universal in scope and can be applied impartially. Permitting exceptions is dangerous because this can erode rules' authority and encourage individuals to exercise their own judgment, which can ultimately help to rationalize deviance. In other words, deontology privileges consistency at the expense of flexibility.

Deontological theories reject virtue ethics' actor relativity and context relativity. Moral rules apply to all people, or at least to all people in certain roles, regardless of character or context. This allows deontological theories to establish clear and coherent standards of conduct that facilitate application by actors and judgments from observers. Treating rules as absolute and inviolable standards that apply universally and impartially also protects them from the whims of individual judgment in particular circumstances.

Deontological theories make weak assumptions about ethics training. They usually only assume actors know the rules and have the capacity to follow them. Knowing the rules is a matter of learning what actions are forbidden, permitted, and required. This knowledge alone is generally treated as being sufficient for promoting good behavior. Consequently, institutions relying on deontological reasoning tend to devote less attention to training actors in the practical wisdom of *phronesis* or in critically evaluating the rules themselves. The primary task of ethics training is to ensure that actors understand the rules, that they are capable of recalling them in practice, and that rules can cover whatever novel challenges may arise.

Although the *form* of deontological reasoning can be defined in terms of rule following, their exact *content* can vary considerably. Philosophers generally favor deontological theories that include one or a few broad rules that can cover many different circumstances.[14] This ensures that rules can apply to the myriad ethical challenges a person might confront, but it comes at the expense of vagueness. The broader a rule is, the more difficult it is to decide what course of action is called for. Armed forces generally pursue the opposite strategy, creating many specific rules to collectively cover an array of challenges soldiers might encounter. This reduces the demand on soldiers for abstract ethical reasoning, although it does require them to memorize longer lists of rules and assumes they will be able to recall them in extremely stressful situations.

The clearest manifestations of deontological thinking in a military context are in the laws governing war, which are collectively known as the law of armed conflict (LOAC) or international humanitarian law. Armed forces operationalize these using rules of engagement (ROE) that reflect legal restrictions as well as narrower ethical and strategic demands. Laws epitomize deontological thinking because they are strict, explicit statements of good conduct backed by institutions and potentially enforceable in a way that moral precepts alone may not be. The LOAC formed from the Geneva and Hague Conventions as well as from treaties and customary law that establish inviolable boundaries of conduct that pertain in all circumstances and for all combatants. The customary roots of some international law suggests an element of pragmatism, with norms gradually accumulating over time until the point they can be said to qualify as laws. This means that, from a historical perspective, LOAC shows a continuity between the kind of pragmatic norm formation I discuss later in the chapter and deontology. However, it is important to note that once the norms are recognized as being customary law, they become fixed and universally binding, losing the fluidity and contextual sensitivity that are hallmarks of pragmatism. This is especially true for soldiers, for whom LOAC has the character of an established doctrine that must be applied in a deontological sense. Soldiers are not directly concerned with the historical development of custom but rather find themselves faced with a code of laws that they tend to see as a rulebook establishing clear boundaries.

The ROE are issued by a specific military and may change depending on context and mission. Soldiers are given ROE that provide instructions on the proper use of force and direct their responses to various types of threats. These can differ a great deal cross-nationally and even within a particular military, depending on its objectives. They are typically short lists that fit onto a single page or onto an ROE card that soldiers can carry, with the rules themselves expressed as short declarative statements about what they may or may not do. For example, one rule from an ROE card used by Americans in Iraq states, "Do not fire into civilian populated areas or buildings unless the enemy is using them for military purposes or if necessary for your self-defense."

A Rule-Governed Approach to War

Deontological theories have three main advantages in military settings. First, rules provide clear standards that reduce the ethical burden on soldiers and facilitate impartial evaluations of their actions. Clear rules reduce the burden on soldiers by ensuring they know what standards they will be held to. Soldiers who want to act ethically can do so by following the rules they are given, without having to anticipate what consequences their actions may have and without being responsible for exercising their own judgment, except insofar as they must choose which rules to follow. Rules facilitate evaluation by others, both inside and outside of the military. It is much easier to see when soldiers have followed explicit guidelines than it is to determine when soldiers are virtuous or when their actions led to the best possible outcome.

Second, deontological ethics education is less invasive than virtue ethics education. From a deontological standpoint, soldiers do not have to have good character, nor do they need to be virtuous, so long as they are capable of following the rules. Thus, recruits do not have to undergo rigorous character reeducation. Their civilian selves may be left largely intact, and contact with the civilian world does not threaten to compromise soldiers' integrity. This also reduces the institutional demands of training, freeing armed forces from the burdens of remaking recruits at a fundamental level or socializing them into a distinctive culture. Lowering the costs associated with transforming civilians into soldiers makes deontological theories particularly attractive for militaries that have limited resources for training, that want to maintain close civil-military links, or that employ soldiers for short periods of time.

Finally, deontological systems may be appealing for civilian administrators and high-ranking military commanders because rules facilitate centralized control. They can be created by those at the highest levels and passed down through the chain of command much easier than ethical theories that depend heavily on contextual considerations or are in some way relativistic. The capacity for centralization is attractive in a military context because it provides commanders with some assurance they will be able to manage their personnel and predict how they will act during deployments.

Deontological theories developed by philosophers tend to be unpopular with military ethicists.[15] They are often regarded as being too abstract and troublesome to put into practice or as being too strict and unforgiving of actions performed under exceptional circumstances.[16] In some situations strict rules may even endanger soldiers, such as when they must follow an escalation of force procedure that may slow their response to a potential threat. Even just war theorists, who attempt to formulate general rules of war, often introduce exceptions that allow their rules to be suspended.[17] These commentators raise an important concern when they say abstract rules may be prohibitively difficult to apply to specific circumstances, particularly when decisions must be made quickly or under pressure.

Even the more narrowly focused deontological ethical systems developed for soldiers suffer from some limitations. Although rules are generally framed as being exhaustive guides, they cannot possibly live up to this goal; they are necessarily incomplete. The ROE provide a prime example of this. The ROE generally state when force can be used, how it can be used, and who may be targeted, but they cannot cover every eventuality.[18] Wars are unpredictable, and events regularly occur that take soldiers beyond what is covered by their ROE. When this happens, soldiers following deontological systems may be left with little guidance unless they can resort to some alternative form of ethical reasoning. And those reasoning skills may be lacking if soldiers have been conditioned to rely heavily on rules without thinking critically about their meaning.[19]

Some rules are frustrating for soldiers who feel that they are poorly formulated or that the rule makers do not understand the experiences of those who are bound by them. During interviews, I regularly heard complaints from soldiers who thought that their ROE prevented them from relying on their own judgment or acting on initiative. Soldiers' narratives are also replete with complaints about excessively strict ROE. The ROE were especially objectionable when they reflected the policies of civilian administrators or high-ranking military commanders who were perceived as being distant from the realities of the battlefield and who were not exposed to the same dangers as frontline soldiers. For example, US marine Michael Golembesky complains that when his unit wanted to call in air support against Taliban fighters, "the rules of engagement and General [Stanley] McChrystal's tactical directive forbade us from doing that, so we'd just have to endure until the situation became just shy of hopeless."[20]

Consequentialism

The defining characteristic of consequentialism is that the morality of an action is judged according to its results, without considering the actor's intentions or character. Guilt or innocence is a function of what a person *does* and not who a person *is* or what a person *meant* to do. Consequentialism comes in many forms that privilege different types of outcomes and provide different ways of allowing potential consequences to guide actions.

The most popular variant of consequentialism in moral theory is utilitarianism, which evaluates actions based on whether they secure the greatest good for the greatest number of people. The greatest good may be judged hedonistically as being simply the greatest aggregate pleasure or according to a more nuanced standard that distinguishes between higher and lower pleasures.[21] Utilitarians also disagree about whether the utility judgment must be applied to every action or whether it can be used to extrapolate rules that identify the course of action that tends to promote the greatest good. These disagreements are extremely important when analyzing utilitarianism as a theory, but in practice the consequentialism employed by militaries is usually not utilitarian in the strict sense because soldiers are not primarily concerned with the maximization of pleasure or happiness.

In a military context, the good that consequentialists use to determine the right course of action is usually proportionality—the tradeoff between lives lost or material destroyed and objectives achieved. An action is considered good or bad depending on whether it offers the best tradeoff of costs and benefits. By this standard, an attack that kills twenty civilians is ethically inferior to an attack that kills ten civilians (assuming they accomplish the same objective), and an attack that can achieve that objective without any loss of life is better still. The reason any killing can be excused is that it is necessary for securing some other desirable outcome ranging from immediate military objectives to more abstract political goals. The consequentialism employed by militaries acknowledges that a range of different goods affect moral calculations, though these goods are rarely given clear values or ranked against each other in practice. This obscures the exact weighting of different courses of action and interferes with evaluating whether consequentialist standards are being fairly applied.

Consequentialism in systems of military ethics also differs from utilitarianism in its particularistic orientation. Utilitarianism is a universalistic theory in the sense that it makes all actors equally responsible for promoting the greatest good for the greatest number of people. It does not privilege particular people or groups, nor does it allow judgments to vary according to actor and context. By contrast, the consequentialism employed in systems of military ethics, at least those I discuss in this book, tend to reject universalism in favor of promoting national interests. This kind of consequentialism, which I characterize as "partisan consequentialism," does not count all people equally when determining whose good should be maximized. Rather, it gives greater weight to the country soldiers belong to. Allies are also important, but usually to a lesser extent. Neutrals follow next, then opponents, whose lives may be worth little or nothing.

Managing the Consequences of War

Perhaps the greatest benefit of consequentialism in military ethics is that it is intuitive. It is appealing to think that norms should help us achieve the best outcomes. If rules of conduct fail to produce good outcomes or if good character does not in any way add value to our lives, then it is unclear why we should want to follow rules or cultivate good character. This intuitive appeal may also make consequentialism easier to implement. We naturally tend to make decisions with an eye toward producing optimal results. Choosing the best course of action does not require a soldier to have good character or to memorize rules. Rather, it only assumes the soldier will be able to assess the good and bad results that actions may have.

Even more important is partisan consequentialism's admonition that normative evaluations can favor certain individuals or groups over others. Opponents of universalistic moral theories like deontology or utilitarianism argue that universalism wrongly treats actors as being atoms detached from group memberships and connections to others. They argue that ethics should reflect our particularistic attachments and that we should be able to give preferential treatment to those who we are naturally inclined to favor.[22] Partisan consequentialism can be defended on this basis. We generally feel special obligations to members of our nation, and we feel special obligations toward co-nationals that we do not owe to others. Soldiers in particular are supposed to be motivated by nationalism. They protect the state and fellow citizens against opponents and kill other people in a collective act of national self-defense. The suspicion of private military contractors is largely premised on claims that they do not feel the right kind of nationalistic attachments. It therefore seems intuitively plausible that soldiers should be partial to their own country and their fellow citizens when making ethical decisions.

The foremost disadvantage of partisan consequentialism is that it verges on not qualifying as a moral theory at all. When ethics are driven by national interests such as protecting the state, its citizens, or its foreign policy objectives, it risks becoming nothing more than a legitimizing narrative for the kinds of practices that moral theories should be designed to prohibit. Norms should be able to impose some restraints on actors, and a theory of military ethics should be able to limit uses of force. If partisan consequentialism becomes so permissive that it can justify any use of force, then it loses its restrictive capacity.

When the protection of national interest is privileged over all else, consequentialism provides a basis for bending or even violating international law. This puts consequentialism in tension with deontological thinking and can lead the two theories to reach divergent conclusions about controversies relating to the use of force. This is why just war theorists, who rely more heavily on deontology, and utilitarians often disagree about fundamental issues related to the morality of war.[23] Deontological theories are capable of setting clear, inviolable limits on certain kinds of conduct. They can prohibit the use of torture, targeted killings, or attacks on civilians. Consequentialism based on national interest, by contrast, can permit virtually anything. If the good that is being achieved is the protection of national interest or saving the lives of members of the home country, then it becomes particularly easy to employ consequentialism as a standard for justifying extreme actions. This is why justifications for practices that are widely considered to be morally reprehensible in any form are often presented in a consequentialist guise.

Proponents of torture routinely justify the practice by presenting ticking-bomb scenarios, in which a bomb is set to explode and the only way to discover it is to torture a suspected terrorist—an action that would ordinarily be considered immoral but that might become permissible because it can save thousands or even millions of lives that arguably count for more than the life of the terrorist being tortured.[24] Consequentialist reasoning also figures heavily in justifications for violating noncombatant immunity.[25] This is evident from the rationale for dropping atomic bombs on Hiroshima and Nagasaki. Those attacks arguably saved more lives than would have been lost if the United States had attempted to invade Japan, making them morally preferable to invasion when judged using consequentialism.[26]

Another problem that not only interferes with partisan consequentialism but also universalistic versions of consequentialism, such as utilitarianism, is that it can be difficult to predict what effects choices may have. Some capacity to forecast outcomes is essential for ascertaining which course of action is right, and any impediments to prediction limit an actor's ability to make an ethical decision. This is a well-known problem of consequentialism that is regularly invoked by its opponents.[27] Predicting the potential costs and benefits of choices made during war is even more onerous than in domestic settings because of the complexity of wartime environments, enemy deception, and the networks of interdependencies between soldiers.

Pragmatism

For pragmatists, norms are not theoretical abstractions but instead emerge out of the practices they are meant to regulate—usually in response to specific recurrent challenges. The result is that ethical systems are not always fully formed guides. Rather, pragmatic ethics exist more as a network of interrelated norms linked together by the collective activities that give rise to them. Pragmatists avoid identifying fixed and unalterable norms and typically reject definitive answers to moral problems. Instead they argue that norms are open to dispute and revision.[28] At the same time, because norms are connected to a group's way of life, the norms may resist change unless there is some major disruption that prompts a search for new protocols. The engagement with specific problems also means that there is not a single version of pragmatist ethics; there may be multiple versions that uphold radically different and even contradictory norms. Even within the military context, pragmatism could take countless forms depending on variations in military doctrine and the roles that soldiers perform. Thus, of the four approaches I identify, pragmatism is the most difficult to systematize and the one that is most heavily grounded in a group's traditions.

Without any universal norms existing outside of practices, pragmatists find it impossible to take a neutral evaluative viewpoint from which different norms can be compared. Separate communities may disagree substantially and have no way of getting beyond their own perspectives. This creates a dilemma when different communities interact: whether to respect other norms as equally valid or whether to reject divergent perspectives even without a strong independent rationale for doing so. The former approach suggests a conciliatory attitude founded on mutual recognition and respect, while the latter suggests the outcome of intergroup contact may be a contest of values that cannot be resolved rationally or with appeals to evidence. It may even lead to violent assertions of one body of norms over another. Which strategy is taken depends on the communities involved and whether their internal value systems urge respect or hostility toward other perspectives.

John Dewey, one of the formative influences on pragmatic ethics, argues that overcoming ethical problems is not merely a matter of altering the world but also changing ourselves and our desires.[29] He says we must distinguish reasonable from unreasonable desires, and we must critically evaluate whether the consequences we hope to achieve remain reasonable. Pragmatists typically acknowledge that norms are always open to revision and that other communities have their own competing norms that are equally valid. This generally leads pragmatists to endorse pluralism, which in turn makes it difficult to justify the kinds of extreme actions that might be sanctioned by partisan consequentialism, such as targeting civilians or torture.[30] However, pragmatism does not require this kind of open-mindedness and may not do so when it arises in military contexts. For armed forces, the emergent values are more apt to be exclusionary and even hostile to other value systems. One especially strong risk is that military traditionalism may hinder efforts to reform a system of ethics, thereby preventing norms accumulated throughout past conflicts from adapting as the nature of ethical challenges shifts.

Pragmatic ethics arise as norms are abstracted out of practices, institutions, and cultures to take on the special status of being ethical guides. A pragmatist ethic will therefore reflect the attributes and practices of the groups that give rise to the norms. The emergent character of the norms means the communities following them may resist the theoretical elaboration of ethics. Any attempt to theorize ethics threatens to divorce it from the practical activities in which it is embedded. Thus, this style of thinking is often at work when organizations describe their ethics as a living and adapting system that cannot be precisely set out in writing. Such systems may be loosely codified but with caveats that preserve this open-ended character.

Emergent Norms

The foremost advantage of pragmatism is that it bridges the gap between theory and practice. Because pragmatic norms are generated by ongoing practices, they are naturally applicable to the situations they are meant to govern without needing any kind of reformulation or operationalization. Pragmatism is also problem oriented. Ethical guidelines are derived from encounters with a particular problem, and once norms have developed they can be consistently reapplied to analogous challenges. Following pragmatic ethics is therefore much easier than following abstract norms, at least in principle. This is a particularly important characteristic in a military setting, as soldiers must make decisions under extraordinarily difficult circumstances that may prevent them from employing complex decision procedures or abstract moral norms but may nevertheless be resolved by relying on established practices for responding to the problem at hand.

Second, pragmatism is likely to have minimal formal training requirements. A pragmatist ethic is one that requires little if any education in ethics as a distinctive subject. Norms can be learned by being a participant in the shared activities that generate them. To some extent this is true of virtue ethics as well, as virtues must likewise be learned through practical activities and enculturation. However, whereas virtue ethics may demand character development to the extent that new recruits virtually become new people, pragmatism can permit a diverse range of individuals and different character types so long as they accept the group's norms and participate in the collective activities that unify the group. That is, pragmatism may call for a convergence of behavior without necessarily requiring all members of a group to embody the same character traits.

As with the other theories I have discussed, pragmatism has some disadvantages. Like partisan consequentialism, pragmatism runs the risk of permitting too much. Any ethic that is abstracted out of ongoing practices may arguably not be moral at all but only the idealization of nonmoral or immoral practices. This leaves pragmatism open to the objection that any guidelines generated pragmatically need to be critically evaluated according to some external standard that can be used to decide whether they should be accepted as moral precepts.

A second problem is that although pragmatic ethical theories overcome the need for translating theory into practice, they are prone to the opposite problem. Pragmatic norms are hard to codify and may therefore fail to provide clear standards of conduct. This raises the possibility that soldiers will be held to ambiguous or unstable standards. It is difficult to evaluate soldiers' conduct or to justifiably punish their misdeeds without having some sense of what they should have done and evidence that they should have known the right course of action. The lack of clear standards is especially troublesome when soldiers encounter novel ethical challenges for which there are no established norms. They may have no way of knowing what others would consider acceptable behavior until after their decisions are made.

Finally, because pragmatic norms are derived from specific practices, they are contextually grounded and reflect existing biases. Richard Rorty, one of the leading proponents of pragmatism, goes so far as to describe his own endorsement of liberal values as ethnocentric because his support for them comes through a specific cultural lens.[31] He and other pragmatists may think this kind of ethnocentrism is unavoidable or even desirable, yet universalists object to this and maintain that ethics should drive us to abandon biases, at least for the purpose of making moral judgments. This problem is particularly important when members of groups with radically different values come into contact, as they do during counterinsurgency operations.

Hybrid Theories and Operationalizing Ethics

Few, if any, armed forces follow a single moral philosophy. Instead, they tend to construct hybrid systems that have affinities with two or more theories, mixing various influences to produce unique constellations of moral thinking. Hybrid systems come in many forms depending on what elements they incorporate and how these are organized. For example, David Fisher advocates "virtuous consequentialism," which combines virtue ethics' reliance on individual judgment and emphasis on habituation with consequentialism's commitment to evaluating the moral worth of actions by looking at their effects.[32] Hybrid systems may privilege a single philosophy while employing others in subordinate roles or they may invoke different norms to govern different types of challenges. As I will show in the case studies, the American and British armies exemplify the former strategy. They incorporate various influences but rely predominantly on virtue-based and pragmatic ethics, respectively. The Israel Defense Forces takes the latter approach by specifying when soldiers should follow rules and when those rules should be suspended in favor of consequentialist evaluations.

Deontology is the most common source of moral guidance because it is embodied in the LOAC. The prohibitions on targeting civilians, abusing prisoners of war, and using weapons that inflict excessive suffering are set out as universally binding norms that soldiers of all countries must follow. The LOAC therefore takes on the status of a fundamental, inviolable code that transcends national divisions and establishes a degree of moral uniformity across the three militaries I investigate. As I show later, this shared deontological framework can account for some of the ethical similarities between militaries, especially when it comes to how they make use of force decisions in combat. Although the laws of war promote cross-national agreement, they are an incomplete guide, only covering some of the myriad dilemmas that soldiers may encounter. This leaves militaries free to rely on different ethical systems to fill in the gaps.

In addition to LOAC, deontological thinking appears in the ROE. These are formulated in accordance with the laws of war, but they go beyond what is contained in them. The ROE attempt to operationalize laws with clear instructions that soldiers can employ when they are in the field. Despite the shared understanding that the LOAC must constrain soldiers, the ROE can vary cross-nationally and even across different units in the same military. They are shaped by the local circumstances, how the law is interpreted, and what aspects of the law are emphasized. The George W. Bush administration's insistence that certain forms of interrogation, such as waterboarding and sleep deprivation, do not qualify as torture illustrates how even a firm legal prohibition can give rise to competing interpretations and, therefore, to contrary applications of the law.

Militaries may even take different attitudes toward how the ROE should be framed. Rules may set broad limits on what actions are prohibited or required while still giving soldiers considerable freedom. When deontology plays this subordinate role, another ethical theory is needed to guide soldiers through the myriad decisions they must resolve without relying on the laws or ROE. In a system more heavily based on deontological thinking, the ROE expand to cover a greater range of contingencies and to restrict soldiers' independence. It is possible to determine whether rules are supportive or the primary source of direction by looking at how expansive the rules are, what exceptions are permitted, and how they are weighted against other sources of guidance.

Despite the prevalence of hybrid systems, it is important to recognize that the appearance of eclecticism is sometimes misleading. The language or concepts of moral theory may be borrowed without that theory having much of a role in practice. In such instances, what appears to be a mixing of influences is only the presentation of one type of moral thinking in the guise of another. The superficial endorsement of certain elements of a theory that really has only limited influence is clearest with respect to virtue ethics. Studies tend to find virtue ethics at work in many armed forces and often cite the widespread use of the language of "virtues," "values," and "character" across the world's militaries as evidence of this. While it is true that virtue ethics influences many armed forces, it is often wrongly attributed to those that employ some of its language without actually incorporating that theory's defining elements.

Contemporary militaries typically affirm codes of virtues or values, yet these are often stated as organizational characteristics, rather than as characteristics of the individuals who are members of the organizations. This is a critical distinction. Virtue ethics is primarily a theory of individual character, and while the appropriate virtues for an individual can be identified by looking at a person's group membership and roles, the individual remains the focus. Attention to organizational characteristics is more indicative of pragmatism, with its interest in how norms arise out of shared practices enacted by multiple actors. Another clue that some talk of virtues is misleading is when it is detached from the substantive character-formation programs that virtue ethics demands. Virtue ethics is not merely a matter of articulating ideal traits but of practicing them so exhaustively that they become embedded in a person's character.

The clearest advantage of hybrid systems is that they may be constructed to overcome some of the limitations characteristic of each of the theories I have discussed, as no theory is without its drawbacks. Those that are more theoretically rigorous may be more difficult to employ in practice, while those that have a more practical orientation may be insufficiently strict and prone to manipulation. Ideally, the right mixture of elements from different moral theories may offer a way of offsetting these limitations and creating systems that provide strong practical guidance without sacrificing their ability to restrict the use of force. For example, Fisher's virtuous consequentialism relies heavily on virtues to guide soldiers through ethical dilemmas but appeals to consequentialist reasoning to resolve dilemmas when virtues conflict or the virtue-based guidance is unclear.[33] Incorporating some deontological elements is important because this can impose clear, absolute limits on how soldiers may act and foster cross-national agreement about what constitutes good conduct. Beyond this, the advantages of hybrid systems depend on which sources are appropriated and how they are arranged. This will become clearer as I explore the different combinations of influences evident from the American, British, and Israeli armed forces.

Although hybrid systems may be used to overcome the limitations of individual systems employed in isolation, they are not without their own failings. Mixing moral philosophies comes at the risk of inconsistency. Each theory depends on fundamentally different and irreconcilable presuppositions. For example, deontological rules are supposed to apply uniformly regardless of the actor, while virtue ethics assumes that different people may justifiably take different actions under the same circumstances. Similarly, virtue ethics' and pragmatism's disagreement between whether moral guidance should come from good character or from group norms may create rifts between individualists and collectivists. The potential for conflict even exists within a hybrid system that is largely pragmatic. Although pragmatism is potentially the most amenable to diversity, it must still resist the influence of totalizing systems of ethics that would impose a single determinant form that would constrain its openness.

Theoretically incoherent systems are not only problematic from a philosophical perspective but may also create problems for soldiers. If soldiers are directed to follow multiple influences, they may be left unsure of which norms to employ. When different systems have equal weight, they also risk being employed opportunistically, allowing soldiers to rely on the one that can provide the best excuse for misconduct in a particular situation. Such opportunism raises the possibility that ethics may lose its power to restrict the use of force and promote good conduct and that it will instead simply become a narrative for legitimizing whatever action soldiers wish to take.

Conclusion

The theories I presented in this chapter are complex and come in an array of variants that are beyond the scope of this book. My overview is not comprehensive but rather an attempt to highlight the general characteristics of the different styles of ethical thinking and to consider how they can be applied by militaries. This provides a basis for analyzing how the theories are deliberately enacted by militaries or how the underlying reasoning appears inadvertently in systems of military ethics. Armed forces do not adopt these philosophies wholesale but rather appropriate elements of them and arrange them into hybrids that bear the marks of different styles. This is why it is important to move beyond the ideal types by giving more attention to implementation. From a philosophical standpoint, the hybrids tend to weaken the theories by introducing contradictions and competing foundational assumptions. Any challenges created by combining various influences are usually inconsequential from the perspective of the armed forces or individual soldiers. Militaries and their members have only an indirect concern with moral philosophy. They rarely invoke the theories they borrow from explicitly, instead relying on less formalized advice or intuitive senses of norms that lack philosophical rigor and can therefore be combined without generating the same puzzles one might find in moral philosophy. Their goal is to develop ethical systems that work—systems that can regularize behavior when commanders are unable to directly observe and control their subordinates.

Whatever their theoretical shortcomings, the hybrid systems reflect efforts to reconcile different moral impulses in ways that realize complementary benefits. In particular, hybrid systems show widespread assent to the LOAC. When it comes to their formalized ethics doctrines, each military included in this study takes international law as an inviolable foundation, framing norms that may be grounded in other perspectives. This is the shared core that produces some consistency in soldiers' attitudes and behavior cross-nationally. Differences between the countries tend to arise when other ethical systems inform actions that are not covered by international law or when they shape the interpretation of laws. These are the instances in which cross-national variation is clearest and most significant.

3

Constraints on Ethical Reasoning in Combat

Wars place people in situations that are radically different from anything they experience in civilian life, disrupting the norms that prevail during peacetime. It is impossible to evaluate soldiers' decisions without considering how the exceptional circumstances of war shape the context of ethical reasoning. Soldiers do not confront ethical challenges as detached observers who are free to carefully weigh their options and arrive at thoughtful conclusions. They are not like the idealized actors of moral thought experiments, who operate in a vacuum and with all of their faculties intact. Rather, they encounter unexpected dilemmas under strict time constraints and while lives are at risk. They make decisions under the weight of powerful structural and psychological constraints that shape what kinds of decision procedures they can employ.

Broadly speaking, there are two types of circumstantial impediments to soldiers' ethical reasoning, which I label "situational constraints" and "cognitive constraints." The former are independent of individual soldiers' mental states and determine the overall context in which decisions are made. They include chance occurrences that are beyond control (which are experienced as luck), information shortages that make it difficult to assess the potential costs and benefits of different courses of action (which are experienced as uncertainty), and institutional constraints on action (which are experienced as the demands of mission performance, obedience to orders, and loyalty to comrades). Cognitive constraints include strong emotions, especially fear and anger, or other cognitive impediments, such as sleep deprivation. Cognitive constraints have external referents and are partly produced by situational constraints, yet they are nevertheless cognitive in the sense that they interfere with moral judgment at its source by influencing how soldiers perceive or respond to ethical dilemmas. The affective dimensions of ethical reasoning are felt directly and often in powerful ways that can interfere with rational calculations.

There is some overlap between the constraints I discuss and the related distinction some psychologists draw between situational and dispositional explanations for individual behavior, especially when it comes to situational constraints.[1] However, dispositional characteristics are often associated with enduring traits like personality, while I am commenting on only short-term cognitive impairments that persist when soldiers are in contested areas. The situational and cognitive constraints I discuss in this chapter are not meant as an exhaustive typology of all the conditions that may inhibit or alter a soldier's judgment. Rather, I focus on the factors that appear to present the most pervasive and serious barriers to ethical reasoning on the battlefield based on my interviews, soldiers' published narratives, and existing research on military psychology. I describe these as "constraints," "barriers," or "impediments" to suggest that they usually impact soldiers without forcing them to act in particular ways.[2] These constraints should be seen as nondeterministic background conditions that influence ethical reasoning and the information that is available but do not exhaust the moral reasoning process.

The situational and cognitive constraints are important to bear in mind when studying systems of military ethics, as any viable system must be able to contend with them. An ethic that fails to account for these constraints would hold soldiers to unreasonable standards and fail to provide effective guidance. The constraints also grant insight into where improvements can be made. The soldiers I spoke with consistently cited epistemic challenges associated with clearly identifying enemy combatants as being the most serious barrier to acting rightly. This uncertainty could be so profound that interviewees sometimes felt they were only guessing at the right course of action. The extent of this problem indicates that normative improvements could be made with efforts to reduce uncertainty (such as with improved intelligence or by avoiding situations in which uncertainty was particularly troubling) or by lowering the costs of missteps (such as by arming soldiers with nonlethal weapons or developing more effective escalation of force procedures).

The first section of this chapter discusses the situational constraints on ethical reasoning, emphasizing the importance of uncertainty as a background condition of ethical dilemmas and discussing some of the scenarios in which soldiers are apt to experience high levels of uncertainty. The second section considers several types of cognitive constraints: acute stress, chronic stress, and sleep deprivation. At times soldiers may be unable to engage in ethical reasoning when they are overwhelmed by these cognitive constraints, but most of the soldiers I spoke to found that this rarely occurred because of the extensive training and preparation they underwent before deployment. Finally, in the third section I argue that in most instances the constraints are not deterministic and that they therefore interfere with ethical reasoning to varying degrees without making it impossible.

Situational Constraints

Uncertainty is a pervasive condition of war. One rarely knows an enemy's intentions or capacity, and a competent enemy is apt to deceive and hinder intelligence collection. The location of civilians and risks to them may likewise be unknown, especially in urban areas and in unconventional conflicts against enemies who attempt to blend in with the local population. Even the position and intent of allies can be uncertain, as evidenced by friendly fire incidents.

Epistemic problems, such as lack of information or inaccurate information, are among the most ethically challenging situational constraints. These had some influence on almost every story I heard from interview participants. Many interviewees discussed scenarios in which they were forced to make decisions involving matters of life and death with insufficient information. Lack of relevant information needed to make ethical decisions was most troublesome for soldiers who guarded convoys or worked at roadblocks, and it was in these instances that "identity uncertainty" (uncertainty about the identity of the people involved in the ethical dilemma) was clearest. Soldiers in these roles continually faced the problem of determining how to respond to vehicles whose occupants could not be identified. Those inside the vehicles were invisible adversaries, leaving soldiers to guess at whether they should be treated as civilians or insurgents. Soldiers guarding convoys or roadblocks had to routinely judge approaching vehicles to make quick decisions about whether to attack, at the risk of harming innocent people, or whether to hold fire, at the risk of coming under attack from hidden gunmen or a suicide bomb. In many instances, there were no clear visual indicators that could help soldiers with this choice, leaving them to make educated guesses about the right course of action.

One American told me about an incident in which he saw a car speeding toward his checkpoint and attempted to stop it using the normal escalation of force procedure: Show, Shout, Shove, Shoot.[3] With only seconds to spare, he moved quickly to the step of firing warning shots. These had no effect, leaving the soldier with just a few seconds to decide whether to fire directly at the vehicle before it could reach him. The soldier said he could not identify the driver or passengers, and he could not bring himself to fire because of his uncertainty about whether they were hostile. When the vehicle reached the checkpoint, the interviewee saw it was a family with children. The father had sped toward the checkpoint even after hearing the warning shots because he thought his family was under attack and wanted to reach safety. The incident stuck in his mind as a clear example of how difficult it could be to identify threats correctly and of the high costs of miscalculations.

Identity uncertainty came primarily from people being hidden inside of vehicles but was compounded by environmental conditions, such as darkness and obstructions in the soldiers' field of vision. Another American was guarding a checkpoint at night and fired warning shots at an approaching motorcycle that did not respond to his verbal warnings.[4] The motorcycle stopped as the bullets passed by, but when the soldier approached it he was horrified to see that what he thought was a motorcycle was actually a car missing a headlight. The warning shots he tried to fire past the vehicle had gone through the windshield and nearly killed its occupants. The interviewee was relieved that he did not injure the passengers but said the incident brought him terrifyingly close to accidentally killing innocent people. As in the previous story, the soldier faced the challenge of guessing who might be approaching, but the situation was even more profoundly affected by uncertainty because he did not even have a clear sense of what type of vehicle was in front of him. These two soldiers, as well as many of the others I spoke with, recounted many incidents like these, emphasizing that uncertainty frequently brought them close to inadvertently killing civilians.

The effects of uncertainty on ethical decision-making can vary in intensity. At times soldiers thought it was only a minor impediment. It might limit the range of options available while still leaving them free to make an informed choice. At other times uncertainty was so extreme that soldiers felt they were unable to seriously consider the moral implications of their actions. The intense stress and time constraints on decision-making added to this. One Royal Marines Commando I spoke with said, "Sometimes you don't have the information to make the decisions when you're in contact. The morality changes in the situation somewhat."[5]

As these examples show, soldiers may have to make decisions without reliable information about what choice they face or who is involved. Each of the theories I discuss in the previous chapter presupposes that actors have some knowledge of a situation before they can apply the reasoning procedure effectively. When they lack essential background information, soldiers encounter what I call an "ethically insoluble dilemma"—a dilemma that cannot be clearly resolved using norms or decision procedures. Ethics may still help in these situations, for example, by urging restraint under conditions of profound uncertainty, yet without providing a clear good course of action. These dilemmas force soldiers to guess at the right decision with virtually no information about the exact ethical challenge they are confronting or the potential consequences, meaning that every decision entails fairly high risk. This plays into deeper feelings of fatalism that are already rampant during war. As Jonathan Shay explains, "Battle creates inexplicable events that soldiers experience as luck. These run from astounding good luck to crushing bad luck that taints the very soul."[6] The psychological cost of having the bad luck of mistakenly attacking civilians or watching idly as comrades are killed is particularly high, leading to feelings of guilt and remorse that increase the pressure to make the right choices.

Cognitive Constraints

Cognitive constraints on decision-making have historically received much less attention than situational constraints and have only recently become the subject of serious study. Before the twentieth century, research on the psychology of war was generally concerned with discussing the virtues appropriate to soldiers or with how best to conduct training.[7] Strategic theorists had little to say about the cognitive disruptions soldiers experience, except insofar as these were presented as personal failings demonstrating a lack of virtue or an abundance of fear. Cognitive constraints only emerged as a major area of research in the twentieth century with increasing interest in veterans' psychological welfare.

One of the formative influences on this field was S.L.A. Marshall's study of combat effectiveness in the Second World War.[8] This raised questions about the adequacy of military training as preparation for combat and called attention to the psychological trauma of fighting. The Vietnam War generated more interest in military psychology, as it led to the widespread recognition of posttraumatic stress disorder (PTSD).[9] Research on PTSD has fueled attention to the many adverse psychological effects of war, which also include depression, anxiety, and substance abuse.[10] Work on "moral injury" has likewise explored the challenges of dealing with trauma and readjusting to the civilian world.

My focus here is on the psychological experience of making ethical decisions and not on the long-term effects on veterans, either in terms of PTSD or moral injury. However, the prevalence of these conditions is evidence of how traumatic war can be, especially when it comes to raising persistent moral doubts that can plague soldiers for decades after leaving service.[11] Research on PTSD and moral injury shows that trauma arises from deeply troubling affective responses to violence that are pertinent here because these could interfere with ethical reasoning at the moment of decision, which is my focus. Among the common psychological impediments to decision-making that studies of military psychology have discovered are the acute stress of being in combat, chronic stress that soldiers experience over the course of a deployment, and sleep deprivation.[12]

Acute Stress

The most immediate cognitive constraint soldiers experience on the battlefield is acute stress from being under fire or in imminent danger. Soldiers describe the experience of battle as a strange mixture of terror and exhilaration—an ineffable feeling so intense that it can only be understood by others who have experienced it directly.[13] Roger Spiller says that "when a soldier moves forward against fire, he steps beyond the boundaries of anything we understand."[14] The special status soldiers receive from experiencing combat firsthand leads some to compare it to their first sexual encounter and to anticipate it with the same desire.[15]

David Bellavia provides detailed descriptions of feeling acute stress in his narrative of the Battle of Fallujah.[16] His squad was ambushed while searching a house, and he became isolated. Alone and without an exit, Bellavia decided to search the house by himself. He admits feeling such powerful fear as he moved to the second level of the house, where insurgents were waiting, that he struggled to move. "Crouched on the stairs, I wait. Waves of fear rock me. I feel unsteady and totally vulnerable."[17] He goes on to describe the struggle of comprehending the events occurring around him and his focus on immediate threats at the expense of his awareness of events happening beyond his field of vision. Bellavia's description is consistent with what many interviewees report and is part of the natural psychological response to acute stress.[18] It causes the redirection of blood and glucose to the parts of the brain that are responsible for perception, and this movement decreases the resources that are available for cognition. As Andrew Steadman explains, "When the limbic system is heavily engaged, as it is during the high-threat stress of combat, it will quite literally steal fuel from the prefrontal cortex, thus handicapping a leader's ability to combat the situation with cognition."[19] He adds that "the prefrontal cortex cannot generate new ideas while stressful events constantly bombard its working memory."[20] Under these conditions, vision, motor skills, and cognition all suffer from the hormone-induced rapid heart rate.[21]

The physiological responses to acute stress have some benefits, including higher pain tolerance, increased strength, and increased endurance. However, these are only positive effects in the sense that they improve soldiers' capacities for fighting. They may interfere with soldiers' abilities to make decisions by leading them to persevere even when they are unable to think critically about their actions. Grossman argues that "individuals under stress are far less capable of doing anything other than blindly running from or charging towards a threat."[22] Similarly, Sebastian Junger reports that "combat jammed so much adrenaline through your system that fear was rarely an issue."[23] Whether this blind reaction to stress improves or degrades a soldier's ability to fight, it is likely to have a negative influence on careful ethical thinking.

Although fear is probably the most common emotion associated with acute stress, it is not the only one or even the one that most hinders ethical reasoning. Soldiers may also feel overwhelming anger and hatred. One American I spoke with told me he once saw a fellow soldier become so enraged that he was unable to think clearly. During a foot patrol in Baghdad, an insurgent ran into the street, shot one of the soldiers in the face at close range, then dropped his rifle and attempted to surrender. The soldier nearest the one who had been killed fired back at the surrendering insurgent. Within seconds both the American who was first shot and the insurgent lay dead. The interviewee said the soldier who had killed the surrendering insurgent was removed from the unit. Rumors circulated that the man was convicted of murder and later served time in a military prison. Nevertheless, the interviewee thought that under the circumstances, killing the insurgent was the right thing to do. He said it was impossible to watch a close friend shot only feet away and to stand idly by as his killer surrendered. Anger can override competing thoughts and feelings, making retaliation feel like the only option.

The literature on acute stress in combat suggests that it temporarily impairs ethical reasoning and other cognitive abilities but that its influence varies considerably depending on the circumstances and its effects can be minimized. The extent to which stress hinders ethical reasoning depends on the perceived threat of injury or death. Higher-ranking officers have more distance from the battlefield and are usually not directly under fire, enabling them to perform more cognitively demanding tasks during battle.[24] The soldiers I talked to were all directly engaged in combat (or in the case of some Israeli soldiers, dangerous patrolling and checkpoint activities in hostile areas that could potentially result in combat). This put all interviewees at high risk of feeling acute stress. Susceptibility to stress also changes over time. Some studies have found that inexperienced soldiers may be less fearful than veterans because they have not yet witnessed death and retain a feeling of invulnerability.[25] Others indicate that veterans may be better able to cope because their experience gives them confidence.[26] Whatever the case may be, the effects of acute stress are not uniform, and their disruption of ethical reasoning is apt to vary considerably.

Some soldiers are so overwhelmed that they are unable to function; they run away, freeze, or refuse to fight.[27] These soldiers could be incapable of making ethical judgments, but their inaction also means they are not active participants in combat. Those experiencing this level of stress may therefore be excluded from the morally important decisions about who to target and what level of force to use. More concerning are instances in which soldiers in combat are consumed by anger that leaves them capable of acting but without the ability to clearly evaluate their choices. Fortunately, these incidents were uncommon in the stories interviewees relayed. Only three of the soldiers reported incidents in which other soldiers seemed to be overcome by emotions and still able to act aggressively. Moreover, the inability to think clearly was attributed to others, while soldiers consistently thought they were in control of their own feelings.

None of the soldiers I interviewed reported feeling that stress had a deterministic effect on their actions, and only a few reported feeling like it determined others' actions. Soldiers felt they were usually able to engage in ethical reasoning even when they were under extreme stress, though their reasoning was not always as clear as it would have been under perfect conditions. Some soldiers who took part in extremely intense or unexpected fighting, such as when they were ambushed, reported reverting to routinized behaviors rather than thinking critically about problems. They also noticed that they might unconsciously make ethical decisions without being able to compare different prospective courses of action. This reliance on learned behaviors could have a positive or negative influence on moral decision-making depending on the circumstances and what kinds of actions had become routinized to the point that soldiers could unconsciously follow them. It also suggests that normative systems that rely heavily on habituation—virtue ethics and pragmatism—may be better guides for soldiers who feel this decline in their cognitive faculties.

Chronic Stress

Whereas acute stress is a reaction to an immediate threat, chronic stress accumulates over prolonged exposure to the conditions of war. It can be caused by acute stress and may in turn magnify acute stress, but it is distinct because it persists over time and may slowly erode soldiers' physical and psychological abilities even when they are relatively safe.[28] It encompasses the feelings of anxiety, dread, and depression that soldiers feel when they are off duty and awaiting their next assignment or even when they have returned home. This type of stress can emerge even without the experience of fighting. Soldiers endure difficult living conditions and culture shock when they are deployed, which can in turn cause loneliness and a sense of isolation.[29]

There are many sources of stress during war: fear of injury or death, physical discomfort, isolation, loss of friends, uncertainty, loss of privacy, boredom, anxiety, lack of individual goals, restricted movement, low individual value, visions of injury or death, and lack of other social outlets.[30] Benjamin Tupper, an American veteran of the war in Afghanistan, describes additional factors that weigh on soldiers and contribute to chronic stress.[31] These include poor nutrition, heat, sleep deprivation, and poor hygiene. Paddy Griffith finds that the number of psychiatric casualties is strongly related to the intensity of fighting but that exposure to any combat over an extended period can lead to psychiatric problems.[32] H. R. McMaster finds that chronic stress can build even without any intense fighting, merely from "the persistent danger of operations" characteristic of irregular warfare.[33] Some research shows a positive linear relationship between the number of firefights someone has taken part in and their chances of experiencing PTSD, suggesting that experiences of distress have a corrosive effect that builds over time.[34] However, there is no clear objective measure of the rate at which soldiers' ability to effectively make decisions declines, making it difficult to say with any certainty when chronic stress begins to affect cognition and when it poses a risk for ethical judgment.[35]

Soldiers' narratives often link the effects of chronic stress to the decline of moral reasoning abilities, but as with acute stress, soldiers usually do not describe chronic stress as having a deterministic influence. In his account of the Second World War, John Babcock reports that fighting transformed many soldiers, disrupting their prewar moral sensibilities and even leading them to commit war crimes. "Some formerly clean, upright, and thoroughly ethical American soldiers occasionally took a shot at an enemy medic; our guys beat up or shot prisoners once in a while; enemy wounded were occasionally left untended for long periods, sometimes out of spite."[36] He attributes these moral lapses to the degradation of compassion after prolonged exposure to terrible conditions, yet Babcock also gives the reassuring report that many of the soldiers' "fundamental values and moral qualities" survived despite the high stress to emerge at critical moments when they were needed.[37] Although he does not clearly explain how these assessments can fit together, Babcock's comments indicate that only certain soldiers became less ethical as they were exposed to chronic stress and that the stress came in varying degrees. As Paolo Tripodi observes, "This does not necessarily mean that the environment is changing the individual and his or her character, but the environment does have the potential to create great confusion."[38]

Chronic stress is probably impossible to eliminate, but like acute stress, it can be managed. Several studies have shown that stress can be reduced by positive influences, such as good leadership, unit cohesion, self-confidence, and confidence in commanders.[39] The soldiers I interviewed cite their own experiences as evidence that although chronic stress may interfere with thinking, it usually does not destroy ethical awareness. Many were involved in deeply troubling incidents—including killing other people and seeing close friends die—yet all said they were able to overcome these experiences to make important ethical decisions when they had to. Most also worked in environments that were more conducive to mitigating the effects of chronic stress; they were able to return to the relative security of forward operating bases when they were not on duty and were frequently rotated in and out of combat areas. Efforts to eliminate stressors were not completely successful but helped to ensure that soldiers did not reach a level of extreme stress that would seriously disrupt their cognitive abilities.

These comments from memoirs and interviewees agree with the characterization of chronic stress in much of the work on military psychology. For example, Zahava Solomon finds that Israeli soldiers showed symptoms of chronic stress during deployments, but this usually did not impair the soldiers' functioning. The soldiers fought through problems with sleeping, nausea, and fear of stigmatization while still being able to perform their duties.[40] Some of the characteristic signs of extreme stress, such as hypervigilance, may even appear to be beneficial to careful thinking under combat conditions, although it is harmful to long-term health.[41]

However, it is important to note that the chronic stress soldiers experience during conflicts may differ from the long-term psychological burdens they bear afterward. Tyler Boudreau reports that returning home triggered some of the most severe psychological trauma because of the dissociation from group bonds and sense of purpose that helped to make life tolerable during deployments.[42] Thus, any ability soldiers have to manage chronic stress to protect their ethical awareness during conflicts may not necessarily reflect the suffering they endure when they are readjusting to civilian life.

Sleep Deprivation

A final cognitive constraint that may interfere with soldiers' ethical judgments is sleep deprivation.[43] Sleep deprivation is extremely common during war, especially for soldiers who are stationed in small outposts and other positions that are exposed to attack or who may be compelled to work long hours to make up for manpower shortages. Moreover, even when soldiers have ample opportunities to rest, they may be unable to sleep because of lingering stress or the fear of attack. In his study of a platoon outpost in Afghanistan, Sebastian Junger reports that few soldiers were able to sleep without the help of prescription sleeping pills and that the heavy use of sleep aids caused some additional cognitive impairment.[44] Jonathan Shay concludes that, with the pervasiveness of threats and possibility of coming under attack at any moment, "the modern soldier's sleep can hardly be said to be sleep."[45]

Studies of sleep deprivation have shown that it leads to significant declines in mental acuity.[46] The most boring or complex tasks are the ones that become most difficult.[47] Error is especially likely when struggling with novel stimuli. "Sleep-deprived members lose the ability to plan, to improvise, to shift targets, and to concentrate on more than one assignment simultaneously, all critical aspects of surviving combat."[48] And sleep deprivation is not an isolated problem. It is both a cause and an effect of chronic stress. It contributes to stress by preventing soldiers from fully recovering from stressful experiences, and it is aggravated by stress, which may further hinder sleep.[49] Sleep deprivation may therefore impair ethical reasoning and contribute to other factors that have this effect.

As with the other cognitive constraints, the extent to which soldiers report suffering from sleep deprivation varies. Some written narratives of combat describe cognitive decline because of sleep deprivation after long periods of fighting, but most of the soldiers interviewed did not report this problem. Lack of sleep sometimes increased soldiers' stress, but it did not (according to their self-evaluations) make it impossible to think carefully about ethical challenges. Soldiers' published narratives give the same impression. Even when exhaustion is identified as a major challenge, as in Junger's work, there is little indication that it plays a decisive role. It was simply one factor among many that made moral reasoning more onerous while still usually leaving soldiers' faculties sufficiently intact for them to be responsible for their choices. Members of elite units are especially well positioned to resist the adverse effects because of their specialized training. Aaron Cohen, a veteran of the Israel Defense Forces' elite Unit 217 says that "sleep deprivation was one of the hardest aspects of army life," but rigorous training helped to prepare him for managing its consequences.[50]

The soldiers I interviewed were also in a stronger position to resist the effects of sleep deprivation than soldiers in previous counterinsurgency operations. Most were stationed in forward operating bases at night and could be reasonably sure of their safety. They sometimes went out on overnight patrols but were rarely exposed to attacks for more than a few days at a time. Thus, like the other cognitive constraints, sleep deprivation is best seen as increasing the burdens of moral reasoning without making it impossible. Its effects will vary considerably depending on the kinds of operations soldiers are involved in and whether they feel secure when they have opportunities to rest.

Conclusion

The situational and cognitive constraints that affect soldiers' ethical reasoning abilities show that context plays an important role in structuring soldiers' decisions and directing them toward certain courses of action. Although context always shapes ethical decisions, including during peacetime, the power of constraints is apt to be greater during war because of the exceptional uncertainty and stress soldiers endure. As I have argued, situational and cognitive conditions can overwhelm soldiers, rendering them incapable of making effective moral decisions or incapable of acting at all. Nevertheless, it is important to avoid describing these constraints deterministically under most conditions. The interviewees felt that cognitive constraints rarely prevented them from making effective ethical decisions and that situational constraints did so only when they had virtually no information about whether an unknown person was hostile.

Both types of constraints can be managed. Uncertainty is likely unavoidable, yet it can be mitigated or restructured to reduce the extent to which they interfere with soldiers' ethical reasoning abilities. Situations that give rise to recurrent dilemmas, such as the decision of whether to shoot unidentified vehicles approaching convoys and checkpoints, can be reconfigured to give soldiers greater opportunities to make effective decisions, more information, or more potential solutions. For example, allowing soldiers to use nonlethal weapons at checkpoints, giving them increased protection from roadside bombs, or minimizing the use of surprise traffic control points that are set up without warning and catch civilians off guard can help to prevent the occurrence of ethically insoluble dilemmas by either lowering the costs of mistakes or eliminating the situations in which they occur.

Cognitive constraints are at least partially the result of alterable living conditions and exposure to danger. Reactions to acute stress can be improved with training, good leadership, and good unit morale. The effects of chronic stress may be reduced with more frequent rotations between combat and noncombat assignments and improved techniques for treating PTSD. Sleep deprivation can be reduced when soldiers are given longer recovery periods between operations and opportunities to rest without fear of coming under attack. Each of the armed forces included in the study has already made considerable advancements in limiting the effects of these constraints, with the United States constructing large and safe forward operating bases, the United Kingdom deploying soldiers on relatively short six-month deployments to limit the psychological toll, and Israel conducting operations within or near its home territory that allow its soldiers to maintain connections with their civilian lives.

4

Ethical Decisions in Counterinsurgency Operations

Counterinsurgency operations present special ethical challenges because they are fought against opponents that openly defy the conventions of war, making it extremely difficult for military personnel to determine how and when to use force. Insurgents dress as civilians, fight in populated areas, avoid pitched battles, and sometimes even use civilians or civilian structures as shields.[1] The ethical issues that arise in counterinsurgency are also broader in scope than those of conventional wars, going beyond issues relating to the use of force to include problems such as interacting with foreign civilians, training foreign security personnel, building governmental institutions, and mediating conflicts between competing factions of a foreign population.[2]

The uniqueness of the counterinsurgency environment is a theme throughout the stories I heard from American, Israeli, and British soldiers. The interviewees frequently discussed decisions that were either specific to counterinsurgency contexts or were aggravated by them. Those in each military usually resolved the dilemmas they encountered while actively engaged in combat based on their perceptions of threat and the possibility of experiencing long-term guilt. When soldiers thought that they or their comrades were in immediate danger, their desire to defend themselves superseded competing obligations. Soldiers therefore usually responded aggressively to apparent threats, except when they anticipated a high likelihood of feeling guilty about the decision later. Potential guilt could make soldiers either hesitate or prefer exposing themselves to danger. This was clearest from two types of cases: situations in which soldiers decided to attack opponents even when doing so would harm adult noncombatants and situations in which soldiers refused to respond to threats because of the risk of injuring children, including child soldiers.

In contrast to ethical decisions in combat, which I define as those that take place when two opposing sides are actively fighting each other, decisions relating to the escalation of force arise when soldiers must decide when to initiate combat, how to interact with civilians, and how to conduct patrols. This encompasses situations in which uncertainty left the soldiers without the requisite knowledge to make informed ethical decisions, where they had to choose whether to attack children, or when facing uncooperative civilians "where it is clearly not appropriate to kill anyone, yet where some forceful action must still be taken."[3] Although soldiers from each military struggled with dilemmas that occurred during combat, most considered those relating to the escalation of force to be the most arduous. These decisions were generally mired in such profound uncertainty that soldiers could not always grasp the true nature of the ethical predicaments they grappled with.

In the first section I explore some of the unique ethical issues that arise in counterinsurgency operations. I argue that the most profound ethical questions emerge because of the contact between combatants and noncombatants and the myriad instances in which soldiers must attempt to distinguish between these two groups. In the second section I discuss the types of challenges soldiers encountered during combat and how they resolved them. Soldiers from each of the countries I analyzed employed similar methods of decision-making when they were actively fighting, usually prioritizing self-defense and defense of comrades. The third section discusses ethical decisions relating to the escalation of force. I illustrate these with examples drawn from situations in which soldiers had to defuse conflicts and those in which they contended with cultural differences. Finally, I discuss the "role strain" that occurs when soldiers who are primarily trained in conventional warfare struggle with the unexpected problems of counterinsurgency.

The Ethical Challenges of Counterinsurgency

Many of the special ethical challenges associated with counterinsurgency are related to the proximity of combatants and noncombatants and the continual interactions between the two groups. Conventional wars are typically fought away from populated areas by opponents who seek to confront each other in open spaces where they can easily maneuver. The American, British, and Israeli militaries in particular avoid fighting in populated areas whenever possible. Each is primarily designed to launch high-tempo combined arms operations against conventional opponents. They are at their strongest when fighting in open areas, where their technological and organizational sophistication can be used to greatest advantage.[4]

Conventional combat between uniformed adversaries in open terrain establishes relatively clear battle lines and shifts the focus of operations away from civilians. Counterinsurgencies, by contrast, are often fought in populated areas against opponents who seek to exploit the combatant/noncombatant distinction. Insurgents attempt to blend in with the civilian population to conceal themselves from attack. They take advantage of fissures in the civilian population by mobilizing competing ethnic and religious groups to fight each other, further destabilizing security.[5] And they attempt to undermine the legitimacy of foreign security forces by inducing them to attack civilians. As Carl Schmitt argues, the irregular fighter "forces his enemy into another space. In other words, he displaces the space of regular, conventional theaters of war to a different, darker dimension—a dimension of the abyss, in which the proudly worn uniform becomes a deadly target."[6] This is an apt description of the basic obstacle that insurgents pose in any context, one that captures just how alien the insurgent strategy can be for regular militaries that expect fighting to follow established patterns of interstate warfare.

Although insurgents deserve most of the blame for the erosion of the combatant/noncombatant distinction in recent conflicts, responsibility does not lie with them alone. States and their security forces likewise disrupt the norms of conventional warfare, especially by imbuing civilians with enormous strategic value. The prevailing view in contemporary counterinsurgency theory is that political, economic, and social objectives must be prioritized, and that efforts must therefore be made to cultivate the local population's support.[7] This ideal of "population-centric" counterinsurgency transforms civilians into a strategic challenge and generates a host of efforts to assist, intimidate, resettle, or cooperate with indigenous populations. Whereas the goal of conventional wars is often to capture terrain from the enemy, counterinsurgency operations seek to dominate what is often called the "human terrain." As I will discuss later, this conception of counterinsurgency has been heavily influenced by British practices, though it is now widely accepted in the US and Israel.

While this counterinsurgency strategy seems to hold many ethical advantages insofar as it prioritizes civilian protection and cooperation with host government forces, it also poses unavoidable challenges that follow from using military units to secure populated areas and forcing soldiers to also act like police officers. As the primary objective caught between opposing forces, civilians are at high risk of attack. They may be inadvertently attacked by soldiers hoping to eliminate the insurgents hidden among them, or they may fall victim to the "spatial violence" of being resettled into cordoned areas.[8] More aggressive security forces even deliberately attack civilians to terrorize insurgents' families and friends.[9] Civilians are also victimized by militants in revenge for collaboration, to compel obedience, to make an example of defectors, or in the name of administering justice for crimes.

The need to win support from civilians has some moral advantages. During conventional operations, militaries can generally disregard the feelings of civilians in neutral and enemy countries; they may even choose to target the citizens of opposing countries when they think that doing so will protect their own people or that it will more quickly end a war.[10] When fighting insurgencies, aggressive tactics—especially the deliberate targeting of civilians—lead to disaster. Misconduct alienates potential supporters and exacerbates instability, which can in turn make it harder for security forces to achieve their political objectives.[11] This puts pressure on soldiers to act with restraint and to privilege political over military goals.

The adverse effects of aggressive tactics can be seen across unconventional wars waged over the past half century. Soviet and Russian militaries followed a pattern of intimidation and a heavy reliance on overwhelming firepower during operations in Afghanistan and the Caucasus, which by most accounts was counterproductive and only fueled local opposition.[12] In Northern Ireland, attacks against civilians and abuse of prisoners during the 1960s and 1970s increased Irish Republican Army recruitment and reprisals.[13] During the Vietnam War, the US undermined its base of support in Vietnam as well as its support around the world with harsh reprisals against suspected communists and overwhelming firepower to eliminate enemy combatants.[14] Israeli mistreatment of Palestinians during the First and Second Intifadas, which included the destruction of civilian property and the use of disproportionate force when attacking civilians, provoked further resistance from Palestinians and drew international censure.[15] Those incidents, and more recent attacks on civilians in Gaza, have left Israel in a persistent struggle to defend its reputation.

When insurgents are defeated, success is often attributed to strategies that combine several key tactics: judiciously using force on a limited scale, separating militants from civilian supporters, building government capacity, and cultivating strong local allies that can share the burden of providing security. John Nagl argues that one of the key differences between the successful British occupation of Malaya and American failure in Vietnam is that the American commanders showed little interest in treating the South Vietnamese people as partners and isolating them from communist influence.[16] Other studies of the Vietnam War suggest that efforts made to build relations with the Vietnamese people during the final years of American involvement could have succeeded if they had been implemented sooner.[17] This is evidence that ethical conduct on the part of soldiers is not only good in itself but is also instrumental for defeating insurgencies. In this context, ethical demands are frequently much different from those of conventional operations, requiring soldiers to reimagine their roles and to make difficult judgments about how and when to use force.

Combat Dilemmas

Interviewees across the three countries tended to encounter the same general types of dilemmas when they were actively engaged in combat. Most of these were related to civilians being in the line of fire. Soldiers from each military reported instances in which they came under attack from insurgents who were near civilians who could be inadvertently harmed or who were based inside of civilian homes where innocent bystanders might be concealed. This compelled the soldiers to consider whether they should retaliate with lethal force or break contact. Soldiers can expect to encounter this challenge in any kind of war. Conventional fighting in urban areas may put civilians at the same risk of being caught in the crossfire. Nevertheless, these incidents are more common in counterinsurgency warfare because of the emphasis on securing the local population. These incidents are also more strategically important during counterinsurgencies because of the necessity of building local support.

Soldiers from each country had similar responses when deciding what to do when civilians were at risk during a firefight. They usually decided whether to continue the fight by considering the extent to which they felt they or their comrades faced an imminent threat. When the perceived risk was high, soldiers fired back in self-defense. When the perceived risk was fairly low, they said it was best to either avoid fighting or to maneuver into a position where the enemy could be attacked without inflicting collateral damage on innocent bystanders. As one American told me, the "top priority is to try to protect yourself. You've got to protect yourself first."[18] Soldiers said they were attentive to the chance of harming civilian bystanders and were more apt to act with restraint when that likelihood was high. Nevertheless, almost all thought that, whatever the prospects of inadvertently harming civilians, their primary motive was self-defense. Thus, self-defense took precedence over civilian protection, but civilian protection was more important than killing insurgents when it was possible to safely break contact and withdraw.

The cross-national agreement in identifying this type of ethical challenge, and the agreement on how best to resolve it, shows the strength of the principle of noncombatant immunity. Protecting civilians is one of the main goals of just war theory and the law of armed conflict (LOAC) as well as the point at which these speak most directly to the experiences of soldiers lower in the chain of command. Of the two primary criteria of *jus in bello*, one—discrimination—is primarily directed at protecting civilians from attack; the other—proportionality—is concerned with reducing the levels of force used so as to minimize collateral damage that could harm noncombatants. Each of these principles is embodied in the LOAC, which means soldiers from each military are under a deontological obligation to not target or endanger civilians. At the same time, the LOAC and the rules of engagement (ROE) employed by each of the militaries acknowledge that soldiers have an indefeasible right to self-defense that permits them to harm civilians incidentally when they must do so to protect themselves. When taken together, the prohibition against attacking civilians and the authorization to act in self-defense create a strong deontological guide for how to treat civilians who are at risk during combat.

One of the best examples of how soldiers may feel they must endanger civilians to defend themselves comes from the Battle of Mogadishu in 1993. Members of Task Force Ranger came under fire from Somali militants who were in the midst of large crowds of unarmed people and inside civilian homes. Mark Bowden describes the soldiers being faced with a clear dilemma of whether they should return fire even at the risk of striking innocent bystanders: "The Rangers were bound by strict Rules of Engagement. They were to shoot only at someone who pointed a weapon at them, but already this was unrealistic. It was clear they were being shot at, and down the street they could see Somalis with guns. But those with guns were intermingled with the unarmed, including women and children."[19] Firsthand accounts of the Battle of Mogadishu reveal that soldiers were conflicted about the right course of action.[20] Some reported they initially held their fire, but attempts to disperse the crowds with nonlethal means, such as low-flying helicopters and flash-bang grenades, failed. As the crowds pushed closer to the American positions and the intensity of the fire from the militants increased, the Rangers and the helicopter gunships supporting them began shooting into the crowds. They attempted to target the armed militia fighters but also hit noncombatants.[21] More recent reports from the wars in Iraq and Afghanistan have accused insurgents of hiding behind human shields, and the Israel Defense Forces (IDF) routinely accuses Palestinian fighters of doing this by living with their families even as they are active participants in the attacks.[22]

None of the interviewees reported dilemmas that were quite as clear as militants literally using civilians as human shields during an attack. Instead, they generally reported scenarios in which they were not sure how their actions *might* affect civilians. For example, several of the British soldiers I interviewed said that while they were deployed in Afghanistan, their forward operating bases and patrol bases repeatedly came under fire from insurgents who attacked from inside nearby homes. Civilians in the area were usually not visible (most would take shelter during attacks), and sometimes the insurgents themselves could not be located, making it extremely difficult for the soldiers to decide how to respond. As in the checkpoint examples discussed in the previous chapter, uncertainty impeded efforts to weigh the costs and benefits of different courses of action. The soldiers' response in these cases was usually to avoid returning fire unless they could clearly see their attackers. Because they were behind the walls of their bases, they did not feel they were at enough personal risk to warrant endangering civilians. Scenarios in which it was possible to take cover inside fortified positions were more likely for the British interviewees because the overstretched British forces tended to be dispersed between bases and lacked the manpower needed for aggressive patrolling.

American and other British personnel (especially the Royal Marines Commandos) told similar stories of attacks that took place when they were patrolling, escorting supply vehicles, or standing guard at a checkpoint. The typical scenario soldiers described was of coming under fire from a nearby building or being attacked with an improvised explosive device—or sometimes both—while there were civilians nearby. In some instances, soldiers who were part of mounted patrols were able to take cover in their vehicles and speed away. They could then allow civilians to leave the area and return with reinforcements, reducing the weight of the ethical dilemmas. When escape was impossible, either because vehicles were disabled or because the soldiers were dismounted, they generally responded by returning fire at their attackers or at areas where they thought their attackers might be located. When doing this, soldiers could rarely see civilians who were at risk of being caught in the crossfire. US and UK soldiers reported finding that they or the air support units that came to their rescue had wounded or killed civilians taking cover inside nearby buildings, although some insisted that under the circumstances it was impossible to tell whether civilians had been hit by coalition or insurgent gunfire.

Other accounts of the wars in Iraq and Afghanistan confirm that similar dilemmas related to the use of air power are routine and that civilians are frequently caught in the resulting blasts. Ben Anderson describes multiple incidents in which soldiers called bombs onto compounds where Taliban were but then found that civilians had been hiding inside. As he points out, "It is impossible to know whether there are no civilians in a compound unless someone can go in and check every room, which they can't do in the middle of a fight."[23] Frank Ledwidge offers several examples of American and British soldiers calling for strikes that accidentally killed civilians, including one incident that resulted in twenty-five civilian deaths.[24] It was a horrific mistake but at the time had felt essential because the British patrol was under attack from two enemy positions.

One Royal Marines Commando I interviewed recalled being involved in a heavy gunfight in a town. He and the members of his squad shot back at the insurgents and darted in and out of cover, moving between civilians' homes. Afterward, they found that several innocent bystanders, including several women, had been struck by bullets meant for insurgents. Killing civilians was not the marines' goal and was counterproductive given their mission of "winning hearts and minds." The interviewee stressed that the intense threat combined with the uncertainty was responsible for the casualties. "Sometimes you just can't tell who they are. They dress in long robes. You can't really see them. You can't really identify someone from beyond 50 meters."[25] When I asked the marine how he chose who to shoot, he said that in combat "the decision is almost made for you. If you're a threat to me, you're going down. You can only think about the ethical implications of your actions later when it comes to situations like that." Thus, he emphasized that the immediacy of threats can force soldiers to prioritize self-defense regardless of the costs.

Only around half of the Israeli soldiers reported being involved in a pitched battle in which they had to make decisions about whether to put civilians at risk. For them, the experience of counterinsurgency operations was characterized by brief altercations with insurgents who were attempting to pass checkpoints, throwing rocks, or evading capture. This put the Israeli soldiers at a lower risk of being killed or injured, yet they were still in danger of coming under attack or failing to prevent future attacks. It was also clear the Israeli soldiers had the same basic understanding of how civilian safety should be weighed against their own safety during combat. That is, the soldiers said self-defense and defense of comrades came first, followed by civilian security, then killing enemies.

The soldiers who recounted seeing civilian casualties in the aftermath of a gunfight said that they regretted having to put civilians at risk, but that this was necessary when acting defensively. They had to put their own security and the security of their comrades first, they insisted. Even those who did not personally experience these types of situations thought they would act the same way under similar circumstances. Whether British, Israeli, or American, the soldiers consistently told me that "nothing can interfere with your right to self-defense"—a line that is even printed on some ROE cards. The uniformity of soldiers' attitudes about civilian immunity and the right of self-defense suggests there may be little difference in how soldiers from these three militaries perceive and resolve ethical challenges that occur in combat. This does not mean that personnel in each military will always act the same way in these situations, only that they are apt to apply similar reasoning procedures that are grounded in the principle of noncombatant immunity and the right of self-defense. As I discuss later, perceptions of exactly when self-defense was necessary differed somewhat, both between militaries and among soldiers in each. This variation shows that even when there is widespread agreement about what deontological constraints should govern the use of force, the interpretation of these rules can vary substantially and call for personal judgments.

Escalation of Force

Uncertainty creates special problems during counterinsurgency operations. Insurgents may intentionally mislead their opponents by blending in with the local population and evading detection. Their attempts to create uncertainty may even be calculated decisions to lead security forces into committing attacks on noncombatants or damaging religious sites, thereby compromising their public image.[26] Uncertainty is further exacerbated when soldiers have limited knowledge of the territory and its people.[27] Lack of background information may make it harder to read the context for clues about how to act and may lead soldiers to misjudge probable outcomes when they must make educated guesses at the right course of action. Most interviewees thought the dilemmas they faced during combat were actually less difficult than some of those that occurred during noncombat activities in which they were at risk of coming under attack, such as when performing guard duty, conducting searches, and going on patrols. These were part of the war effort, yet they were not combat activities in the strict sense of being performed during gunfights with insurgents. Rather, they were activities that required escalation of force decisions—decisions about when to use force, what level of force to use, and how to prevent hostilities from intensifying.

Escalation of force decisions can be more demanding than use of force decisions in combat for two reasons. First, these require soldiers to think and act in ways that are beyond the scope of their training, or at least outside their core competencies. Whereas soldiers in combat arms units spend most of their time preparing to fight uniformed opponents and to respond to the ethical dilemmas that occur during combat, escalation of force decisions tend to occur during operations that are more related to policing. This brings them into unfamiliar territory. Second, escalation of force decisions generally involve much greater uncertainty than use of force decisions during combat. Soldiers in combat are affected by inadequate information, yet they at least have some sense of how seriously they are threatened and by whom. By contrast, when soldiers are not actively fighting, they have to constantly evaluate potential threats, anticipating which are real and showing restraint when they are ambiguous. This leaves the soldiers mired in uncertainty and interferes with their efforts to apply norms.

Traffic control points (TCP) were the most frequently mentioned setting for the escalation of force decisions that interviewees described. Soldiers guarding them have to continually decide whether to attack the oncoming vehicles whenever they failed to stop, and this is a common occurrence, as people in contested areas often have good reasons for ignoring or missing the checkpoints. "Snap TCPs" that are set up for short periods of time and without notice are especially troublesome. Intercepting traffic by surprise is a way of catching insurgents off guard, yet it has the unfortunate side effect of also surprising civilians. One US soldier recalled a time when his unit shot at an unresponsive vehicle. Inside they found an unarmed man who had been wounded by the shots that disabled his car. When questioned by a translator, the driver said he was illiterate and unable to read the checkpoint's warning signs. The warning shots then caused him to panic, so he did not stop the car. The interviewee emphasized that this kind of incident was common during his two deployments and that civilians who came under fire generally had reasonable excuses for failing to stop (if they survived), such as being drunk, mistaking the warning shots for insurgent or celebratory gunfire, and being unfamiliar with local TCP rules when traveling through an area. This particular story stood out in the soldier's mind because he later heard that the driver died from his injuries. "I was there to help people," the soldier told me, "we all were. But you still have to protect yourself if you want to make it home."[28]

Determining whether to attack people approaching a TCP is made even harder by the time constraints. According to a US Army Traffic Control Point Operations Smartcard published in 2010, checkpoint guards have around 11.6 seconds to stop a vehicle if they can see it approaching from 300 meters away.[29] That leaves around 10 seconds to go through the escalation of force procedures and decide whether to attack an unresponsive vehicle. In urban areas, the time is further reduced by limited visibility. This is often insufficient time to make an informed decision about whether to use force. One British marine said that "there is a gray area in ROE with the inherent right to self-defense and applying the escalation of force. Rarely can you say 'stop' and fire warning shots. It's rare that you can actually go through all of the steps, so it's really down to the right of self-defense."[30] As he and many others said, the decision to shoot at a vehicle had to be made in seconds and was largely based on whether soldiers could intuitively feel that there was a threat. This left the soldiers with an extremely demanding and recurrent ethical obstacle that often led to violence being misdirected against innocent people.

The experiences of interviewees are substantiated by narratives that other veterans have published.[31] Tyler Boudreau describes soldiers stationed at a checkpoint called the "Mixing Bowl" being fearful after seeing the terrible effects of a car bomb exploding and this shaping their subsequent responses to any vehicles that seemed threatening.

> From that moment on, they didn't hesitate. They shot at any car that didn't stop because they remembered, all too well, what we told them. But Mike and Tony found that sometimes the good guys don't stop either. Sometimes Mike and Tony and them would blaze away into a car, and

> then they'd come to find out that there were no bad guys inside, just dead, unarmed civilians. But the car didn't stop, and Mike and Tony and them couldn't, for the life of them, figure out why.[32]

Like the soldiers I spoke with, Boudreau goes on to emphasize that this kind of mistaken violence against civilians was common. "For every actual car-bomb attack in Iraq, there were dozens more innocent people shot at checkpoints like the Mixing Bowl."[33] He finds that these incidents were virtually unavoidable because each time a suicide attack reached a checkpoint or was intercepted by the guards, it reaffirmed their worst fears and legitimized every mistake.

Frank Ledwidge, a former British Army officer, reports seeing the same pattern during his deployments to Iraq and Afghanistan. He explains that "from the perspective of the nervous young soldier at a checkpoint, anyone who drives out of line is a potential suicide bomber."[34] He describes accidental attacks as being routine but seriously undercounted because of the lack of attention they received. Even in one especially terrible incident he describes being unable to find any reports about "the baby, accidentally shot by a British soldier at a checkpoint, whose blood-covered body I had seen in Helmand."[35] Thus, even without clear metrics for judging how many innocent people have been mistakenly killed at checkpoints, there is a pattern of veterans recounting these incidents as being some of the most common and challenging ethical dilemmas that arise during counterinsurgencies.

Soldiers protecting convoys encountered similar situations, as they were tasked with shooting unidentified vehicles that appeared to be hostile. They were usually unsure of whether the approaching vehicles contained civilians or insurgents and were rarely certain of this even after attacking because the standard operating procedure was to speed away from contact to avoid being ambushed. As one American infantryman told me, "We shoot the cars because we might be under attack, and if you're in the middle of an ambush you can't stop everything for an investigation."[36] The same soldier described an instance in which he refrained from shooting at an approaching car, even when ordered to do so, but watched others in his unit open fire. Later he learned that a team investigating the incident discovered two unarmed adults, a man and a woman, inside the vehicle. The evidence suggests the casualties were civilians. The private said he had a guilty feeling of relief from this evidence. He did not, as he had worried, put himself and his comrades in danger by not shooting, and he was not responsible for killing innocent people. When I asked him whether he was concerned about the possibility that he might have harmed civilians during other encounters when he did choose to fire, he explained, "You just can't take the risk. You have to defend yourself when someone's a threat. We don't know when they're armed, so if they're acting threateningly, you know, if they're not responding to our warnings and ignoring our warning shots, then they're a threat." The soldier went on to cite the inherent right of self-defense as authorizing him to attack potential threats.

As with the incidents at TCPs, there is considerable evidence from soldiers' published narratives and journalistic accounts that convoys in Iraq and Afghanistan frequently launched misdirected attacks against vehicles and pedestrians. Chris Hedges and Laila Al-Arian relay the experiences of one American National Guardsman who ran over a child in 2004 rather than stopping his convoy and of two other soldiers who did the same to adults—in each case at direct orders from superiors.[37] Although these pedestrians were clearly not threatening, the risk of stopping was judged as being too high. The authors also report on many interviewees saying they participated in or witnessed incidents of convoys firing on civilians, noting that "dozens of veterans said they had witnessed or heard stories from those in their unit of civilians being shot or run over by convoys. These incidents were rarely reported."[38]

Facing Child Soldiers

Some of the most troubling escalation of force decisions occurred when soldiers had to decide whether to attack children who were armed or who appeared to be armed. Soldiers threatened by children have the same right to self-defense as they do when confronting adults on the battlefield. However, acting defensively may come with a much higher price than when soldiers defend against adults. Shooting a child can have severe psychological repercussions for a soldier who must live with the guilt of having killed someone who seems to be intrinsically in need of protection. Harming children can also be more damaging to relations with the local people than harming adult noncombatants, making encounters with them profoundly important for broader strategic and political considerations.

Fortunately, the experience of confronting child soldiers was uncommon among my interviewees. Only two (both Americans) described incidents in which children seemed to pose an immediate threat that they would have ordinarily countered with lethal force. One said he had to decide whether to shoot at a young boy who pointed a gun at the soldier while he was on patrol in Baghdad. The boy appeared suddenly, coming out from an alley and pointing a pistol directly at the soldier. The soldier felt vulnerable because he was ahead of the other men on his patrol and in the middle of a street where he did not have cover. Nevertheless, he decided he could not shoot a child. He knew he would rather be shot than attack the boy because he would be overwhelmed by the guilt. "I couldn't do it. I knew I couldn't shoot a kid. I couldn't go back home after doing that."[39] The soldier made his decision and prepared to feel the bullets strike him, but the boy turned and ran away in the direction he had come from. With the immediate danger gone, the soldier decided he should try to disarm the boy. The soldier chased after and caught the boy, then pulled the gun from his hands only to find that it was a realistic toy. There had been no real danger, but the soldier made the decision not to shoot when he was faced with a plausible threat and had decided his conscience would not permit him to kill a child.

Although this story was the only incident of an interviewee confronting a child who appeared to be armed, it is not an isolated incident. Ledwidge tells a nearly identical story. "When I served as a soldier in Iraq I very nearly shot a teenage boy during a patrol. The boy was aiming a toy rifle at us from a street corner. Fortunately, that morning we had been warned in briefings that there were realistic toy guns on the street and to be careful."[40] Such a dilemma cannot be solved by simply acting in self-defense. The interviewee and Ledwidge would have been justified in attacking, yet they recognized that the problem called for more careful thinking relating to the escalation of force against uncertain threats. Stephen Coleman reports an even more extreme version of this scenario in which three Australian soldiers confronted a boy armed with an AK-47 and none were prepared to fire.[41]

Another interviewee faced an almost identical dilemma, except that the young boy was holding a real gun and firing it. Like the first interviewee, this one said he knew he could not live with the consequences of killing a child. He described this as an unreflective feeling, as though there were a psychological barrier that would prevent him from aiming. For a moment, the soldier hesitated, struggling with this feeling. Then he saw the opportunity to shoot the outstretched rifle, which he did. The bullets struck the weapon as well as the boy's hand, seriously wounding him and requiring urgent medical attention. This allowed the boy and the soldier to survive the encounter, though with the former losing a hand. The soldier reported he was satisfied with his decision afterward, and he thought it was the best possible outcome.[42] It allowed him to protect himself and the members of his squad without killing a child. I asked the soldier whether he would have killed the boy if he had been unable to shoot at his rifle, and he said he probably would have refrained from shooting and hoped the boy would miss.

When explaining their motives when facing armed children, the interviewees I spoke with did not say it was absolutely wrong to shoot or that their mission demanded restraint. They thought they had a right to defend themselves, even against children. In these cases, the soldiers judged the potential consequences in terms of what Bernard Williams calls "agentic regret"—the regret for a state of affairs one caused or failed to cause.[43] As Williams argues, and as these stories confirm, the experience of agentic regret plays an important role in moral thinking if the risk of a guilty conscience prevents action. When the anticipated agentic regret is extremely high, it has the power of overriding soldiers' interest in self-preservation and leading them to either avoid escalating the level of force or to do so cautiously. Similarly, these cases might result in what Rita Brock and Gabriella Lettini call "moral injury": "Moral injury results when soldiers violate their core moral beliefs, and in evaluating their behavior negatively, they feel they no longer live in a reliable, meaningful world and can no longer be regarded as decent human beings. They may feel this even if what they did was warranted and unavoidable."[44] Ledwidge and the two soldiers who reported encountering child soldiers all seemed to have a strong, intuitive feeling they were perilously close to sustaining this kind of injury if they chose to use force too freely.

IDF veteran Aaron Cohen describes encountering the feeling of moral injury following one mission in which he was forced to make the difficult decision of whether to shoot a fifteen-year-old boy. The teenager surprised Cohen during a raid against a Hamas leader's home, opening fire as the entry team passed through a doorway. Cohen instinctively shot six times at the young Hamas courier but then later felt guilty. "It was a tough night: known Hamas courier or not, this wasn't what I enlisted for. I didn't sign up to kill kids."[45] Although Cohen ultimately returned to active duty, the shooting clearly had an impact on him, even shaking his identity as a soldier. It is therefore understandably a decision that soldiers struggle with and that may haunt them long afterward.

Responding to Cultural Differences

Escalation of force problems can arise because of cultural differences between the soldiers and the civilians they interact with. Soldiers who are ignorant of local customs sometimes mistakenly interpret benign actions as hostility. Steve Fainaru describes one incident in which US soldiers on patrol in Iraq mistook celebratory gunfire for an attack. "There was a familiar pop-pop-pop, and, as they moved through the village—two dozen adobe houses set back from the road—the Americans poured gunfire in the direction of where they believed people were shooting at them."[46] Later the soldiers discovered that the shots were fired to celebrate a wedding. The convoy's retaliation killed several civilians and wounded others, including a nine-year-old girl. The incident could have been easily avoided if the soldiers had recognized the possibility that they might hear nonhostile gunfire and waited to respond until they could determine whether the shots were directed at them, but they were unaware that such an accident could occur.

The soldiers I interviewed did not report any incidents in which misunderstandings directly caused casualties, yet many told stories of cultural differences aggravating strained relations with local civilians. A common complaint from the Americans was shock at how women in Iraq and Afghanistan were treated. A first sergeant who took part in the invasion of Iraq in 2003 said he regularly saw men publicly beating women. His initial response was to intervene. The first time he saw such an incident, he screamed at the man and threatened to shoot him if he hit his wife again. The first sergeant explained his response by saying, "As an American soldier you don't like to see a man doing something like that."[47] However, after ending several beatings in this way, he was instructed to avoid preventing domestic violence. It was, he told me, an order that reflected a growing belief that soldiers needed to show greater respect for the Iraqi culture and that efforts to reform it would be counterproductive. After receiving those instructions, he avoided intervening to protect women from domestic violence, although he found it difficult to stand by and watch the abuse. It was something he had to reluctantly endure and to rationalize as best he could. He emphasized that "it was hard to deal with, but there are just some things that you aren't going to correct." He went on to say, "You're part of the army, part of a group. You can't intervene just because you think it's wrong."

The first sergeant's experience was not unique. Five other Americans mentioned seeing beatings or rapes during their time in Afghanistan and Iraq. They recounted similar experiences of first being eager to intervene and then later being ordered to not do so on the grounds that it went against the demands of cultural tolerance. One American sergeant said that when he was on patrol in Baghdad he saw women and boys being abducted on several occasions.[48] He explained that although the rapes did not occur in the open, he could see them beginning when a man or group of men would appear to push a woman or a boy into a nearby building. Nevertheless, he and others who saw beatings and sexual assaults were prohibited from intervening. Similar incidents, including sexual assaults of children and between soldiers in local security forces, have been reported in other published narratives.[49]

These incidents involved escalation of force decisions because they occurred outside of combat and required the soldiers to choose whether and how to respond. The decision of whether to prevent domestic violence and rape was not simply that but also involved a decision of whether to show cultural sensitivity and whether to follow orders to avoid interfering with interpersonal conflicts among civilians.

To the US Army's credit, the challenges of reconciling security with culture have come up more prominently in *FM 3-24/MCWP 3-33/5: Insurgencies and Countering Insurgencies*.[50] Although the manual does not offer a clear solution, it does take a more critical position on culture by recognizing that certain types of predation like rape and assault may not truly be culturally sanctioned but rather are temporary features of conflict settings because of the lack of security. This note of caution lays the foundation for a more nuanced approach to what cultural practices should be respected and which ones should not, or, indeed, which do not count as "cultural" at all. The warning acknowledges the kinds of stories the interviewees reported, but it ultimately leaves them with the challenge of making the difficult ethical judgments when it comes to deciding whether and how interactions between civilians should be regulated.

Counterinsurgency and Role Strain

Throughout my interviews, veterans recounted the trouble they had interacting with civilians and how this took them beyond the conventional military roles they had been trained for. In almost every instance, those from combat arms specializations (infantry, cavalry, or special operations) commented on the role strain they experienced when confronting escalation of force decisions. They were trained to fight conventional enemies in battles based on maneuver and the use of overwhelming firepower. Once deployed, they were given jobs that were more suitable for police officers—jobs for which they were untrained and that actually contravened much of the training they had received.

This sentiment was less common among the British personnel because more of these soldiers were inclined to say that counterinsurgency operations were within the scope of the roles they had been trained for. They were generally more confident about being prepared to think about counterinsurgency as a distinct type of operation apart from conventional war. Nevertheless, even with this greater perceived comfort with counterinsurgency, seven of the seventeen British Army soldiers I interviewed felt they had not been adequately prepared for the challenges specific to Iraq and Afghanistan and experienced role strain from intercultural misunderstandings.

Many soldiers articulated their experience of role strain by saying they felt as though they were working as police officers. One IDF soldier's comments capture the general sense that certain counterinsurgency tasks fall beyond the scope of what soldiers should be doing: "I strongly believe that the IDF or any army should not be engaged in operations among civilians. Operations such as checkpoints, roadblocks, and disengagement should be reserved for law-enforcement and not the military. This, I feel, is a huge source of ethical dilemmas and unclear Rules of Engagement and conduct."[51] The parallels soldiers draw between counterinsurgency and police work are informative because they are correct in sensing that soldiers who had police training were generally better prepared for the most sensitive aspects of counterinsurgency. Two Americans who served as military police officers reported a higher degree of confidence operating checkpoints and protecting government buildings than the many interviewees from each country who were part of infantry units. Their work was made more arduous because they were overextended and often obliged to work alongside soldiers who were untrained at interacting with civilians and who could therefore be just as difficult to manage as the local civilians.

An American military police officer (MP) provided an example of how soldiers could become overwhelmed when acting in a role they were unprepared for and how the resulting stress could cause overreactions.[52] It was also an instance in which this was a liability for military police officers who had to manage the resulting chaos. In 2003 she and two other female MPs were assigned to work with a cavalry unit guarding an Iraqi government welfare office in Baghdad. They were tasked with providing security for the building, which was distributing paychecks to Iraqi civil service workers. The three police officers were needed to search Iraqi women entering the building, as male soldiers in the cavalry unit were not permitted to do this. Although the building was well protected and encircled with barbed wire, the Americans guarding it felt threatened by the growing crowd. Thousands of Iraqis waited to enter and became restless when the doors failed to open on time. After several hours, announcements were made that the building would not open that day because there were insufficient funds to issue payments. The anger intensified, and the people in the back of the crowd began pushing forward, driving those in the front into the barbed wire around the building.

The Americans found themselves in a very difficult position. They were being pelted with rocks and their perimeter was in danger of being breached as people surged forward. The cavalrymen responded violently—falling back on their training to use force when they felt their personal security was at risk and having no sense of how to disperse the crowd nonviolently. The MP reported watching in horror as the soldiers pulled bats from their vehicles and began striking the Iraqis in an attempt to drive them back. This was ineffective, as those in the front ranks of the crowd were being pushed forward against their will. Still, the soldiers continued beating the Iraqi civilians in a desperate attempt to regain control. The situation continued to devolve as more people were pushed into the barbed wire only to be trampled by those behind them or beaten by the Americans.

The MP said that, while the cavalrymen's response to the threat was to escalate their level of force, she saw there was a better way of dispersing the crowd. She called in reinforcements from their quick reaction force (QRF), which was composed of MPs trained in riot control, and directed the reinforcements to break up the crowd from the back. This eliminated the pressure driving the front rows into the barbed wire. As the QRF worked to break up the mob, the three MPs did their best to restrain the other US soldiers and prevent them from attacking more civilians. Thus, the soldiers who had the task of providing security for the welfare office were confronted with an escalation of force decision for which they were unprepared because their training had been focused on conventional combat. With no relevant training to draw on, they made their best attempt at solving this unexpected problem and overreacted to the threat.

Although the Israeli and British soldiers I interviewed did not report seeing any instances in which role strain caused violent reactions on the same level as those reported by the American MP (and even that story was exceptional for US interviewees), there is ample evidence of similar incidents involving soldiers from those militaries, even ones occurring under similar circumstances. For example, the IDF used excessive violence in dispersing crowds on multiple occasions during the First Intifada, resulting in civilian casualties. As Ahron Bregman explains, this had much to do with the IDF's method of scattering crowds by firing at them: "The high toll amongst children was the direct result of them taking an active part in the revolt, but it was also because the practice of Israeli troops was to shoot at the legs of the demonstrators in order not to kill them—which for small children was lethal."[53]

Attacks may also be more accidental, occurring not because of a clear policy for how to use force against civilians but instead because inadequate procedures are in place. This was the case when US marines shot Esequiel Hernández, an eighteen-year-old American who appeared to be shooting his rifle toward the marines' concealed position during border protection operations in 1997. Stephen Coleman observes that this mistake of thinking the rifle fire was an attack "illustrates some of the problems that can occur when military personnel are required to perform operations that would routinely be the role of the police."[54] Being trained to fight conventional opponents, told they have an indefeasible right to self-defense when threatened, and armed with rifles and machine guns as their only means of responding to hostile civilians, soldiers may feel they have no alternatives to shooting. They lack training in the range of options open to police officers and therefore fall back on what they have been trained for, which is usually conventional warfare.

These instances of soldiers confronting escalation of force decisions that cause them to overreact are examples of a task-induced form of acute stress that is directly related to role strain. This happens when the demands of a task exceed a person's capacity and lead them to resort to other abilities in an attempt to find some way of coping with the situation.[55] As David Horner explains it, role strain occurs "if the individual's role is ambiguous (i.e., if there is a lack of clarity in work objectives)" and when "there are conflicting job demands, or if different superiors make different demands."[56] The role strain in these instances is the result of soldiers trained for conventional warfare making ethical decisions about the escalation of force in counterinsurgency operations. Without adequate training in nonlethal crowd control, the soldiers were left with difficult decisions that led them to overreact by employing greater force than was warranted.

Conclusion

Based on my interviews and other firsthand accounts from American, British, and Israeli veterans, it appears that soldiers in each military encounter structurally similar challenges when they are fighting. The most common dilemma to arise during combat is deciding whether to return fire against known enemy threats when there is a risk of harming civilian bystanders. In these cases, soldiers from each military say they respond by judging the threat to themselves against how their actions might affect noncombatants. Soldiers generally weight their own lives and those of their comrades above those of civilians and justify their actions with reference to the inherent right to self-defense. Across the three countries, they agree that soldiers are permitted to defend themselves using lethal force even when doing so might harm innocent people. The soldiers generally prioritize civilian protection when they feel secure, even if this means forgoing an opportunity to kill insurgents or accomplish mission objectives.

The agreement between soldiers from different countries when resolving the ethical challenges arising in combat has much to do with their shared commitment to complying with the laws of war. The LOAC imposes fairly clear restrictions on who may be targeted and how, which facilitates the establishment of cross-national norms about how to act during combat. It helps that soldiers are usually able to gauge the location and nature of threats when they are actively fighting. Having this awareness allows them to make informed decisions about whether they can safely break contact with enemy fighters to reduce the risk to civilians in the area. Soldiers have more trouble deciding how to respond to ambiguous threats when making escalation of force decisions. When making these judgments, there is a great deal of cross-national variation, as soldiers employ the reasoning procedures particular to their respective militaries. This makes it important to explore what these differences are, why they exist, and how they shape soldiers' actions.

5

The US Army and Virtue Ethics

Embodying the Warrior Ethos

The US Army can be best characterized as following a system of rule-bounded virtue ethics. Soldiers are trained to embody a warrior ethos and to make decisions reflexively, based on ingrained character traits. Virtue ethics receives support from the Army's professionalism, voluntary service, and long-term membership, all of which enable the Army to subject soldiers to the extensive socialization that virtue ethics requires. Rules play an important part, though they do so by setting limits on the scope of action without serving as a comprehensive guide. Although I describe the US Army's ethics as a "system," I use this term loosely. It is a heterogeneous doctrine derived from multiple sources: American cultural values, international laws regulating the use of force, mission demands, and the Army's professional identity.[1] The diversity of influences is unavoidable given the Army's emphasis on character as the source of good conduct. Character formation is a life-long process that inevitably takes place through various cultural practices and institutions.

Of the three armed forces I consider, the US Army is the most interested in monitoring the effectiveness of its ethics training and routinely attempting to improve it. The Army follows a pattern of continually revising its ethics doctrine and reforming its training procedures each time it experiences a crisis of its moral identity. It is especially eager for reform following high-profile incidents of misconduct, such as the My Lai Massacre. Just as the Army attempts to counter future threats via constant technological innovation, it attempts to counter future ethical crises with ongoing reforms. This dynamism should not be misconstrued teleologically, as a process of improvement directed at a clear goal. Rather, it is an unsteady process of reorienting the Army to overcome the stigma of past mistakes and to face the next anticipated challenge.

The US Army offers an important case study for understanding military ethics. First, virtue ethics is widely regarded as the most popular inspiration for military ethics, especially among Western countries.[2] This makes the study of how virtue ethics is operationalized an essential starting place for understanding contemporary military ethics beyond the three cases I discuss in this book. Second, because the US military is continually engaged in operations around the world, the conduct of its personnel is of international significance. Soldiers' actions affect people in contested areas and help to determine the fate of nascent governments in countries where the US military is involved in nation building, making the conduct of soldiers an important influence on international politics. Finally, the US provides training assistance to many countries working to establish more professional armed forces, which includes exporting its military ethics.[3]

The first half of this chapter provides a brief overview of the history of the US Army's ethics doctrine, devoting special attention to the post-Vietnam "renaissance" in military ethics. This history shows a continual effort to reassess and revise the Army's norms, usually with a renewed emphasis on individual virtue. The influence of virtue ethics waned during the 1990s with the introduction of stricter rules of engagement (ROE) for peacekeeping operations. However, virtue ethics regained its status in 1998 when the Army formulated its seven values, and it remained the dominant influence throughout the wars in Iraq and Afghanistan. The second half of the chapter discusses contemporary Army ethics training for officers and enlisted soldiers, focusing on efforts to instill virtues. I contend that the ROE set limits on how soldiers may act but that individual virtue and good character remain the primary sources of guidance. I conclude by discussing the importance of professional identity and a group-based conception of virtue for informing soldiers' identities and reasoning.

US Army Ethics until Vietnam

Prior to the Korean War, the US Army was designed to be an expandable force. It was kept small during peacetime and then quickly inflated by new recruits and conscripts during war.[4] This is a function of the United States' distance from threats and its relative security. The Army has had the time to reconstitute itself before confronting enemies rather than being compelled to defend itself against imminent threats. This policy also reflects a perennial suspicion of the government and standing militaries. The practice of continually expanding the

Army during war and reducing its size during peacetime gave few opportunities for military ethics education. Training had to be directed at teaching practical skills as quickly as possible. We can see from the Lieber Code—the landmark attempt to develop norms for soldiers fighting in the American Civil War—that the US military has long recognized that its soldiers need some normative guidance. However, the Lieber Code reveals an effort to impose moral rules without the corresponding virtue-based education that now characterizes the Army's ethics.

The Korean War initiated a radical transformation of the US military, which had been unprepared for war and was slow to mobilize, resulting in a series of humiliating early defeats.[5] The defeats made it clear that, as a global power, the United States could no longer allow its military to contract during peacetime. Instead it would maintain a large standing force that could quickly respond to threats. Although this decision did not immediately transform US military ethics, it helped to create the structural conditions that allowed the Army to develop an aretaic system. Despite increasing the size of its peacetime force, the Army had to follow its previous pattern of expanding rapidly during the Vietnam War because it had to fight there while still containing the spread of communism in Europe and around the world.[6] As the conflict intensified, there was limited time for providing new recruits and draftees with ethics education.[7] Once again, soldiers were rushed into service as quickly as possible, with training focused on imparting the skills that would make them effective in combat. "The intense escalation of the American war in Vietnam between 1965 and 1970 necessitated a rapid increase in the size of the Army, with a corresponding decrease in attention paid to ethics education and training."[8] The loss in Vietnam reinforced the lessons of Korea: that the Army had to remain powerful even during peacetime and that its ranks had to be filled by professional volunteers who would be more effective and reliable than conscripts.

In Vietnam there was greater emphasis on small-unit operations and interacting with civilians than in many of the Army's previous wars—precisely the kinds of operations that are apt to raise challenges and shift the burden of decision-making to soldiers lower in the chain of command. Further aggravating the ethical problems was the Army's heavy use of airmobile tactics, which were based on moving American units in and out of contested areas by helicopter to launch quick strikes.[9] This prevented soldiers from establishing strong relationships with the local people, thereby increasing mutual suspicion and impeding efforts to distinguish combatants from civilians.[10] The Army also attempted to wage a war of attrition that depended on mass devastation of the environment and infrastructure.[11] This is itself ethically questionable, as it places the emphasis on killing and wounding enemy soldiers rather than on achieving objectives with minimal loss of life. This contributed to the strain between civilians and soldiers by encouraging disproportionate uses of force.

The US Army had to contend with serious cognitive problems that disrupted the formation of a strong corporate ethic. These included dissent among the soldiers, low morale, and poor adherence to regulations.[12] The practice of rotating soldiers in and out of units, rather than maintaining unit integrity throughout the conflict, contributed to low morale and the lack of oversight by leaders, aggravating the other challenges that interfered with the Army's ability to maintain moral standards. Without good unit cohesion, many soldiers felt that they were alone and that their highest priority was to simply survive.[13]

The Vietnam War showed the harm that could be inflicted by a powerful military with poor ethical restraint. Soldiers at all levels of the chain of command carried out disproportionate attacks, intentionally targeting civilians and the civilian infrastructure and using weapons that caused long-term environmental damage.[14] The most famous among these, and the incident that played the largest role in forcing a shift in the Army's ethical consciousness was the My Lai Massacre, in which soldiers from the 23rd Infantry Division killed somewhere between 347 and 504 Vietnamese civilians, in addition to raping and torturing many.[15] My Lai became a symbol of the horrors that could be caused by individual soldiers. It was also a reminder of the good that soldiers with strong ethical judgment could do, as at least three of the soldiers who were present risked their lives to save civilians. These examples of good and bad conduct drove the US Army to reinvent itself in the following decades.

The Renaissance in Military Ethics

According to many histories, the Vietnam War marked a turning point in the development of the Army's military ethics doctrine and training, giving rise to a postwar "renaissance" characterized by greater moral sensitivity.[16] Studies by Army personnel support this narrative, as they generally suggest that the Army perceives its own transformation as a reaction to the Vietnam War. In the words of one officer, Vietnam helped to initiate "a period of serious introspection as to what are our fundamental values as a profession."[17] This narrative of Vietnam transforming the Army's ethics has a degree of truth, but it is frequently overstated. The Vietnam War did not alter the basic character of Army ethics, which was primarily virtue based before and after.

The US Military Academy's Honor Code of Duty, Honor, and Country started as an elite code for the country's professional officers but has long functioned as a de facto code of conduct for the entire Army. These three values were adopted as an official guide in the lead-up to Vietnam with the publication of the manual *Character Guidance Discussion Topics: Duty, Honor, Country* (DA PAM 16-3) in 1962. In 1965 the Army issued regulations in its *Character Guidance Program* (AR 600-30). Then in 1968, at the height of the war, the Army republished DA PAM 16-3 as DA PAM 16-5, which affirmed the importance of honor, authority, sense of duty, and marriage as well as the values of duty, honor, and country. Other guides that tangentially addressed moral concerns were also issued for officers and chaplains. There was therefore no shortage of efforts to define the Army's values. Moreover, officers who underwent training at West Point and other service academies went through rigorous programs of character building and values internalization constructed according to the virtue ethics model. Jeffrey Wilson finds that the debates over military ethics throughout the 1960s and '70s assumed that some type of virtue ethics was essential. The central issue was whether "Duty, Honor, Country" provided sufficient guidance.[18] And studies from the postwar period indicate that the ethical struggles during Vietnam were interpreted as failures to live up to the existing ethical standards rather than as indicating some problem with the standards themselves. For example, one internal review of the Army's performance in Vietnam concluded that there was "a significant difference between the ideal values and the actual or operational values of the Officer Corps."[19] That is, the fundamental problem was not with ethical guidelines but with implementation.

In terms of ethics doctrine and training procedures, the post-Vietnam reassessment of moral standards was less a "renaissance" in the Army's ethics than a reaffirmation of the virtue-based guidelines that were already in place. Among the top priorities in rebuilding the Army's image were developing its theory of virtues in more detail and standardizing training procedures. A 1977 report found that Army schools had been conducting ethics training without consistent standards and that ethics training within units was left to the discretion of commanders.[20] The service academies were the first to address this weakness with greater systematization. During the 1970s, each academy developed mandatory classes on morality and war.[21] These formalized elements of the virtue ethics curriculum had been largely implicit and provided a model of character training that spread to the regular Army over the following decade.[22]

General John Wickham, the Army Chief of Staff from 1983 to 1987, initiated a campaign to improve military ethics in 1985 and intensified it over the following years.[23] He declared 1986 the "Year of Values" and started several new projects, including the creation of an hour-long video that all members of the Army—active, reserve, and national guard as well as all civilian employees—were required to watch. Wickham's *Guideposts for a Proud and Ready Army* presented four soldierly qualities that he considered essential: commitment, competence, candor, and courage.[24] Wickham reaffirmed the importance of individual virtue in *Values: The Bedrock of Our Profession* in 1986, then again with *Values: A Handbook for Soldiers* in 1987.[25] In these works, Wickham developed more sophisticated definitions of the Army's values. He also helped to establish the Army's style of teaching ethics by telling stories about how historical figures solved their challenges. Each of Wickham's efforts reflects the interest in reinforcing and formalizing virtue ethics that characterized the post-Vietnam era.

Renewed attention to ethics following Vietnam was essential for rebuilding the Army's image. However, the reforms had several limitations that prevented them from being as sweeping and transformative as the image of a "renaissance" would suggest. First, and perhaps most serious, was the failure to reassess the philosophical foundations of the Army's ethics. There seems to have been little study of whether virtue ethics was indeed the best model or of the limitations of this approach. Second, many of the new training programs reflect a degree of naïveté about how easily the problems of Vietnam could be overcome. The hour-long training video in particular was a woefully inadequate response to the serious human rights abuses perpetrated in Vietnam. Third, there was little attention to enlisted soldiers and noncommissioned officers. Most studies conducted in the aftermath of the war, including the Army's first study of professionalism, were exclusively interested in officers.[26] The new programs for ethics education were likewise largely directed at officers. Enlisted soldiers were excluded from most studies of ethical awareness and from many of the new training programs.

Changes in the structure of the US military were even more important than the new ethics guidelines and training programs. First came the transition to an all-volunteer force in 1973, which made it possible to establish a much stronger sense of professionalism and cohesion among soldiers and to construct a distinctive military culture with its own stable norms. This was a precondition for strengthening the Army's virtue ethics because character formation is a demanding process that often takes years, which is therefore difficult to enact when soldiers are drafted for short terms of service as they were during Vietnam.

Second, suspicious of the American civilian population following Vietnam and eager to establish a distinct ethical consciousness, the Army distanced itself from the civilian population. As Richard Lock-Pullan says, "Once [the military] was withdrawn from Vietnam in 1973, its rebuilding relied on developing its own and independent norms within the context of the American culture."[27] The attempts to improve standards contributed to the separation of the military from the civilian population, as the Army's ethics were framed as being unique to the military profession.[28] The Army's virtues were virtues that civilians and draftees could not embody. General Wickham's reforms played a critical role in this, as one of his overriding goals was to define military service as a profession and to create an ethos surrounding it.

Post–Cold War Operations

The US Army has traditionally devoted little attention to what it calls "operations other than war," and the new guidelines developed during the 1980s failed to include adequate instructions for these. The threat of war with the Soviet Union dictated the Army's training regime, including on ethical matters. However, during the 1990s, the Army's primary mission changed from conventional war fighting to counterinsurgency and peacekeeping.[29] Wilbur Scott and colleagues estimate that "the U.S. military carried out 106 actions on foreign soil between 1990 and 2003. Of these, 101 (95.3 percent) were evacuations, peace or relief efforts, contingency positioning, or shows of force. The 5 combat actions were all against quasi-military groups."[30] The US military's success in the Gulf War overshadowed its increasing involvement in unconventional operations and diverted attention away from training soldiers for the unique ethical demands of counterinsurgency. The quick and overwhelming victory gave the impression that the military was in perfect form, with little room for improvement. Moreover, because the victory was secured with the help of high-profile air strikes and new weapons technologies, the strategic discourse of the following decade was dominated by discussions of whether ground forces would be relevant in future combat operations.

Although the Army has generally been preoccupied with a virtue-based approach to ethics since before the Vietnam War, it has gone through brief periods during which rules have become stronger and more prominent. The Army had to cope with massive reductions in strength, undergoing a net loss of 133,000 soldiers in the year following Operation Desert Storm.[31] In this context, ethics education was marginalized. Faced with budget cuts, size reductions, and a change in priorities, the Army became more heavily invested in rule-based ethics that required less demanding socialization and training. This was a time when "ethical training in preparation for combat was centred on the Law of War."[32] Moreover, with the Army's mission shifting from conventional warfare to peacekeeping, stricter standards seemed essential. Based on comments from soldiers I spoke with, this reduced their effectiveness and put them at greater risk. It produced a backlash against deontology and caused the Army to strengthen its commitment to virtue ethics in the years leading up to the War on Terror.

Five of the soldiers I interviewed, on active duty during the 1990s, noticed changes in ethics education during the American intervention in Bosnia. They experienced a brief period in which the Army's involvement in peacekeeping operations led rule-based ethics, especially rules having to do with civilian protection, to become the dominant influence. One first sergeant said that "during Bosnia, most of the training was policy oriented."[33] It dealt with the Law of Land Warfare, the Geneva Conventions, the Code of Conduct, and the importance of protecting civilians. However, he reported there was very little practical application of these rules and virtually no discussion of how soldiers should exercise their own judgment, leaving him unsure of how he and his subordinates should conduct themselves. He described being frustrated by the strictness of rules throughout his time in Bosnia and by the Army's overall inflexibility when it came to peacekeeping operations.

Mark Viney recalls that "in the opinion of many Quarterhorse [the name of his squadron] junior officers, tactical actions in Bosnia were more centrally planned, executed, and controlled than was warranted."[34] He also describes this as conflicting with tactical decentralization and permitting officers to exercise their own judgment. An interviewee who was an infantry platoon commander in Bosnia from 1995 to 1996 said that the emphasis on deontology hindered operations because the rules were too broad and inflexible.[35] His ROE stated that he could not allow anyone under his command to open fire with heavy weapons like the .50-caliber machine gun without explicit consent from the company commander. This led to some uncomfortable situations in which he and his subordinates had to endure enemy fire and could only protect themselves with their rifles as they waited for requests to use heavier weapons to be radioed to their company commander and approved. He also said that throughout much of the conflict his subordinates were not allowed to have magazines in their rifles or rounds in the chamber without instructions from him. This moved the burden of decision-making upward and reduced the soldiers' freedom to act in self-defense.

Moreover, because the Americans were more heavily armed and armored than the peacekeepers from other countries, they looked aggressive and had trouble interacting with the local civilians. The same officer explained that "putting on the body armor gives you a different mentality, makes you think more aggressively" and that "it's hard for people to trust you when you look like you're going to kill them." This was compounded by the predeployment training, which was still preoccupied with conventional military operations against the Soviet Union.

The Army shifted back to virtue ethics education in the late 1990s, culminating in an official list of seven Army values in 1998. These values, which are still the Army's core values, are loyalty, duty, respect, selfless service, honor, integrity, and personal courage.[36] This list is abbreviated using the acronym LDRSHIP, which is a mnemonic for remembering the values and a way of emphasizing the connection between them and good leadership. The Army's values are defined in terms of individual character attributes and ethical attitudes—a strong indication of the influence of virtue ethics. For example, the definition of loyalty says that "bearing true faith and allegiance is a matter of believing in and devoting yourself to something or someone."[37] The definition of selfless service tells soldiers to "put the welfare of the nation, the Army and your subordinates before yourself."[38] And the definition of honor emphasizes the habit of good character in saying that the greatest soldiers are those "who develop the habit of being honorable, and solidify that habit with every value and choice they make."[39]

The most complete descriptions of the values are found in the *Army Field Manual FM 22-100*. That manual also states the values' underlying intent. They are not merely meant to ensure that soldiers act appropriately but that soldiers have the right kinds of beliefs and good character. Several passages in the manual explain this:

> Beliefs matter because they help people understand their experiences. Those experiences provide a start point for what to do in everyday situations. Beliefs are convictions people hold as true. Values are deep-seated personal beliefs that shape a person's behavior. Values and beliefs are central to character. . . .
>
> Ethical conduct must reflect genuine values and beliefs. Soldiers and Army civilians adhere to the Army Values because they want to live ethically and profess the values because they know what is right. Adopting good values and making ethical choices are essential to produce leaders of character.[40]

The manual echoes Aristotle by describing how habituation to virtuous conduct helps to cultivate good character, and by arguing that soldiers must not only make good decisions but also have good character. For example, it says that "consistently doing the right thing forges strong character in individuals and expands to create a culture of trust throughout the organization."[41] Statements like these establish that the purpose of the Army's ethics education is to go beyond training soldiers to obey orders or to refrain from abusing their power. It aims at nothing less than transforming recruits into good soldiers who can be trusted to act properly out of habit.

The Army's New Ethics Doctrine and Training

Since the invasion of Afghanistan, the US Army has solidified its commitment to virtue-based training by placing greater emphasis on character formation and value internalization. It has also revised its ethics doctrine several times in ways that have strengthened its commitment to virtue ethics. Starting in 2007, all active-duty enlisted personnel are required to undergo initial ethics training within 90 days of starting active duty or within 180 days for newly enlisted personnel.[42] To encourage personal identification with the Army's values, recruits are required to carry a card listing the seven values.[43] Training staff routinely check to ensure that recruits have their cards and that they can recite the values from memory.

The case study method of demonstrating good or bad conduct is the most common way of teaching ethics at all levels.[44] This typically consists of two parts, which are the same regardless of whether the lessons are being presented by a textbook, training manual, or instructor. First, there is a discussion of how a person or unit should act, described abstractly in terms of what the Army values demand or what the ROE are. Second, there is an illustration of the value or rule in practice, either with historical or fictional examples meant to resemble common dilemmas. Many texts also include quotations from famous commanders that distill a lesson's central ideas. This style of teaching links abstract values to real situations and people who can be emulated. By providing historical examples, the books give new recruits role models—exemplars of virtue—who can provide an enduring reference point as they strive to become good soldiers.

The language of training materials is strongly virtue based, calling attention to the importance of good character and of intuitively grasping moral challenges. For example, one Reserve Officers' Training Corps (ROTC) textbook says:

> It's often said that human beings have a "moral compass" inside—an invisible mechanism that automatically points people toward the right thing to do. You can certainly ignore your moral compass; sometimes circumstances shake it so badly that, for a time, it no longer points true. But when you reflect on your values, the compass needle always seems to return to the right course. That's where Army Values help. They give each individual, team, platoon, company, division, and the Army an orientation for moral decisions in everyday life, especially during stressful situations.[45]

The wording used to explain the Army values frequently emphasizes the difference between the ethical demands for soldiers and civilians. The ROTC textbook quoted above affirms that "Soldiers must live these values more intensively and professionally than most others live them in civilian life, because Soldiers serve to protect this nation and the values upon which it was founded."[46] This attitude reflects the actor and context relativity of virtue ethics. Because the meaning of virtues and good character depend on one's status, ethical instruction must continually reaffirm the uniqueness and moral exceptionalism of US Army soldiers.

The Army's concern with developing virtuous soldiers is also evident in the many ethical guidelines it has developed to supplement its statement of values. The Soldier's Creed, which was established in 1998 and later reformulated in

2003 as part of the Warrior Ethos program, is framed as a personal affirmation of good conduct. Both versions of the creed are written in the first person, so it reads as a personal statement of values that is the same for all members of the Army. The main difference between them is that the new version of the creed simplifies the original language to more clearly operationalizable principles of conduct. It replaces the complex sentences of the previous version, such as "as a soldier, I realize that I am a member of a time-honored profession—that I am doing my share to keep alive the principles of freedom for which my country stands,"[47] with a series of short declarative statements like "I will never quit" and "I am an expert and I am a professional."[48] Both versions of the creed reflect the Army's goal of transforming the character of its members and making them embodiments of its warrior archetypes, though the short, simple directives of the new version make it sound even more like a series of personal affirmations.

Four lines of the Soldier's Creed have been given the distinction of constituting the Warrior Ethos: "place the mission first, never accept defeat, never quit, and never leave a fallen comrade."[49] Although these are stated as absolutes, they are contextualized as being the type of actions that characterize a particular ethos, meaning that they are better seen as consistent standards of behavior that follow from virtuous character than as rules. Other official publications refer to the Warrior Ethos and describe it as the most fundamental statement of a soldier's identity. For example, the *Foundations of Leadership* says, "The Warrior Ethos embodies the professional attitudes and beliefs that characterize the American Soldier. This ethos is a reflection of our nation's ideals and values by the profession charged with protecting those very values."[50] The Warrior Ethos has an important place in Army training and is taught using the nine "warrior drills": react to contact, avoid ambush, react to ambush, react to indirect fire, react to chemical attack, break contact, dismount a vehicle, evacuate injured personnel from a vehicle, and secure a halt.[51] It also serves as the basis for the Warrior Tasks and Battle Drills, a series of basic skills that all soldiers are supposed to be able to complete.

By being attached to these combat activities, the Warrior Ethos is given a practical dimension but one that, as these combat activities indicate, focuses on aggressive operations against regular opponents. Here we can see that even as the Army revises its ethics doctrine and develops a more complex integration of norms and fighting skills, it remains focused on the challenges of conventional warfare. This suggests the Army may have overcome the poorly implemented virtue ethics that characterized the post-Vietnam era and the rigid rule-based guidance of peacekeeping operations during the 1990s, but it retains its focus on operationalizing norms in the context of conventional fighting against state military forces.

Constraining Virtue

Soldiers have a great deal of freedom to resolve ethical challenges by relying on their own judgment, but the scope of their action is always supposed to be constrained by inviolable rules that establish boundaries within which soldiers can exercise their own judgment. At the broadest level, the boundaries are captured by the Uniform Code of Military Justice (UCMJ) and the law of armed conflict (LOAC). The UCMJ establishes a system of military justice and a body of law that applies to military personnel. It covers an array of offenses, including fraud, desertion, disrespect toward superior officers, and making false official statements. Among these are regulations specific to combat, such as penalties for murder, theft, and sexual assault. The LOAC is composed of international agreements about the use of force, such as the Geneva and Hague Conventions. This provides more specific guidance about how soldiers should navigate the ethical challenges of war and serves as a cross-national ethical reference point at the core of American, British, and Israeli military ethics. Critically, both the UCMJ and the LOAC are concerned with criminal offenses and largely used for prosecution. They are therefore minimal guidelines establishing rules that soldiers cannot break, but they do not provide much in the way of affirmative guidance that would direct soldiers in how to respond in situations where the law is ambiguous, where the legal issues at stake are not clear, or where moral decisions do not lead to criminal misconduct.[52]

The UCMJ and the LOAC inform the ROE that are designed to guide soldiers through ethical challenges. When a decision is made to engage in combat operations on any scale, the combatant commander of the theater, a general or admiral, works with lawyers from the Judge Advocate Generals Corps to create the operational ROE. These rules must be approved by the secretary of defense and the Department of Defense general counsel. This may result in some changes to the rules but not to the extent that they will interfere with the commanders' intent for the operation. Once the ROE pass the secretary of defense and go into effect, they remain classified but must be known by soldiers at all levels and closely followed. Lower-level commanders may also issue their own ROE. For example, air or naval units may need special instructions that differ from those given to ground forces. However, the ROE can only become stricter—never less strict—as they filter downward. This helps to ensure that the ROE continue to reflect the overall mission intent and legal requirements even as they are adjusted to meet narrower operational demands.

Although the ROE and escalation of force procedures are rules rather than virtues or values, they are frequently stated in conjunction with discussions of values and character, which show an effort to link these rules to the Army's virtue ethics. For example, the *Soldier's Blue Book* describes them as rules that a person with good character follows. "Our leaders conduct operations in accordance with laws and principles set by the U.S. Government, and those laws together with Army traditions and Values require honorable behavior and the highest level of individual moral character."[53] This description suggests that the rules soldiers are required to follow reinforce virtue-based ethics, giving them a supportive role in structuring soldiers' moral consciousness. The Army's rules are so closely related to its virtue ethics that they have an implicit aretaic content. They require and encourage virtues like obedience to the rules, loyalty to the authorities that make them, and duty to follow the absolute limits they set.[54] In this way the restrictiveness of rules is reconciled with more permissive virtue-based thinking.

Evaluating the Efficacy of Ethics Training

Most of the American soldiers I interviewed said they received limited ethics training when they joined the Army, and it primarily consisted in lessons on the Law of Land Warfare, how to follow the ROE, and the rules regulating professional conduct, such as what a person is allowed to do while in uniform. Almost all said their training did not alter their existing values. Most found that the Army's ethics instruction cohered with the values they learned in civilian life and reported that if training had any effect on them, it was to reinforce and clarify the values they had before joining the military. Only two of the soldiers credited Army training with affecting a significant transformation of their thinking about ethics. For both, the effect was to lead them to reflect on their values more than they had in the past and to force them to define these more explicitly. Thus, based on the interviewees' self-assessments, training had a limited effect on reshaping their ethical sensibilities.

The main reason soldiers gave for the weak influence of training was that, despite the Army's efforts to continually revise its education, soldiers received little formal ethics training. This sentiment was especially common among the enlisted soldiers, many of whom were unable to recall taking part in ethics classes. Around a third of the soldiers also commented that the problem of limited ethics training was aggravated by the separation of that training from combat exercises. The soldiers who could recall their training underwent ethics education in a controlled classroom setting, without the lessons learned being explicitly brought into their field exercises. Although there have been few systematic studies of Army ethics training, those that have been conducted suggest that the interviewees' experiences are representative of general trends. Joe Doty and Walter Sowden estimate around only 10 percent of officers' education in ROTC is explicitly directed at character formation, and this number drops to somewhere around 5 percent among noncommissioned officers and officers during their Army training.[55]

Although soldiers thought that training explicitly focused on ethics was not very useful, many reported undergoing a profound change in their attitudes and identities during their careers. Almost all the interviewees said they experienced a powerful identity shift that took them from an individualistic orientation to a collective orientation. This led them to think less about their own interests, though these still mattered, and more about the interests of other soldiers and of the Army as a whole. The defining moment of the transformation came when they began to consider themselves soldiers before all else, which is to say, when membership in the Army became their defining identity. This transformation was an intense experience for the interviewees—one they were usually able to describe in great detail. One captain said he once thought only of what was best for himself and had little concern for others. Joining the Army initiated a shift in his values. As his identity changed and he came to see himself as a member of the Army, his values likewise became more altruistic. "When you sign the contract for the Army, you're giving up your personal rights to help other people have their freedoms."[56] Another soldier cast this in terms of what it meant to be a member of a profession, saying, "Professionalism gives you pride in service, gives you pride in helping people, instills you with a sense of pride in what you're doing."[57]

Most of the interviewees reported that their reasons for joining the Army were not noble or altruistic. They had self-interested motives, such as the desire for a good job, for an education, for revenge against al-Qaeda, or simply because of uncertainty about the future. This was even true of some of the soldiers who attended the US Military Academy. A few of those who went to West Point said they decided to go to the academy because they had visited it and were impressed by the architecture, the uniforms, and the history. One officer said he did not even realize he was required to join the Army until he was nearing the end of the application process.[58] Others reported that they joined because of a bad employment market or because they were not satisfied with their jobs. They were attracted to military service because it offered excitement or job security.

Around a third of the enlisted soldiers told me they joined because they grew up in neighborhoods that did not offer many opportunities for employment or because they were worried they were headed down a bad course in life that had to be interrupted before it was too late. This is consistent with the Army's own recruitment strategy during the time these soldiers joined, which emphasized the transformative effects of service allowing people to find direction in their lives and make their families proud. A few soldiers said they chose to join because of a role model—either family members who were in the Army or characters they saw in movies or on television. Popular action movie heroes like John Wayne were especially influential role models, inspiring more than one interviewee to begin a career in the Army. This is consistent with what other researchers have found using more systematic methods. For example, Richard Homes reports that over half of marines in a class at Camp Pendleton in 1960 admitted joining because of John Wayne movies.[59]

Whatever their initial motives for joining, the soldiers described becoming heavily invested in the Army's corporate identity over time. For most, the transformation was not caused by training. Rather, it developed slowly over the course of several years, resulting from cumulative experiences. Almost all participants said that as they adjusted to the Army life, they began to enjoy it and their motives for military service changed. They were proud of their membership in the "profession of arms" and quick to differentiate themselves from those who did not make a similar commitment. The interviewees sounded as though they were describing different people than those who had initially joined the Army. This self was one that soldiers invariably described while making references, sometimes tacitly and sometimes explicitly, to the values and character traits embedded in the Army values.

The soldiers showed a strong desire to clearly distinguish insiders from outsiders. There was a sense that it was easy to pick out the soldiers who had yet to undergo the transformation that would make them true military professionals. Those soldiers were still outsiders to some extent. This sentiment was most often directed against members of Reserve and National Guard units, though even active-duty soldiers were sometimes characterized as lacking a deep commitment to the Army. There was an even stronger feeling that those outside the American military, especially civilians, were fundamentally different. Even American civilians were treated as an Other that could not comprehend or appreciate the military and the soldiers themselves.[60]

Soldiers described their corporate identity with reference to a concept of professionalism that unified all members of the Army. They felt strong personal attachments to their friends and members of their unit, but their professional identity and the associated values were linked to the Army as a whole. Initially, this revelation was difficult to reconcile with claims that ethics training was ineffective. As the soldiers explained their personal journeys becoming members of the "profession of arms," I found myself wondering how they could have the same ethical sensibilities before and after training even as they professed to be fundamentally different people because of their time in the military. I came to see that soldiers did experience a shift in awareness, but it was the result of enculturation and cumulative efforts to change identities rather than the product of any explicit ethics training. They transformed as they came to see themselves as members of a distinct group with its own culture and values and as they internalized those values.

The soldiers' descriptions of the effects of enculturation fit with Alasdair MacIntyre's account of how virtue ethics functions within a community. He describes virtues as being connected to a group's way of life. Virtues are attached to social context and social roles.[61] He argues that systems of virtue ethics exist only within this group context, as the group must define what qualifies as virtue and give virtues their substantive meaning. Virtues do not exist in the abstract but always within a specific practice. With MacIntyre's point in mind, it makes sense that explicit ethics training presented in a classroom setting, outside of the context of normal group life, would seem ineffective to many soldiers, especially for new recruits before they undergo the identity shift that leads them to become members of the collective for which the virtues are meaningful. The Army's culture, its sense of professionalism, and its virtue ethics are therefore mutually reinforcing. The organization's strong professional identity serves as a basis for its distinct way of life and the formation of a unique set of values. These values in turn reinforce the belief that the Army is a profession in the strongest possible sense, with its own way of life that is different from that of the American civilian population.

Conclusion

The US Army has a history of relying on virtue ethics as its primary source of guidance going back to the decades before the Vietnam War, when the elite codes of American military academies became the basis of military ethics for all soldiers. The virtue-based reasoning the Army employs is bounded by rule-based ethics, which shows up most clearly in the ROE, yet soldiers are afforded a great deal of freedom to use their own judgment when making decisions, and individual character is invariably treated as the ultimate source of good and bad conduct. As I show in this chapter, the Army's ethics doctrine and training are designed to shape the character of those who become members of the Army not only through explicitly virtue-based education but also with the more subtle and powerful practice of affecting a change in how soldiers see themselves. Soldiers become members of the Army and take on the values perpetuated by the military culture as they undergo an identity shift to become members of the military profession.

The most serious issue for the US Army as it engages in counterinsurgency warfare is reconciling a culture based on warrior virtue with operations that often require soldiers to act with restraint. This problem has continually emerged since the Vietnam War as the US military goes through cycles of reaffirming its virtue ethics and reconnecting it to conventional operations in response to failures in counterinsurgency only to find that its ethics are inadequate for the next unconventional war. During the peacekeeping operations of the 1990s, rules became more salient and strict, severely limiting soldiers' autonomy. However, dissatisfaction with constraining the ROE and a sense that these are inimical to mission success and force protection led the Army back to virtue ethics. Throughout its wars in Iraq and Afghanistan, the Army has sought to innovate and adapt to the challenges of counterinsurgency. A central part of this adjustment has been the gradual strengthening of virtue ethics, especially through more sophisticated training techniques and more detailed guidance about how the Army values and good character should be enacted.

6

The US Army in Afghanistan and Iraq

Warrior Virtue in Asymmetric Wars

In this chapter I continue analyzing the US Army, this time focusing on the extent to which the ethics training I discussed in chapter 5 informs soldiers' conduct in practice as well as the consequences of using virtue ethics as a guide for counterinsurgency. The interviews I conducted reveal that virtue ethics was the strongest ethical influence on US Army soldiers fighting in Afghanistan and Iraq. This is evident from the importance they attributed to values and character when describing their reasoning processes. When faced with demanding choices, soldiers emphasized their reliance on intuition and personal judgment. This is characteristic of a virtue-based approach, as it suggests that soldiers acted according to habits that had been so deeply ingrained that they could be followed unreflectively or that dilemmas could be resolved by employing a kind of judgment akin to Aristotelian *phronesis*.

The first and second sections evaluate interviewees' attitudes toward ethics. Although soldiers drew ethical inspiration from various sources, their primary reference points were the Army values and a sense of professional identity. For most, values and character informed all actions, making virtually every decision an ethical decision to some extent. The soldiers tended to describe deontological norms (the laws of war and their rules of engagement [ROE]) as being restrictions on how they could act but not as providing positive guidance. Almost all the soldiers I interviewed said that when they were deployed and acting as members of the US Army, they placed their obligations as soldiers before all others, leading them to act according to what they considered to be good character for a US Army soldier. At times they found that their military obligations conflicted with other moral feelings, yet they usually prioritized the former.

The third section considers several of the stories soldiers told me to illustrate their good conduct. They described making intuitive moral judgments or acting based on deeply held values. Many of the actions soldiers were most proud of were performed when the ROE were open to interpretation or despite possible bad consequences, which put them beyond the scope of deontological or consequentialist reasoning. In the fourth section I discuss situations in which soldiers made or observed decisions they thought were questionable or unethical. As with good actions, bad ones were generally linked to character attributes and values. Misconduct was never an isolated event but rather a symptom of "bad character." The fifth section also considers some of the potential explanations for misconduct among US Army soldiers. Commentators blame infractions on poor ethics training programs, badly formulated norms, unit subcultures, and the pressures of conformity. These explanations probably have some degree of truth, as the soldiers I spoke with were unimpressed by the quality of formal ethics training, sometimes had trouble deriving clear guidance from the Army's abstract values, and reported inconsistencies in standards across units. Nevertheless, these issues were symptomatic of more fundamental problems.

In the final section I argue that the strengths and weaknesses of the Army's ethics, both at an institutional level and in the reasoning of individual soldiers, are closely linked to how the Army's ethics are framed. Because the system is based on values that are only loosely defined, the US Army's virtue ethics is extremely flexible. The Americans interviewed seemed to be skilled at finding their own solutions to unexpected dilemmas. Even when faced with unanticipated situations, they were quick to take decisive action and confident in their choices. Soldiers admitted to a tendency to overreact to threats or misidentify civilians as enemy combatants. This was especially clear when it came to interactions with civilians. Compared to the Israeli and British soldiers, the Americans were generally the most inclined to see counterinsurgency in terms of conventional warfare and to interpret noncombatants as being hostile. This was a barrier to good civil-military relations. Also concerning was that many of the soldiers had feelings of exceptionalism, seeing themselves as distinct from and morally superior to civilians, both in the United States and in the areas where they were deployed.

Attitudes about Ethics

The US Army soldiers I spoke with had greater difficulty than British and Israeli soldiers in identifying whether an event qualified as an ethical dilemma. When prompted to recall ethical dilemmas they had encountered or to explain their reasoning processes, they generally needed some further explanation of what I meant and what types of situations might qualify as ethical challenges from my point of view. I quickly found that this was not a reflection of poor ethical judgment but rather an effect of a virtue ethics perspective. For someone who is trained to see actions through this lens, everything is in some way related to one's character, being guided by character and reinforcing or reshaping it. All actions have an ethical dimension to some extent. The difficulty interviewees had when recalling dilemmas was therefore not a sign that they were incapable of ethical reasoning or that they were uninterested in the deeper implications of their actions but rather that they were used to thinking about ethics in ways that make it hard to approach ethics in counterinsurgency as a distinct subject apart from larger issues of professional identity.

The interviewees were highly attuned to the importance of values. As I discuss in chapter 5, they tended to narrate their careers and the personal transformations of becoming part of the military profession by talking about shifts in values and changes in their character. They also tended to describe the world in terms of different value systems when characterizing interactions with foreign civilians or enemy fighters. They would say, for example, that Americans value life and soldiers in non-Western militaries do not, or that they were surprised at the different values of the foreign populations they encountered. The use of personal values as the language to describe ethics reflects a strong preference for this character-based way of thinking. This language divides the world into groups with irreconcilable codes of conduct.

Interviewees usually invoked the Army values when describing their character traits or explaining decisions they made. These were often considered so important that they could outweigh competing norms and interests. Almost all participants described themselves as religious. Most were Christian, which reflects the Army's overall composition, although I also interviewed one Muslim soldier and three Jewish soldiers. Around a third of the soldiers said religion had a significant influence on their thinking. However, most felt that it would be unprofessional to rely on religious values as the primary source of norms when they were acting on behalf of the Army. One Muslim officer said he prided himself on placing his membership in the Army above all else and doing this conspicuously to set a good example of what Muslims could be like for his fellow soldiers. He also felt it was his responsibility to educate others about his religion and to help them understand it for strategic purposes. He wanted to educate others in the religion not so they would become converts but rather so they would be better able to accomplish their military objectives. That soldier went on to say his primary guide when resolving ethical challenges was his sense of duty to follow orders.[1]

Soldiers also described some instances in which their obligations as "members of the profession of arms" forced them to suppress discomfort about their mission. One member of a civil-military affairs unit reported that he was given the task of funding reconstruction projects and paying sheikhs for cooperation, work that often required him to suppress his own sense of right and wrong.[2] Construction money went toward infrastructure development, including work on sewer, water, electricity, academics, trash, fuel, and hospitals (SWEAT-FH). These projects had the potential to rebuild communities damaged by the fighting, but commanders responsible for distributing the money gave the most to leaders who disliked the Americans, in an attempt to win new allies to the American cause. The soldier said he was upset whenever he received orders to pay sheikhs who criticized the Americans and were even suspected of carrying out attacks. The hostile sheikhs would claim credit for reconstruction projects and undermine the American war no matter how much money they were given.

The interviewee described one very disturbing incident in which he had to continue providing assistance to an uncooperative sheikh who was using the American funding to seize control of a pro-American sheikh's neighborhood. He used the money to pay for various construction projects, thereby increasing his prestige when rivals who aligned with the United States lacked the resources to compete. Mismanagement of funds is a common complaint in soldiers' narratives and journalistic accounts of the wars, but what was striking about the soldiers' story was how he responded to these problems.[3] He felt he had little choice but to report this concern to his superiors and then follow his orders. He was among the most disillusioned and cynical of the soldiers I spoke to, describing the war in Iraq as "a big fucking mistake." Nevertheless, he emphasized that he was obliged to do his duty to follow orders even when they were seriously flawed. It was revealing that someone so strongly opposed to the war and how it was managed still felt that the bond with his comrades and loyalty to the Army must dictate his actions.

Others reported similar value conflicts when assisting local fighters in Iraq and Afghanistan. Five interviewees recounted stories of giving weapons or training to local fighters who promised to support American operations, only to later find those weapons on the bodies of dead enemy fighters or to see former trainees joining the insurgency. The soldiers expressed disgust over the decision to arm and train enemy militants, yet each said he continued to follow orders when told to distribute weapons or to help train a new group of local security forces. This problem of weapons and training being used against coalition forces has been borne out in other research and appears to be a systematic hindrance to US counterinsurgency operations.[4] The soldiers emphasized that they did not understand how the weapons were advancing American interests in the country or promoting stability but thought it was their duty as members of the profession of arms to follow the orders they were given.

When soldiers described taking guidance from sources other than the Army values and their professional identity, they nevertheless framed their actions in terms of values and character. This was evidence that even if soldiers disagreed about what constituted good conduct, they tended to share a virtue ethics orientation and subordinated personal feelings to their professional obligations. One member of a National Guard unit deployed to Iraq made this particularly clear. He held his identity as a soldier in high regard but said his religious identity as a Christian provided his most basic and important moral guidance. This was in sharp contrast with what most soldiers told me. However, it was revealing that this man still described his ethical outlook in terms of character traits. He said he did not employ specific rules from Christianity but rather attempted to be a good Christian, allowing that identity to direct him toward the right course of action. His conception of virtue therefore deviated from those the Army attempts to inculcate, though the style of thinking remained the same. This coincides with Martin Cook's research on US Air Force personnel, as he finds that Christian morality heavily informs soldiers' ethical sensibilities but that it tends to do this by reinforcing the military's character education. In particular, it discourages moral relativism and emphasizes the importance of treating morality as part of personal identity rather than simply a matter of producing good effects or following institutional norms.[5]

Applying Personal Judgment

Just as the soldiers had trouble distinguishing ethical from non-ethical decisions, they found it difficult to articulate an explicit method for resolving dilemmas. Again, this was a by-product of the virtue ethics tendency to treat all types of action as being a reflection on character and the related aversion to formulaic approaches to decision-making. Throughout the interviews, I listened to story after story illustrating good or bad conduct and then asked the soldiers why they or others acted as they did. Most characterized their decisions as being unreflective, instinctive, or intuitive. The soldiers rarely stopped to weigh the potential consequences of different courses of action, nor did they apply a clear decision procedure. They generally thought that such rigid approaches to ethical reasoning were laughably unrealistic in most cases—far too slow and cognitively demanding when they were on patrol in a dangerous neighborhood or under enemy fire. They also did not describe applying specific Army values as though these were rules. They never explained their decisions by saying something like "the value of courage says to do X, so that is what I did." Instead, soldiers generally described their ethical reasoning in terms of personal judgments.

Whenever their stories of specific incidents reached a moment of choice—the point at which the soldier was forced to resolve an ethical challenge—soldiers said they used "judgment" to determine the right course of action. Judgment played the central role in directing soldiers, especially when facing ambiguous threats or uncertainty. They described their decisions by saying things like "I made a judgment call" and "it was up to me to use my best judgment." This is what we should expect from soldiers who have internalized a set of values and a warrior ethos. These values rarely provide soldiers with direct guidance but rather are meant to give them an intuitive sense of good conduct that can guide them on a pre-reflective level. Judgment operated as *phronesis*, the practical wisdom that virtue ethics prizes above all else—the wisdom to simply *know* what to do when an ethical challenge arises.

Soldiers often described judgment as being "personal judgment," or they personalized judgment in some way by calling it "my best judgment." However, they also made it clear that judgment had a collective aspect. It was their judgment because they exercised it as individuals and because they felt it was a part of their ethical identity. The personal judgment that soldiers relied on reflected norms derived from their group memberships, especially their membership in the Army. The soldiers did not make judgments as lone individuals; rather, they attempted to act according to collective values shared by all members of the profession, which they had personally internalized. Above all, their judgment was informed by a sense of how good soldiers were supposed to behave.

The importance of judgment for these soldiers was not a personal inclination. It was a policy decision embodied in the ROE and the instructions provided by superiors. Interviewees refused to discuss their ROE in detail because these were classified, but they mentioned that the ROE always opened with explicit instructions that nothing they contained could prevent self-defense. For example, an ROE card used in Iraq in 2003 said, "Do not fire into civilian populated areas or buildings unless the enemy is using them for military purposes or if necessary for your self-defense."[6] The authorization to act defensively was understood as permission for soldiers to exercise independent judgment. Although they would have to justify any use of force decisions, they were ultimately responsible for deciding what qualified as legitimate self-defense and felt they were given the benefit of the doubt when invoking this. When asked to explain why soldiers protecting convoys would shoot at unmarked vehicles that strayed too close, one said, "It's right there in the ROE. We are authorized to defend ourselves, and sometimes we have to."[7] As this comment illustrates, the ROE create a deontological boundary within which the soldiers felt they were free to make their own judgment calls.

Soldiers also reported being given explicit instructions to use their own judgment if they had to make any difficult decisions. One interviewee, who had been a philosophy major in college, said he would often ask his commanders for more definite guidance about how to act when faced with a "what if" scenario because he was so concerned with the ethical implications of his decisions. The commander's response was always the same: "use your best judgment."[8] Others had similar experiences of commanders stressing the importance of personal judgment and refusing to give definitive answers about how they should respond to any general problems. David Bellavia's narrative of fighting in Fallujah confirms this, as he says that "part of being a leader means you trust your subordinates to do their jobs, and that requires trusting their judgment."[9] He also tells several stories in which he instructed subordinates to trust their judgment.

There is some danger in this admonition to rely on personal judgment. As Mark Osiel points out, it raises the possibility of commanders sanctioning misconduct through omission.[10] It is all too easy for officers to issue vague instructions and then deflect responsibility for how their subordinates behave. A few of the soldiers I spoke with confirmed this assessment by cynically describing the command to "use your judgment." One soldier even characterized this as a way for his superiors to avoid taking any responsibility for their instructions and to shift the ethical burden onto him. "They just push everything on to you. You have to make the call. Then they're safe and they can come after you if you make a mistake."[11]

At the same time, soldiers were protective of this authorization and frustrated whenever guidelines were too specific; the encroachment of deontological reasoning was a persistent concern. They sometimes resented the commanders and lawyers who second-guessed the judgments soldiers had to make in the field. Their comments were mixed with a touch of hostility toward the "REMFs" (rear echelon mother fuckers) and "fobbits" (soldiers who rarely left the forward operating bases), passing judgment on those in the field without enduring the same hazards. One infantryman who was deployed to Iraq said that every time he came in from patrol, the first thing he and other members of his unit had to do was be interviewed by an officer to determine whether the ROE were followed.[12] Even lightly wounded soldiers had to submit to questioning before being given medical treatment. This scrutiny of events that happened beyond the safety of the base by commanders who were rarely in any danger felt like a hypocritical affront to the trust in individual judgment that soldiers were conditioned to expect. Thus, there was a delicate balance between permitting soldiers to act on their own initiative without excessive scrutiny and providing clear enough boundaries to ensure that soldiers would stay out of trouble.

Guiding Values

Most of the soldiers I interviewed supported the wars in Afghanistan and Iraq and were proud of what they and their comrades had accomplished. They offered stories of extraordinary courage in which the norms they had internalized led them to disregard their own security to help others. The stories of right conduct were informative. First, they gave a sense of what kinds of actions soldiers understood as epitomizing good character. These were invariably instances in which soldiers performed supererogatory actions—actions that were not required by any rules and that put them at extreme danger. The more dangerous and selfless the act, the more it exemplified ethical conduct. Second, soldiers emphasized the role of values and good character in these cases. Sometimes they referred to the Army values or to the Warrior Ethos, other times to nonmilitary sources of guidance such as "the value of life."

One of the most experienced soldiers I interviewed was a sergeant major who was a veteran of operations in Somalia, Iraq, and Afghanistan. When asked to recall challenges he had faced, the first example he gave was having to decide whether to provide assistance to an injured civilian after an ambush. During a mounted patrol in Baghdad, an improvised explosive device (IED) exploded, damaging several of the vehicles but not destroying them. The blast also struck Iraqi civilians who were passing nearby. The convoy raced out of the blast area to avoid being caught by additional IEDs or ambushed by militants who might have been waiting in the surrounding buildings. Clearing the area as quickly as possible was standard operating procedure; remaining in a kill zone could invite follow-up attacks on the survivors and emergency responders. Once they were a safe distance away, the Americans regrouped to assess the damage. Several soldiers had light wounds, but nothing required immediate attention. At this point the sergeant major decided to return to the site of the attack to help the wounded civilians. The decision was difficult, he said, because it put his subordinates in danger. There was a good chance that insurgents were still in the area and waiting for a second opportunity to strike. Nevertheless, "the value of life"—a phrase he repeated a dozen times throughout the interview—compelled him to go back.[13]

Upon reaching the blast site, the sergeant major faced a difficult decision. One of the civilians was seriously wounded and seemed to be near death. The medic performing triage said the man's wounds were fatal and he would soon be dead. Insurgent small-arms fire erupted from across the road, prompting calls from the medic and other soldiers to flee the area. The sergeant major said he again decided "the value of life" required him to do the best he could to save the injured man, even if the effort was futile. He ordered the medic to provide treatment and called for reinforcements. He and his subordinates managed to defend the area until help arrived and the insurgents withdrew, but the civilian died.

Although the sergeant major arguably put his subordinates at greater risk by returning to the scene of the attack and directing medical supplies away from others to someone who might have been too injured to save, he acted based on a concern for an innocent person. Acting this way because of "the value of life" and disregarding contrary opinions, even those of a medic, are characteristic of a virtue-based style of thinking. The interviewee displayed initiative, a willingness to endure danger in a supererogatory display of virtue and to persist in acting virtuously, and a disregard for the consequences of doing what seemed right. The same action would probably be considered wrong, or at least misguided, from a consequentialist perspective. After all, the sergeant major put his subordinates at risk and got them into a firefight without saving any civilians in the process. The choice also went beyond what was required by the ROE, especially because these urge soldiers to prioritize self-defense and unit defense above all else.

Another soldier told me that despite doing two tours in Iraq and helping to recapture Fallujah in 2004, he was terrified of IEDs every time he left the forward operating base. The hardest decision he could recall making was overcoming that fear when it threatened to overwhelm him. During his second tour in 2005, his unit was continually conducting patrols in Ramadi and the surrounding countryside. One day the vehicle he was in was hit by an IED. The blast sprayed the vehicle with shrapnel but failed to wound anyone. Shaken, he and the others inside resumed the patrol only to get hit again. This time one soldier was killed and several others wounded. When the soldier returned to base, he was the only man in his vehicle who did not require medical attention, but he was psychologically traumatized. "I spent hours trying to calm down," he said. "It took me forever just to stop shaking. The toughest decision I had was whether to get back in the Humvee the next day."[14] I asked how he was able to keep going after that. "It's my job. If I didn't do it, then someone else would have to." Professional responsibility and a sense of duty compelled him to persist despite intense fear.

Comments about the importance of having good character at times like these provided insight into the soldiers' ethical reasoning processes. On the surface, these remarks seemed fairly superficial and even silly given the weighty decisions at hand. One soldier told me he was very careful about firing his rifle in urban areas because "good guys don't hurt civilians. Good guys try to protect people."[15] Another said he modeled himself on John Wayne and other action movie heroes he had idolized as a child.[16] The soldier who went on patrol the day after sustaining two IED attacks said that "a good soldier doesn't let other people take over the dangerous work. He just keeps going, even when he's scared." They felt more comfortable when they could emulate a role model, even a fictional one; soldiers have a ready supply of models from popular culture and the many historical exemplars featured in the ethics training materials I discuss in the previous chapter.

The Effects of Character

All the soldiers I spoke with said they consistently tried to act ethically. They even attempted to defend themselves when they did things that would seem to be wrong to an observer, such as hitting a prisoner or crashing into a civilian's car. In these instances, they cited extenuating circumstances that compelled their behavior. Usually it was self-defense compelling otherwise questionable acts. Self-reported misconduct was rare, although soldiers recounted many stories of their comrades committing infractions. With misconduct always coming from someone else, it was difficult to get a clear account of why it occurred. Nevertheless, the examples were instructive because of how soldiers explained the reasons for moral deviance.

Among the most shocking examples of deliberate wrongdoing came from a corporal in the infantry who told me about how his squad leader enjoyed harassing Iraqi civilians. Early in 2004 the interviewee was tasked with guarding a checkpoint in Baghdad that controlled access to the Green Zone. The checkpoint was extremely important because of the risk of attacks on those commanders and because many of those passing through it were influential Iraqis cooperating with the Coalition Provisional Authority. One of the regulars at the checkpoint was a sheikh who had been crippled by an American bomb earlier in the war but who was nevertheless committed to working with the American military. The interviewee reported seeing the sheikh kicked, hit, and verbally abused by the sergeant commanding the checkpoint; despite reporting the incidents to his platoon leader and other superiors, nothing was done to remove the sergeant.

The interviewee was able to speak with the sheikh on several occasions and asked him why he continued to cooperate with the Americans. The man's answer was that he would not allow one bad soldier to dissuade him from doing what was best for the future of Iraq. The soldier also explained that the reason the checkpoint came under few attacks compared to others in Baghdad was that the sheikh used his influence in the neighborhood to promote peace while also providing American commanders with details about insurgent activity in the area. That relatively peaceful arrangement changed the day the sheikh passed through the checkpoint with his wives, who the abusive sergeant insisted on searching personally. This was a serious breach of Army rules and of Iraqi norms because the sergeant was a man, and he was deliberately invasive as he touched the women. Although the sheikh had been willing to endure some insults, he felt humiliated by the improper search of his wives. It was the last time he came through the checkpoint and the last day the checkpoint went without an attack for several weeks.

This story is significant for three reasons. First, the sergeant in command of the checkpoint was able to act inappropriately without sanction because the decentralization of command gave him a great deal of freedom to operate the checkpoint as he wished. Second, the soldier who told the story emphasized that the sergeant's misconduct intensified hostilities. The soldier felt his life was threatened by the unethical conduct. Finally, the soldier said that although the lack of oversight aggravated the situation, the sergeant's actions were rooted in a personal ethical failing. In other words, as the interviewee saw it, the underlying cause of the misconduct was not that the ROE were unclear or that there was something wrong with the mission. The sergeant's bad character was to blame.

This was an exceptional story among soldiers I spoke with. No others recalled instances of such blatant abuse of authority. Nevertheless, this is not an isolated event. For example, two Iraqi civilians, Marwan and Zaydoon Fadhil, died when American soldiers forced them into the Tigris River as an ad hoc punishment for being caught outside after curfew. That incident confirmed the same points as the sergeant's story. The soldiers involved had considerable freedom of action and the trust of their commanders to take their own initiative. Their commander, Lieutenant Colonel Nathan Sassaman, echoed the sergeant I spoke with in saying of a soldier involved in the incident that he had "a single lapse in judgment."[17] And once the incident was publicized, it triggered anger in the local community.[18] There was also the case of five American soldiers raping and murdering a fourteen-year-old girl in Iraq, which began with the soldiers at the nearby checkpoint drinking alcohol and plotting their attack. In the weeks leading up to the incident, the soldiers at the checkpoint had continually harassed the girl to the extent that family members and neighbors were worried about her safety.[19] In that instance, too, there was little oversight of the soldiers involved, the perpetrators were criticized for having poor moral character, and the Mujahideen Shura Council was able to exploit the attack for propaganda purposes.

The language interviewees used to describe misconduct is revealing. Whenever they told stories like the one above and reflected on why a fellow soldier acted wrongly, they invariably described the guilty parties as having bad character, poor judgment, or not living up to the Army's values. For example, one military police officer said she saw Special Forces operatives abusing prisoners in the facilities she helped to guard. By her account, "they showed a lack of character."[20] This is a recurrent theme when US Army soldiers reflect on instances of misconduct. In an attempt to rebut claims that he was partly responsible for murders carried out by his subordinates, Colonel Michael Steele said the attacks were the "result of an individual soldier's judgment call."[21] Moreover, as I mention in chapter 5, soldiers routinely criticized comrades who they felt had not internalized the Army's values, and they described those people as being outsiders even though they wore Army uniforms. This criticism came regardless of whether these people actually did anything wrong; the character failing was treated as being inherently problematic regardless of whether it actually caused any bad outcomes.

Although soldiers did not describe their own actions as being unethical, some did confess regretting their choices. Two interviewees mentioned feeling this way the first time they were tasked with searching homes. Both were enlisted infantrymen in the 82nd Airborne Division who had done multiple tours during the early years of the occupation of Iraq, and they recounted virtually identical experiences.[22] They would receive reports about insurgents and then raid their homes in the middle of the night to make arrests and search for weapons. These raids initially seemed like an ideal way to take the fighters by surprise, and several even turned up small numbers of weapons. However, the strategy ultimately failed. As the searches continued, the soldiers came to realize that many of the people were innocent and were unfairly traumatized by heavily armed foreigners storming their houses in the middle of the night. They thought the searches were counterproductive because they inspired anger and fear, especially from men, who would feel obligated to protect their families. The soldiers were revolted by the searches and their own participation in them, yet they were compelled to continue because of their professional obligation to follow orders. They felt they lacked grounds for disobedience because they were not being asked to do anything illegal.

A similar problem arose when soldiers had to deliberately attack civilians while conducting vehicle mounted patrols. During the early years of the occupations of Iraq and Afghanistan, patrols typically lacked armored vehicles and were vulnerable to IEDs and small-arms fire. Every time soldiers got inside a vehicle, they became easy targets. This was especially true in urban areas. Narrow roads and obstructions penned the patrols in, giving them limited space to maneuver and forcing them along paths that were easy to attack. Civilian vehicles further reduced mobility and were sometimes used to block escape routes. To avoid being ambushed, the Americans would ram civilian vehicles blocking the roads and race away as quickly as possible.

Several interviewees reported deliberately ramming or shooting vehicles that they knew belonged to civilians; in some instances they recalled the looks of terror from the drivers as they took the impact of a Humvee. Soldiers' narratives and journalists' reports corroborate that such aggressive tactics were routine.[23] The US military has also documented dozens of instances in which this practice caused civilian casualties.[24] Soldiers rarely stop to assess the aftermath of the attacks—this would defeat the purpose of knocking the vehicles out of the way and exiting potential ambush sites—but they knew that civilians were seriously injured and killed. Michael Schwartz even reports one incident in which a driver was punished for making the dangerous decision of stopping to help a young girl who had been run over.[25] The interviewees who talked about ramming civilian vehicles said they usually reacted instinctively and with the goal of protecting themselves. It was only afterward that they reflected on the ethical implications of their actions and felt remorse. Nevertheless, the soldiers consistently said they had no choice—they had to defend themselves even if it meant prioritizing their safety over that of civilians. The authorization to act in self-defense took precedence, with soldiers insisting that they should have broad personal control over when it was legitimate to invoke this defense.

The Army's Current and Future Ethical Challenges

Despite the US Army's continual efforts to revise and improve its ethics doctrine and training programs, it faces many challenges. The wars in Iraq and Afghanistan were marked by a series of highly publicized unlawful killings and human rights abuses. And my interviews suggest that these incidents are not exceptional. Most of the soldiers I spoke with could name at least one instance in which they saw comrades committing some kind of serious infraction (shooting at surrendering insurgents, disregarding civilian welfare, disrespecting civilians, or abusing prisoners). Most expressed a strong commitment to upholding the highest ethical ideals and were genuinely interested in helping the people of Iraq and Afghanistan, yet their stories suggested there is a disconnect between these intentions and the way soldiers sometimes acted when they were deployed.

Surveys of military personnel have discovered that many have attitudes indicating a high risk for misconduct in the future. One study conducted by the Army's Office of the Surgeon General in 2007 found that, of the 1,767 military personnel surveyed (1,302 Army soldiers and 447 marines), "approximately 10 percent of soldiers and Marines report mistreating non-combatants or damaging property when it was not necessary. Only 47 percent of the soldiers and 38 percent of Marines agreed that non-combatants should be treated with dignity and respect."[26] These numbers are consistent with what interviewees told me. Around half expressed some hostility toward foreign civilians and thought they deserved harsher treatment because of collusion with the insurgents, though all denied acting on these feelings because they were prohibited by the ROE.

Timothy Challans, a professor of philosophy at the School of Advanced Military Studies, reports that many of his students have disconcerting beliefs that could potentially lead them to act unethically or illegally: "The vast majority of military students I have personally taught in the classroom have many malformed moral beliefs. For example, most justify the exhorbitant [*sic*] degree of collateral damage. They also justify harsh and coercive interrogation measures, even after understanding the manifestly illegal nature of such actions."[27] Challans concludes that these attitudes are symptoms of systematic failures in ethics training, and he is not alone in drawing this conclusion. Another study involving interviews with twelve officers who served as brigade commanders in Iraq and Afghanistan found a general consensus that the Army does not do enough to train soldiers in ethics, that classroom ethics education is ineffective, and that they regretted not devoting more attention to these subjects before deployment.

One explanation for unethical attitudes and misconduct is that the Army's system of virtue ethics may be fundamentally flawed. Challans argues that some of the values endorsed by the Army are potentially dangerous, that the emphasis on values is insufficient as a guide for military ethics, and that definitions of the values are superficial.[28] These are related problems, as the inappropriateness and insufficiency of the virtues arises from the lack of deep reflection about what the Army's values should be. As Challans says, "Most discussions about values remain utterly vacuous because people do not reflect upon them enough to figure out what they really are and what metaphysical assumptions they are positing."[29]

Brian Imiola and Danny Cazier argue that the Army's values are inadequately developed. "While values are essential to morality, expressions of values are too vague by themselves to provide guidance for action. For example, the value of 'respect' provides no guidance unless it is further articulated and developed."[30] The values must always be explained and contextualized beyond what is contained in their definitions. Other studies suggest that whatever the strengths and limitations of the Army's ethics doctrine, training practices need reform. Joe Doty and Walter Sowden maintain that the Army's lists of values do not really give soldiers an idea of what a virtuous person should be like and do not amount to a coherent guide. "The primary problem is that the Army does not have a model for character and leader development. We have a piecemeal, catch-as-catch-can training checklist that attempts to teach Soldiers character and ethics."[31] Worse still, they argue that existing instructional techniques are relatively passive and encourage memorization of abstract principles and consideration of scenarios without any real engagement with the underlying ideas.

Another concern is that certain units form subcultures with their own sets of values, which may contradict those of the US military or the civil society.

Dick Couch, a former Navy SEAL officer who has experience with the subcultures of elite units, argues that initial entry training programs across the armed forces give recruits a strong understanding of the values of the US military but that the units to which they are assigned may have different cultures that promote contrary values.[32] Unit subcultures are often dangerous because they can be far more coercive than the larger military culture. Recruits in training are numerous, undergo training as a large group, and are closely supervised. They are more susceptible to peer pressure when they are the new members of the unit and outnumbered by veterans who have an existing social network. For newcomers who are alone, outranked, and desperate to fit in, the costs of failing to conform or of reporting misconduct are high. Couch argues that "moral insurgents" may pressure other members of their units to join their misdeeds or they may succeed in mobilizing tacit approval for them. Douglas Pryer reaches a similar conclusion and uses the Abu Ghraib prisoner abuse scandal as evidence.[33] He argues that those responsible were ethical insurgents who pressured other members of their units to cooperate with them and, in doing so, spread moral corruption.

Lieutenant Colonel Nathan Sassaman's cover-up of two Iraqi deaths in 2004 illustrates just how powerful group loyalties can be.[34] Upon learning that his subordinates had sent two Iraqis into the Tigris River as punishment for being out after curfew, which led to the Iraqis' drowning, Sassaman told them to report the incident "except for the water." Members of his battalion later said that Sassaman had also known about other instances of abuse but had failed to report these or even suppressed them.[35] As he later explained in a memoir, he felt a responsibility to care for his subordinates and protect them not only from threats on the battlefield but also from those who would second-guess their decisions and put them at risk with more restrictions. He expressed concern with the incompetence of senior leaders and the hostility of the media that rationalize this kind of insularity while casting loyalty to fellow soldiers as the highest ethical obligation.[36]

Training for the Wrong Kind of War

The foregoing explanations of why soldiers may take on aggressive attitudes have some merit, but they can be best appreciated by looking more carefully at how the ethical system creates a context in which these problems may arise. Virtue ethics' openness to individual judgment leaves it vulnerable to charges of being too permissive or of leaving guidelines poorly defined. Its reliance on group socialization processes highlights the risk that peer pressure could have a negative impact that goes against broader institutional values. There are also deeper problems with the content of the ethics training soldiers are given—specifically, with its orientation toward conventional military operations and its assumption of American military exceptionalism. As I show in chapter 4, conventional armed forces engaged in counterterrorism and counterinsurgency operations face considerable role strain as they struggle to reorganize and adapt.[37] Soldiers who are inadequately prepared for the unique challenges associated with counterinsurgency, especially delicate escalation of force decisions, are apt to fall back on their training when they experience the intense stress of the battlefield. This is particularly true when their ethics training emphasizes the use of personal judgment, as virtue ethics does.

The US Army's culture has formed in response to the demands of large-scale, high tempo, and extremely destructive operations that can devastate enemy field armies. Analysts of the US Army's conduct during the War on Terror have critiqued its slow adaptation to the demands of counterinsurgency, especially a tendency to use excessive force.[38] Even many senior figures in the US Army have acknowledged this lack of preparedness and advocated greater restraint. The revised counterinsurgency doctrine that was released in 2006 and reaffirmed in 2014 reflects this sentiment and illustrates a desire to reform the Army's culture.[39] Yet many of the soldiers who were tasked with implementing that doctrine were socialized into a much different type of army, and the unit subcultures that Couch and Pryer describe are largely shaped by the most experienced veterans who have a stake in the old ways of thinking. These soldiers were trained to embody warrior values, which may be appropriate for regular warfare but are problematic in the context of counterinsurgency operations. This orientation encourages overreaction in escalation of force scenarios and can inspire a sense of contempt for the civilians or ostensibly inferior soldiers who are seen as not living up to ethical ideals linked to conventional warfighting.

Tyler Boudreau perfectly captures this orientation from a marine's perspective when he says that "for all our talk of gaining popular support, for all our long speeches, we didn't train like we meant it. We didn't focus on establishing rapport or helping a languished people left with no government or infrastructure.... Combat came first."[40] The importance of combat is built into the Army's culture, and a desire for it has led soldiers to seek out opportunities for fighting. In one particularly shocking case, Colonel Michael Steele, a veteran of fighting in Somalia and one of the most experienced brigade commanders in the Army, called on his subordinates to increase the number of attacks on military-age males and promised trophy knives to soldiers who killed insurgents.[41] Steele was reprimanded when Army investigators determined that his aggressiveness helped to incite the murder of four Iraqi men who had been captured.[42]

The conduct of Sassaman's battalion offers further evidence of this mentality's pervasiveness. In an interview with him, Dexter Filkins reports, "He sent his men into the Sunni villages around Balad to kick down doors and detain their angry young men. When Sassaman spoke of sending his soldiers into Samarra, his eyes gleamed. 'We are going to inflict extreme violence,' he said."[43] Sassaman also commented on the extremely different roles soldiers were asked to perform: "By day, we're putting on a happy face. By night, we are hunting down and killing our enemies."[44] Paul Robinson correctly observes that Sassaman's failure to show the right sensibilities highlights the gap between training and expectations, especially the mistake of thinking that ethics training for combat will naturally equip soldiers to make qualitatively different ethical judgments outside of combat.[45]

Virtue ethics demands the pursuit of excellence in whatever is identified as virtuous. If virtues are defined to fit conventional military operations, then the excellence soldiers are encouraged to pursue is based on applying destructive force. This is the challenge that virtue ethics' context and role relativism presents. Ideals of ethical conduct in a conventional war may be poorly suited for counterinsurgencies, and even if ethics training is revised, the socialization processes and culture accumulated for the conventional war orientation take years to change. Thus, regardless of virtue ethics' value as an overall framework for military ethics, great care must be taken when deciding what exactly qualifies as virtuous conduct and what kind of characters soldiers should aspire to.

Civil-Military Interactions

The disconnect between virtues developed for combat and the demands of counterinsurgency appears to be most pronounced when it comes to the strained relations between soldiers and civilians. Because virtues are oriented around a particular community and the Army's virtues are specific to the profession of arms, the Army's system of ethics encourages soldiers to differentiate themselves from civilians. Civilians are outside of the Army and unable to live according to its values, which means civilians are in a sense intrinsically less ethical. A persistent complaint among the soldiers I interviewed was a mistrust of foreign civilians. Over half of the interviewees told stories of civilians secretly supporting the insurgents or of civilians harassing soldiers with nonlethal attacks or verbal abuse. The tendency of insurgents to hide among civilians added to this, with many soldiers telling me about instances in which they were convinced that a civilian was secretly an insurgent.

One specialist in the 10th Mountain Division told a story of coming under heavy fire from rifles and a rocket-propelled grenade while he was at a Special Forces firebase in Afghanistan.[46] When the firing ended, he went with a patrol to find those who had launched the attack and encountered a group of unarmed men in the area from which they had received the fire. The men denied having seen anything suspicious and provided no useful information. The specialist was frustrated that he could not arrest the Afghans or force them to cooperate. He was sure that they knew more than they admitted and that they were either insurgents or collaborators. Reflecting on the incident, the soldier felt it was necessary to put more pressure on suspected insurgents to prevent them from hiding among civilians. He said that attempts to show restraint made it easier for civilians to disrespect soldiers and for insurgents to carry out attacks with impunity. The solution, as he saw it, was to loosen the ROE in a way that would permit greater scope for exercising personal judgment.

At least a dozen other soldiers told similar stories of finding men who they just knew were guilty of an attack and who they thought were only pretending to be civilians, and roughly a quarter of the soldiers I interviewed expressed some dissatisfaction about having to interact with civilians at all. This was because working with civilians felt like a much different job than the one soldiers thought was appropriate. One said that in his company, "everyone was tired of being told to smile and shake hands and give candy away."[47] Another said he felt more like a police officer than a soldier, especially when working at checkpoints. As he put it, "We were all just beat cops in a foreign country . . . that's not what I signed up for."[48] One US soldier recalls in his book hearing another soldier "complaining about the type of moral character that was seemingly inherent in the locals, that ill-bred sort who pushed and shoved to become first in line."[49] Later the author describes the Afghan civilians being duplicitous in claiming to support the Americans only to secretly cooperate with the Taliban. Another soldier writes of his platoon sergeant, "He'd had a rough tour in Ramadi in 2004 to 2005 and hadn't gotten over a visceral distrust of most Iraqis."[50] Chris Hedges and Laila Al-Arian report interviews with soldiers in which they admit attempting to punish civilians because of frustration at being unable to find the combatants hidden among them.[51] This is not to say these soldiers acted inappropriately, only that suspicion of civilians was relatively common and helped to entrench a sense of moral exceptionalism.

Another interviewee said he felt the roles he and his comrades were asked to perform were inappropriate, unfair, and lead civilians to disrespect the Americans.[52] Although the soldier was trained for combat, he found himself spending much of his time distributing food and giving candy to children. These were attempts to build public support, but he found that such measures had the opposite effect. Distributing candy encouraged children to surround the soldiers and to pull at their uniforms and equipment. They learned they could harass Americans with impunity and "they lost their fear of us." The same interviewee reported that some attempts to win hearts and minds were counterproductive given the cultural context. As the Iraqis became accustomed to the American presence, they learned what kinds of responses to expect and realized that as long as they were not violent, the soldiers would not respond.

The soldier reported that he and members of his unit were verbally harassed by civilians, even women, on multiple occasions. Allowing women to yell at them without responding lowered the status of the Americans in the highly traditional Iraqi society. The soldier said he wanted to be able to respond to these incidents in the way that an American police officer would. As he explained, one cannot touch a police officer or verbally harass one without punishment, yet the American soldiers were not allowed to detain people for doing these things. He was especially upset about requiring US soldiers to repair the damage done by IEDs. In one particularly troubling incident, his unit was attacked by an IED that wounded several Americans. The next day they were asked to return to the scene of the attack to repair the destruction caused by the bomb and to repair a nearby building that was damaged in the subsequent gunfight. The interviewee compared this to a woman being raped and having her head smashed through a window and then being forced to return to the scene of the crime to fix the window.

As these examples indicate, many of the soldiers I interviewed reported antipathy between themselves and the civilian populations of Iraq and Afghanistan, and published narratives tend to agree with this assessment. Some hostility is likely to exist during any foreign occupation, yet it was aggravated by the soldiers' dissatisfaction with policing roles and their tendency to see civilians as insurgents in disguise. This should come as no surprise from looking at the Army's ethics and the culture that soldiers are socialized into. Before the wars in Iraq and Afghanistan, training overwhelmingly dealt with conventional military operations, with little preparation for counterinsurgency.[53] And even during those wars, as training expanded to include more work on counterinsurgency and civil-military affairs, the values soldiers were trained to embody remained those associated with conventional war fighting. They were taught to embody a warrior ethos and to follow ethical guidelines that were primarily illustrated with the help of examples drawn from conventional wars. To be a good soldier was to perform well in combat, making combat the highest moral test—a test that soldiers actively pursued. And even after changes to the counterinsurgency doctrine, ethics training remains dominated by the warrior ethos.

For many soldiers—especially ardent supporters of the wars in Iraq and Afghanistan—the mistrust of civilians included American civilians. Most of the Americans I interviewed considered themselves to be morally exceptional. They continually described themselves and their values in contrast with civilians and emphasized the importance of soldiers' sacrifices for the country. To some extent, this may be a consequence of the controversy over these wars and the fact that the wars have had little perceived influence on the civilian population. Some interviewees resented civilians' lack of awareness of how the wars affected members of the military. They were especially angry at how the American public could easily forget about the country's ongoing wars. Many described feeling a sense of betrayal when they returned home to find a general lack of awareness of and concern for the struggles military personnel soldiers endure. Even more upsetting was the strong antiwar sentiment. Roughly two-thirds of the soldiers I talked to supported the wars in Iraq and Afghanistan, and most of these soldiers were very critical of American civilians who opposed the wars and called for an end to them.

Numerous studies conducted over the past two decades have also found a significant gap between civilian and military worlds.[54] My interviews confirmed this and revealed that this gap extends to the ethical domain, with soldiers feeling they are ethically different from and better than civilians. Soldiers see themselves as being ethically superior as citizens because they made the choice to join the military—an act the interviewees tend to see as one of selflessness unmatched by the general population. This feeling of exceptionalism is at least partly the result of the Army's own efforts to maintain a separate, professional identity. A divide between insiders and outsiders is a natural consequence when members of a large institution claim to have a different set of values, different way of life, and different identity than those who are not members.

Other investigations of the military culture have found similar evidence of a gap between civilians and soldiers rooted in a sense of moral superiority. James Fallows argues that members of the military feel civilians do not care about their sacrifices and show little support beyond superficial displays of patriotism. He quotes a retired Air Force general as saying, "I think there is a strong sense in the military that it is indeed a better society than the one it serves."[55] Richard Kohn reports a "wide-spread attitude among officers that civilian society has become corrupt, even degenerate, while the military has remained a repository for virtue, perhaps its one remaining bastion, in an increasingly unraveling social fabric, of the traditional values that make the country strong."[56] Challans says that "military doctrine claims to have domestic moral superiority over American society at large."[57] These feelings show that virtue ethics and the culture that supports it can promote insularity and a potentially dangerous sense of opposition to outsiders.

Conclusion

When character and values play the primary role in structuring military ethics, virtually all aspects of life become ethical in some sense. This makes it difficult to clearly identify discrete ethical decisions that could be resolved with deontological or consequentialist thinking, yet it also integrates ethics more holistically with other aspects of life. The Americans I interviewed emphasized the role of character, values, and judgment in informing their decisions. These were guided by the ROE and some consequentialist concerns about balancing goals against each other; yet when it came to the difficult decisions that had to be made quickly, personal judgment arising from character built through years of enculturation in the Army took precedence.

This conception of ethics holds many advantages. It encourages individuals to take the initiative to do what is right and gives them the freedom to act with confidence when they cannot rely on instructions from their superiors. In some instances, the pursuit of soldierly excellence can manifest itself in heroic efforts to save wounded comrades or protect civilians. At the same time, virtue ethics introduces some risks. Trust in personal judgment and the freedom soldiers have to make their own decisions makes it more difficult to clearly identify misconduct or to restrict soldiers who are apt to abuse their authority. It is extraordinarily difficult to say when a person's character is good and when it is flawed. Moreover, virtue ethics encourages an us-versus-them mentality by creating sharp lines between members of moral communities who share the same values and the outsiders who do not. And because this line is drawn with reference to fundamental differences in character, it can appear insuperable. This results in military ethics being grounded in opposition to the civilian world—an opposition that is potentially dangerous when soldiers perform roles that require extensive civil-military interaction.

The kinds of stories the soldiers told reflect the importance of these ethical influences while also showing that they were anchored in conventional warfare. Values do not exist in the abstract. They may change considerably depending on what kinds of behavior are identified as being salient. The values that take priority in the US military are informed by traditional conceptions of how soldiers should act, which is reflected in references to a "warrior ethos," the use of classical figures like Achilles and Hector as archetypes in training, and the importance soldiers place on distinguishing themselves in combat.[58] The heterogeneity of influences, lack of systemization, and periodic reforms mean that the various pieces of the Army's ethics do not always fit neatly together. The Army's ethics develops rapidly, changing in response to new challenges and new intellectual influences. This dynamic character gives it enormous potential to adapt, but only if the Army can maintain the system's overall coherence and ensure that it is inculcating the kind of ethic best suited for the missions soldiers will be called on to perform.

7

British Military Ethics

Pragmatism and Minimalism

The British Army (BA) and Royal Marines provide a second example of how a system of military ethics can be structured and how a military's history and strategic challenges help to determine the form of its ethical system. British ethics are only loosely articulated and do not have a definitive statement. Instead, ethics are established pragmatically with norms emerging out of ongoing practices and being reformulated as those practices change.[1] Pragmatism has some affinities with virtue ethics, as both systems rely heavily on informal mechanisms of socialization in training and hold individual initiative in high regard. The British Army is even sometimes analyzed in terms of virtue ethics.[2] However, there are important differences between the two styles of thinking. Whereas socialization into the US Army works primarily through integration into a culture sustained by members who derive their identities from shared military values and membership in a profession, British ethics are more rooted in operational practices. British soldiers learn to trust established techniques developed over decades of unconventional warfare and to rely on that doctrine as their main source of guidance.

British Army and Royal Marine ethics are inseparable from the British counterinsurgency doctrine. That doctrine is not itself a system of ethics; it lacks a theoretically sophisticated description of values or rules and was not designed with ethics in mind. Nevertheless, the counterinsurgency doctrine elaborates practices of defeating insurgents that embody ethical attitudes. The central ethical guidelines inherent in the counterinsurgency doctrine are minimalism, cooperation with foreign supporters, and respect for foreign cultures. These are mutually reinforcing components that are analytically distinguishable, but they are enacted together as mutually supporting components of the British practice of unconventional warfare that are designed to promote the kind of conduct that will look attractive to civilian audiences. This approach is epitomized by one of the section headings in Joint Doctrine Publication 3-40: "Lose Moral Legitimacy, Lose the War."[3]

Minimalism appears in both a tactical and a strategic sense. Tactically, the British counterinsurgency doctrine is based on using the lowest levels of force that will accomplish a mission. Tactical minimalism is based on the belief that violence frequently generates backlash and must therefore be employed judiciously. Strategically, the British military is minimalist in the sense that it tends to avoid nation building and other objectives that require sweeping reforms. Instead, the British military strives to leave local institutions and local security forces intact to the greatest extent possible while also enlisting their help in defeating insurgents. This leads the British military to cooperate extensively with foreign security forces in the country of operation as well as to rely on the support of Britain's foreign allies. Finally, the British counterinsurgency doctrine is based on respect for cultural differences, which is essential given its extensive cooperation with foreign institutions and security forces. This sets British pragmatism apart from the US Army's virtue ethics. Whereas virtue ethics tends to promote an exceptionalist attitude, with members of the community being ethically superior to outsiders, pragmatic ethics are generally more open to new values and norms.

In the first section of this chapter I discuss the British Army's and Royal Marines Commandos' involvement in counterinsurgency operations, emphasizing how experiences shaped their institutions and culture. I argue that the most important British military norms emerged out of decades of fighting small wars and confidence in established techniques. Operations in Northern Ireland and Bosnia were particularly important for informing soldiers' sense of how they should behave in Iraq and Afghanistan. Thus, whereas the US Army's ethics is grounded in an effort to escape the legacy of Vietnam through continual reforms, the British military attempts to capitalize on lessons learned from past missions that are generally considered to be successful. In the second section I turn to recent efforts to formalize a British ethics doctrine. I show that these statements of ethics lack a strong basis in any particular type of moral thinking and are instead an attempt to formalize an ethical system that has hitherto been implicit. The third section analyzes the four central norms embedded in the British approach to counterinsurgency: tactical minimalism, strategic minimalism, cooperation with foreign personnel, and respect for cultural differences. These reveal the pragmatic orientation of British military ethics, demonstrating a close association between what is considered ethical and what is tactically/strategically effective.

The Practice of Fighting Insurgents

The British military is extremely active, having taken part in twenty-one conflicts since 1946.[4] These have been waged around the world, in countries such as Northern Ireland, Kenya, Cyprus, Yemen, Oman, and Malaya, and have in most cases put the British military in a counterinsurgency role. Moreover, these wars were fought using many of the techniques learned from the small wars Britain waged to acquire and protect its colonial dominions: strengthening local allies, working with indigenous security forces, learning about foreign cultures, and building political institutions. "Asymmetric or low intensity conflict was the norm for the British Army for nearly every year of the twentieth century, this despite recent assertions that it is a hallmark of the twenty-first."[5] This extensive experience waging small wars has established practices of counterinsurgency and repertoires of action that the British military continually draws from when it is deployed to new theaters.

The British confidence with unconventional warfare is important from an ethical perspective and helps to explain why the British military has not attempted to formalize its ethics to the same degree as the American and Israeli militaries. The American and Israeli militaries became increasingly interested in military ethics, and especially in developing formal ethics doctrines, in response to jarring ethical crises that occurred during counterinsurgency missions that they felt unprepared for. Unexpected moral and strategic challenges disrupted existing institutions and organizational cultures, causing a loss of confidence and the disruption of identity. These experiences in turn generated the need for new operating procedures and new ethical standards capable of withstanding unconventional warfare. Without undergoing similar crises of confidence, the British military has not endured similar periods of ethical disorientation and has instead developed a more implicit ethic over time. The British Army has sought to preserve its practice of counterinsurgency warfare and to resist innovations that might interfere with its established practices.

Past involvement in counterinsurgency is not in itself evidence that the contemporary British military is better prepared for future operations of the same type. Among the soldiers I interviewed, the experience level of the British and Americans was roughly the same. Most of those in both armed forces had no background in counterinsurgency operations before 2001 and were on their first deployments when they were sent to Afghanistan or Iraq. Some of the British soldiers were veterans of Northern Ireland, Bosnia, and the First Gulf War, but I found just as many Americans who had fought in the First Gulf War, Bosnia, and Somalia. However, it is significant that the challenges of counterinsurgency operations *felt* more familiar. The British soldiers I spoke with expressed far less dissatisfaction with policing, civil-military affairs work, and infrastructure reconstruction than the American and Israeli soldiers. These missions fell within the scope of what they had expected from military service and what they thought their training prepared them for. Moreover, training materials, official histories, and soldiers' memoirs routinely affirm the British military's comfort with small wars and its successfulness, thereby solidifying this identity.

The US Army's ethics training reveals a continual effort to overcome past mistakes and, in particular, to escape the legacy of Vietnam. It is preoccupied with its missteps and eager to chart a new course at each opportunity. It actively works to develop new techniques or borrow them. The British military, by contrast, looks to its past as a source of guidance, seeking continuity rather than change. It is particularly sensitive to maintaining tradition and resisting innovations that might interfere with them.[6] As Hew Strachan says, "to an extent unparalleled elsewhere it enjoys the benefits of continuity."[7] The BA doctrine expresses this sentiment by emphasizing its historical roots, saying, "The British attitude to conflict and warfare derives from a deep national martial tradition and a pragmatic fighting culture that stretches back centuries, in both narrative and popular sentiment."[8] As this statement reveals, the British Army not only strives to preserve its tradition and values but does this self-consciously because of its confidence that the lessons of the past continue to matter.

Maintaining tradition is especially important when it comes to counterinsurgency, as the British military is widely considered to be the world's most successful counterinsurgency force. The British military prevailed in most of its colonial wars and is among the few militaries credited with defeating insurgencies since the end of the Second World War. Even when it experiments with different strategies, it usually returns to those that have succeeded in the past.[9] Admiration from strategic theorists and members of other armed forces further contributes to British confidence in their traditions and enthusiasm for maintaining established practices, along with the ethical attitudes embedded in them. Many American strategic theorists and officers advocated for or sought to emulate British techniques during the early years of fighting in Afghanistan and Iraq.[10] This endorsement contributes to the sense that the British approach is best and, by extension, helps to ensure that the British Army continues to employ its well-tested counterinsurgency doctrine as well as its embedded ethical guidelines.

British Army Ethics

The British Army conducts little formal ethics training and avoids any explicit philosophical guidance.[11] The statements of ethics come from the British Army's strategic doctrine and *The Values and Standards of the British Army*.[12] Anthony Clayton says of the latter, "Values and Standards is perhaps the most important statement of British military conduct for 200 years."[13] These sources state the same basic ethical commitments and the same list of values. They also jointly affirm the necessity of acting in a way that upholds the reputation of the British Army and maintains its traditions. Although these sources offer lengthy discussions of soldiers' duties, they usually do so in language that avoids theoretical commitments. Patrick Mileham says of these manuals, "None of them appear to draw on any situational sources of moral philosophy."[14] Without a clear grounding in moral theory, commentators struggle when attempting to categorize BA ethics.

Iain Torrance describes the British Army in terms of Alasdair MacIntyre's virtue ethics, which holds that morality emerges from communities and is inseparable from the ways of life that give rise to them.[15] Torrance's comparison with MacIntyre is apt given the extent to which the British Army understands itself within the context of its traditions and group identity. However, the British Army's ethics fit imperfectly with MacIntyre's because they are not primarily virtue based. Many of the characteristic signs of virtue ethics that are so clear from the US Army are absent. In particular, group standards overshadow individual character, there is generally much less talk of "values," and individual judgment is not the main source of good decisions. References to character are uncommon in moral guidelines because of the class connotations of this term.[16] There may be good reason for this concern when virtue ethics is so often connected back to the kinds of elite codes I discussed earlier. The British Army attempts to strike a more egalitarian note by emphasizing institutional processes over traits that may set certain individuals over others.

Paul Robinson argues that *Values and Standards* is a contradictory mixture of virtue ethics and utilitarianism because it favors virtue ethics but then urges soldiers to use a utilitarian service test. He concludes that "consultation with a moral philosopher could have avoided this contradiction."[17] Robinson's guess that no moral philosophers were consulted when writing the manual is likely true, given the many contradictions in the British Army's statements of ethics and its anti-intellectualism. However, the influence of utilitarianism is far weaker than virtue ethics. There is little evidence of any effort to maximize the greatest good for the greatest number. The British Army clearly prioritizes its national obligations above such cosmopolitan sensibilities. Its thinking bears more resemblance to what I characterized as partisan consequentialism because of its prioritization of national concerns, yet even this label is not adequate because it fails to capture the extent to which accumulated counterinsurgency practices shape current operations. Consequentialism has a synchronic orientation that treats each decision as a discrete event detached from previous events, whereas the British Army's identity and approach to counterinsurgency are inseparable from its history.

In the absence of theoretical grounding, official statements of ethics draw their legitimacy from tradition. The *Values and Standards of the British Army* instructs soldiers to honor "the reputation of the British Army" and to recognize the existence of "collective responsibility" for maintaining high standards of conduct.[18] In doing so, the manual affirms the British Army's identity as a traditional force. It describes joining the ranks of the British Army as a kind of symbolic exchange. The army's reputation, it says, is sustained through the actions of every soldier contributing to a larger collective. Each soldier has the chance to become part of a prestigious institution, and in return the army expects a high level of self-discipline and professionalism that will uphold its standards.

Those standards are embodied in its six core values: selfless commitment, courage, discipline, integrity, loyalty, and respect for others. The language of values and the values that are selected give the appearance that the British Army uses a version of virtue ethics similar to that of the US military. However, the values are framed much differently. Most are stated as *collective* values that describe the British Army as an institution rather than as *individual* values that can be expressed by soldiers acting independently. Whereas the values of the US Army tend to emphasize individual judgment and initiative, those of the British Army emphasize participation in collective practices. The BA *Land Operations* manual even defines morality as "the ability to act in accordance with a shared view of what is right."[19] This is further evidence of a reluctance to frame ethics in ways that would support the same kind of elitism or insider-versus-outsider thinking that may arise from virtue ethics.

Explanations of the British Army's values tend to be vaguer than the US Army's. Most are stated in broad terms that do not give any specific examples of what the value might mean in practice or how one could apply it. However, they are clearly less focused on conventional operations than the American guidelines. The values are not characterized as forming part of a "warrior ethos" or using other language that suggests they are unique to the battlefield.

Selfless commitment affirms that soldiers must follow whatever orders they are given, even when these are unpleasant or dangerous. The definition starts by stating how the British Army is structured. It then informs soldiers that they must allow themselves to become part of that structure in whatever capacity is required, saying, "On joining the Army soldiers accept a commitment to serve whenever and wherever they are needed, whatever the difficulties or dangers may be. Such commitment imposes certain limitations on individual freedom, and requires a degree of self-sacrifice."[20] The definition of discipline reiterates many of the same points. The operations manual explains that the Army can only be effective when commanders can trust that their orders will be followed and when soldiers can trust their comrades. The functional necessity of ensuring that the British Army operates effectively as an institution therefore takes priority over the exercise of individual virtue.

Self-discipline is described as "innate rather than imposed," albeit with the somewhat contradictory claim that "the Army draws it out through education and training."[21] Courage is somewhat more informative. The manual states that soldiers must be willing to use lethal force, but this force should be controlled and restrained, even when restraint increases the risk to oneself and one's comrades. It also explains the importance of moral courage, saying, "the courage to do what is right, even if it is unpopular," may be more important than physical courage in battle.[22] Here we see that ethical conduct is explicitly detached from combat and that combat is therefore not cast as the primary test of good conduct. Integrity is defined as a person's willingness to subordinate their needs to the needs of the group, to minimize their conflicts with their comrades, and to build trust. It "requires adherence to a code, based on common values and standards, and honesty."[23] Again, the value stresses the shared identity of BA soldiers and encourages individuals to look for guidance from other members of their unit.

The definition of loyalty restates the same commitments as the preceding values and explains that loyalty is what unifies the army and builds trust between soldiers. However, whereas selfless service is described in terms of a bottom-up commitment of soldiers to the state, loyalty is characterized by a top-down commitment of commanders to their subordinates. As with integrity, trust is central to this definition. Effectiveness in war depends on trust at all levels. Each member of the army must be able to trust that all others will obey their orders and complete their objectives. Finally, respect for others means soldiers must respect those in their chain of command and people in general. It is a matter of "putting others first."[24] It also explains that soldiers must care for wounded people, including prisoners and civilians, humanely. This is one of the rare places in the definitions that there is a clear statement of what kinds of actions the value entails.

As with the US Army, the rules of engagement (ROE) provide a boundary for acceptable conduct without clearly directing all actions. The "Yellow Card," as it is commonly known, is a brief list of broad instructions that pertain primarily to use of force decisions—instructing soldiers to only use minimal violence to kill enemy fighters, to only attack clear enemy threats, and to fire warning shots whenever possible. The rules forbid actions that are clearly immoral or illegal but still give soldiers extensive freedom of action.

The Royal Marines Commandos' Ethics

When it comes to ethics, the Royal Marines Commandos are similar to the British Army. They follow comparable ROE, which create a deontological boundary within which the soldiers can make their own choices. Like their army counterparts, the marines said their formal ethics training consists almost exclusively in lessons on the ROE. The Royal Marines Commandos also share an anti-intellectualism in their approach to ethics. Their training materials give little attention to moral theory or to articulating a systematic approach to ethics. Like the soldiers, the marines I interviewed have a great deal of confidence in established practices developed over decades of small wars and take a pragmatic approach to determining what they should do when facing dilemmas. For example, avoiding civilian casualties is important not just because harming civilians is illegal or wrong based on some moral theory but because it is counterproductive; it would undermine the mission and could ultimately lead to defeat. Similarly, marines stressed the importance of being polite when interacting with foreigners and of not inflicting property damage, yet they generally said this is essential for building local support, not as an absolute moral imperative.

The marines I talked to emphasized the role of identity and unit integrity when describing their compliance with norms. One said there are two levels of ethics: "the policy level, and the level soldiers are actually on." The latter "is more about identity. They tell you marines do that, or marines don't do that. Marines don't shoot civies."[25] This comment encapsulates the sense that ethics cannot be reduced to deontological or consequentialist decision procedures. The interviewee was clearly aware that international law forbids attacks on civilians, yet his compliance with this restriction was motivated by a sense of self rather than legal oversight. Such references to identity bear some resemblance to virtue ethics. However, in formal statements of marine values and in the interviews I conducted, the language of "values," "character," and "judgment" that heavily inform US Army soldiers is largely absent. As with British soldiers, the marines eschew such individualistic normative reference points.

Interviewing BA soldiers and Royal Marines Commandos revealed the extent of interservice rivalry even when it comes to ethics. The marines said they had much higher standards than their comrades in the army, and although they recognized a shared bond with co-nationals, most felt they had more in common with elite members of the American military than with the rank-and-file members of the British Army. "A different kind of person joins the army" one marine told me, "they just don't have the same standards we do."[26] Another marine said the problem for BA soldiers was that, without the same degree of training as the marines, they were more inclined to panic and misidentify threats.[27] Thus, the marines thought that they had superior training and that their operational skills would naturally translate into superior conduct.

It is revealing that skill itself seems to include an ethical component in the few places where official materials explicitly address the importance of norms. For example, *The Royal Marines Vision* states, "Excellence mitigates risk. Quality expands choice. The quality of Royal Marines Commandos ensures an effective first response and dynamic, ethical adaptation to unforeseen world events."[28] The potential to reduce risk and expand choice by developing higher standards agrees with the interviewees in thinking that more elite fighters should be able to in some way avert or control the ethical challenges they encounter. This prioritizes skill and effectiveness in accomplishing missions over moral reasoning—a point underscored by the notion of "ethical adaptation." Here it is evident the Royal Marines share the British Army's sense that ethics is best approached pragmatically by linking norms to efficacy to the point where these seem to be inseparable.

Elements of Counterinsurgency

The British counterinsurgency doctrine is not an ethical code; it is a political and military strategy for defeating insurgents. It is therefore important to recognize that the British counterinsurgency doctrine is not intrinsically moral even though it serves as an ethical guide. A persistent mistake in commentaries on the British military is the supposition that the British approach to counterinsurgency is more moral or more humanitarian than strategies employed by other states. Some British techniques are morally questionable. In particular, British forces have asserted strict control over civilian populations, used indefinite detention, destroyed civilian infrastructure, and deliberately intensified ethnic divisions to control contested areas and to deprive their opponents of resources.[29] The political uses are also morally questionable, as the British military frequently applied its counterinsurgency doctrine in wars to protect colonial interests or to support corrupt governments. The British approach to counterinsurgency provides guidance not because it is inherently moral but rather because it establishes norms of conduct that govern how soldiers should act when making decisions.

The four most important norms underlying the British counterinsurgency doctrine are tactical minimalism, strategic minimalism, cooperation with foreign forces, and respect for cultural differences. Each of these is primarily driven by strategic necessities rather than a concern with morality, and they are rarely explicitly labeled as being ethical guiding principles in BA publications. Nevertheless, these characteristics of the counterinsurgency doctrine inform the way soldiers respond to challenges when they are deployed and therefore constitute a pragmatic ethic.

Tactical Minimalism

At every level, the British counterinsurgency doctrine embodies a spirit of minimalism—a commitment to achieve objectives using the least disruptive means available. For analytical purposes, it is helpful to distinguish minimalism in the use of force (tactical minimalism) and minimalism in the overall military and political objectives (strategic minimalism). The former is based on using low levels of force in combat and attempting to avoid escalating nonviolent security operations. This directly addresses the escalation of force problem I raised earlier, with a commitment to prevent the intensification of hostilities wherever possible. Thus, it goes beyond the principle of proportionality, which applies to use of force decisions, to encompass the myriad low-level, noncombat actions essential to counterinsurgency operations. This sense of minimalism is frequently cited as being one of the most basic and distinctive characteristics of British counterinsurgency. As Robert Cassidy points out, "Since at least 1945, the basic principle of minimum force has underpinned the British Army's approach to operations short of war."[30] Eitan Shamir notes that "the British variant of mission command is a fundamentally cautious philosophy of applying minimum force, avoiding escalation and stressing the relevance of both action and inaction."[31] Similarly, Frank Ledwidge, a British officer who served in Bosnia, Kosovo, Iraq, and Afghanistan, says that "a 'minimum force' philosophy has long been a feature of British military culture."[32]

Minimalism more is a matter of necessity than a moral choice. Given its small size and its dispersion around the world, British ground forces are rarely in a position to use overwhelming firepower to defeat opponents. Even when expecting combat, British soldiers are routinely outnumbered. This was a common problem throughout the wars in Afghanistan and Iraq. The British military must use force judiciously to overcome numerically superior opponents. It must also avoid inflicting disproportionate harm on civilians or civilian infrastructure, which may draw vital local supporters away from the British cause and even lead them to join the insurgents. The history of British counterinsurgency is therefore characterized by a heavy reliance on small-scale operations, a propensity to only attack the most important targets, close cooperation with foreign militaries, and a preference for separating insurgents from civilian populations.

The emphasis on minimalism sets the British Army apart from the US military, which generally strives to use overwhelming force against its enemies to achieve decisive victories. This was especially true early in the wars in Iraq and Afghanistan, before the more restrained US counterinsurgency doctrine went into effect in 2006. The opening years of the Iraq War provide a particularly good comparative look at two different approaches to counterinsurgency and the extent to which these shaped the actions of individual soldiers. American and British militaries were assigned to regions with different problems and different opponents. Most notably, tensions between ethnic groups were generally higher in the American areas of Iraq than in the predominantly Shia areas controlled by the British military.[33] Nevertheless, the circumstances of their deployment were similar enough to permit comparison.

The British military draws a sharp line between conventional and unconventional operations, transitioning quickly from one to the other as the circumstances demand. The British Army and Royal Marines fought a series of conventional actions against regular Iraqi units during the first week of the war. In the following weeks it was quick to abandon its matériel and technological advantages in an effort to deescalate hostilities. It sacrificed security in the interest of building trust with local people by falling back into tactics taken straight from operations in Northern Ireland, as described in this account: "On 8 April the British began to adopt a postwar mode. Anxious to reassure the Shi'a population that they had come to stay, they took off their helmets and flak jackets, dismounted from their armoured vehicles and began to mingle with the crowds. Soon afterwards General Brims withdrew his armoured vehicles from the city centre altogether, leaving his soldiers to patrol on foot, with orders to smile, chat and restore the appearance of normality."[34] Three of the BA soldiers I spoke with and two of the marines who were in Iraq during the invasion confirmed Keegan's description. They described a strategy of deliberately making themselves look as little like invaders as possible. One interviewee said "the goal was to treat Basra like Belfast"[35]—as a dangerous place where one could get into a gunfight but was foremost a civilian area. They patrolled without armored vehicles (and did so on foot in many instances), stopped carrying heavy weapons, worked in small groups, and abandoned their personal body armor. The soldiers made an effort to become part of the local community while stationed in the city. They even went so far as to visit local restaurants and shops when they were off duty.

One particularly interesting feature of the post-invasion strategy was the way structural constraints were imposed to promote compliance with norms. Because they were denied heavy weaponry or armored vehicles immediately following the invasion, soldiers were given fewer opportunities to use firepower that might inflict collateral damage on Iraqi civilians. This did not determine how soldiers would act, but it did limit the scope of action to make abuses of force less likely than if soldiers had access to heavier weaponry. These kinds of restrictions constrained the available options more than ROE alone. ROE can be ignored or forgotten, but soldiers cannot use weapons they do not have, nor can they afford to alienate local people when their survival depends on cooperation. Some interviewees also described feeling a priming effect such that their attitudes to the local civilians and sense of mission priorities changed along with changes in armament. Therefore, to some extent, the conduct of British soldiers may have been due to the doctrine of restricted war established by senior leaders and directly informed by precedent.

British journalists and even some officers from the British Army issued harsh assessments of the American military's excessive use of force in Iraq. Patrick Cockburn says of the American military early during the Iraq War that "there was massive overuse of firepower. Military tactics had not changed since Vietnam, with success calculated by the number of supposed insurgents killed, weapons captured and suspects taken away with bags over their heads."[36] Brigadier General Nigel Aylwin-Foster, who worked closely with Americans, said Americans showed a shocking level of cultural insensitivity, and the overuse of heavy weaponry helped to strengthen the insurgency.[37] These comments reflect the British view that unconventional conflicts should be waged using low levels of force and that they are fundamentally different from conventional conflicts. They also reveal a tendency to define the British approach to counterinsurgency in opposition to what are seen as excessively violent alternatives.

It is important to be clear that the British Army's strong commitment to minimizing violence is foremost a strategic decision when it is described in official publications or in work on strategic theory. It is a way of avoiding confrontation when possible, and of subordinating the military objectives to the more important political mission.[38] Nevertheless, this pragmatic decision is ethically significant. In principle, it directs British soldiers to limit the level of harm they inflict on civilians and the civilian infrastructure. The practices of conducting dismounted patrols and not carrying heavy weapons also provides greater opportunities for relationships of trust to form between soldiers and civilians as well as for soldiers to feel a sense of empathy for those civilians.

The soldiers I interviewed emphasized the importance of the British policy of using minimal levels of force and generally exercising restraint in tactical matters. Their goal was to accomplish their objectives without inflicting much harm and to avoid disrupting the local civilians' way of life. They described the ethical imperatives of acting proportionately and not harming civilians as being a means of stabilizing the areas under their control and preventing further violence. Ethical and practical goals were inextricably linked and mutually reinforcing. The soldiers made many of the same complaints about excessively strict ROE as American soldiers did, with many wishing they'd had more freedom of action. There was sometimes even a touch of jealousy when remembering Americans' superior protection or greater scope for exercising personal judgment, yet it did not dampen the overall sense that the British approach to counterinsurgency was more effective and ethically defensible.

To be clear, I do not mean to suggest that the narrative of British superiority and ethical restraint is accurate, and I challenge this narrative in the next chapter. The British Army's strategy of using minimal force and restricting what weapons were available to soldiers did not prevent disproportionate attacks and other types of misconduct. James Fergusson, a reporter who witnessed many of the battles between the British Army and Taliban in Helmand Province, writes, "In truth, the British were probably not as good at exercising 'proportionality of response' as they thought they were."[39] Ian Rigden, a colonel in the British Army, describes "the use of minimum force" as a myth because "what constitutes minimal force is determined by tactical circumstances and the strategic objectives, and will not necessarily be the lowest force option."[40] Nevertheless, tactical minimalism is held up in British doctrine and by the soldiers I interviewed as a guiding ideal—a goal that they should aspire to and a part of their identity—even though it was not always satisfied in practice. That is to say, tactical minimalism provides ethical guidance that may be imperfectly realized, or even deliberately violated, in the same way as other norms.

Strategic Minimalism

Strategic minimalism comes from the British military's pursuit of comparatively modest political and military objectives as well as from the decision to subordinate the latter to the former. The ultimate goal of its counterinsurgency operations is generally not to remake an occupied area in substantial ways but to restore security and promote British political interests in the least intrusive way possible. This approach has deep roots. During the eighteenth and nineteenth centuries, the goal of colonial occupations was to either take control of existing institutions and use them as the basis for its administration or to develop new governmental institutions that could be operated by foreign officials who had British backing.[41] This permitted Britain to protect its interests in foreign countries without maintaining a large force presence. This strategy persists in the British counterinsurgency doctrine, which is likewise based on strengthening or reconstructing political institutions without attempting to redesign them in the substantial ways characteristic of nation building or democratization.

Although strategic minimalism is pursued at the highest levels of command by those who are in a position to determine what the strategic objectives are, it was also reflected in the attitudes of individual soldiers toward their deployments to Afghanistan and Iraq. The British soldiers described their reasons for taking part in the wars in Iraq and Afghanistan differently from the US soldiers. Over half of the Americans I spoke with claimed that fighting terrorists abroad prevents them from carrying out attacks in the United States. They echoed President George W. Bush's assertion that Americans must "fight them over there, so we don't have to fight them here." Other common justifications were that the wars were retribution for the 9/11 attacks or were important efforts to democratize other countries. This also reflects the American strategic culture, which is characterized by "a strong and long-standing predilection for waging war for unlimited political objectives."[42] Only three of the Americans thought the wars were unjustified when they were initially deployed, and those who afterward felt the wars were misguided generally objected to how the wars were *managed*—not to the overall goals.

The British soldiers were more skeptical about the motives for the wars, especially in Iraq. None I talked to thought that nation building was a good idea in principle, and almost all said the political objectives in Iraq and Afghanistan should have been more modest. Most doubted it is possible to remake a country's government by force, especially when the country has a much different culture and lacks many of the social institutions that serve as the basis for democracy. Most also felt that political reconstruction intrudes too much into affairs that should be left for local governments to determine. They favored taking an advisory role in counterinsurgency operations—providing security and helping to rebuild institutions and infrastructure without dictating exactly how these have to be remade or what system of governance should be used.

Other firsthand accounts from soldiers and journalists interviewing them often express the same skepticism about the political objectives, especially democratization. Stephen Grey writes, "The new Afghan war is being fought also in the name of the new 'democratic' Afghan government. But soldiers know this government is corrupt and often reviled by the local population."[43] He argues that the war was really about drugs and that even this was futile because the government participated in the drug trade and would use security checkpoints to regulate shipments. Kevin Mervin, a veteran of the Iraq War, argues that "democracy and freedom will only work if the Iraqi people are left to use it in their own way."[44] As he sees it, foreign military support could help to create a context for political change but cannot be its true source.

The soldiers also did not feel that the outcomes of the wars in Afghanistan and Iraq would affect British national security, only that they would shape foreign policy. Again this was in sharp contrast to the Americans, many of whom joined because of 9/11 and wanted to prevent another attack, and to the Israelis, who felt they faced an intense and persistent security crisis. The British soldiers' feeling that the stakes of the wars were fairly low supported the attitudes of detachment and minimalism. Without a deep personal or national investment in the conflicts, the soldiers did not think they had to completely destroy their opponents or fundamentally remake foreign polities.

It was enough to kill or capture key enemies and to empower more moderate local forces. This fed the soldiers' hopes of accomplishing their objectives with as little destruction as possible. It also promoted respect for the cultural and political autonomy of those living in the contested areas, as the British soldiers felt there was no need to transform the identities of Iraqi and Afghan people in pursuit of nation building.

Reliance on Foreign Support

The British military has long been a diverse institution that incorporates many noncitizens and works closely with foreign personnel. Ian Rigden says it "is inherently joint in its focus."[45] Like tactical and strategic minimalism, this is a matter of necessity. The country's relatively small population and its military dispersion around the world makes it impossible to fulfill all security obligations without foreign support. However, this necessity is one that the British military has transformed into one of its greatest strengths. It has proven to be very successful in including foreigners into its ranks, employing large contingents of soldiers from South Africa, Fiji, Gambia, Malawi, Kenya, and the Caribbean.[46] During the wars in Iraq and Afghanistan, roughly 12 percent of the British military personnel were born outside the UK.[47] The British military also includes the Brigade of Gurkhas, which is primarily composed of soldiers from Nepal. Virtually every major campaign of the past two hundred years has drawn on assistance from foreign soldiers who distinguished themselves by working alongside UK natives.[48]

The British military also cooperates extensively with local security forces in the areas where it is deployed. Foreign auxiliaries are generally used either to supplement the regular British military to increase its numbers or as specialists who can perform roles for which British soldiers are poorly suited. Each of these modes of inclusion is evident from the Malayan Emergency (1948–60), which is often cited as being the country's greatest counterinsurgency victory and an archetype for future conflicts. "During the first three months of the insurgency some 24,000 Malays were enrolled into a special Constabulary and used for static guard duties, freeing troops for mobile patrols as the constables were trained."[49] Later it created a force of almost 250,000 Home Guards.[50] British soldiers were unskilled at jungle warfare and relied on assistance from Sarawak Rangers, who were recruited from Borneo, to lead their patrols. The British even created the Special Operations Volunteer Force, which was entirely made up of rehabilitated enemy fighters.

In Iraq and Afghanistan, the British arranged for local militia groups to help provide local security. In Iraq, they had assistance from the Mahdi Army and other militias, and their dependence grew as the size of the contingent there shrank.[51] When the British withdrew from Basra in 2007, it did so with assistance from the Mahdi Army—a controversial decision that resulted in a brief reign of terror by the militia once it was left in control. They then depended on the Iraqi Army to liberate Basra from the oppressive militias and restore order. In contrast to past collaborative efforts, this was generally considered to be a humiliating defeat. As Christopher Elliott notes, "The British might have been right in the long term that prompting the Iraqis to solve their own problems was the best solution, but it was at the cost of huge reputational damage for the British and the lives and disruption of many Baswari citizens."[52] The attempt to emulate previous operations by providing cooperative security and gradually increasing the burden on local forces ultimately failed. By extension, the implicit ethic of granting local autonomy ended up having disastrous consequences.

In Afghanistan, British forces worked alongside the Afghan National Army (ANA) and Afghan National Police (ANP) to compensate for their numerical weakness. This was similar to what it had done in Malaya by cooperating with local auxiliaries and in Northern Ireland, where it worked with Protestant militias and police forces such as the Royal Ulster Constabulary.[53] Although most of the Afghan forces were trained by the United States and other International Security Assistance Force (ISAF) partners, the British military provided some specialized training and conducted joint operations with the ANA and ANP. As I discuss in the next chapter, many interviewees worked alongside these local forces and found that this collaboration introduced unexpected ethical challenges.

Respect for Other Cultures

The norms of tactical minimalism, strategic minimalism, and cooperating with foreign personnel are made possible by, and also help to reinforce, an underlying attitude of respect for cultural difference. The British military has developed in a way that has made it highly conscious of foreign cultures, in large part because it has been involved in so many different countries for so long. Its colonial operations gave it extensive experience in cultivating civil-military cooperation in dozens of settings.[54] Successful commanders became adept at understanding unfamiliar people, their cultures, and their values as this knowledge was the key to building strategic relationships and deciding how foreign populations could best be controlled and administered. Since the Second World War, the British Army's orientation in unconventional conflicts has shifted from maintaining colonial rule to protecting allied governments or enacting regime change, yet knowledge of foreign cultures remains a key instrument of control. Respect follows from this knowledge, both because learning about foreign cultures fosters insight into how others think and because cooperation with foreign populations requires that knowledge of their culture be used to facilitate good relations with them.

The British Army resembles the US Army and is distinguished from the Israel Defense Forces (IDF) in the distance from civilian populations that is characteristic of all-volunteer forces. It has its own culture, dress, and language. It also has distinct military values that diverge from those of the public at home and in areas where it is deployed.[55] However, whereas the US Army's system of virtue ethics is premised on a strict separation of soldiers from civilians, the British Army attempts to minimize this difference with efforts to bridge the gap between military professionals and outsiders. It strives to reduce the distance between soldiers and civilians by having soldiers live among foreign civilians, meet locals during patrols, and work alongside foreign government and security personnel. This is reflected in the efforts to discard heavy weaponry and armor, which I discussed in relation to tactical minimalism. The goal is to create a sense of understanding that can be more effective in maintaining security than coercive force.

Joint Doctrine Publication 3-40 affirms the importance of understanding the local culture and transforming this knowledge into a strategic asset: "People from different cultures both behave and think about the world in different ways. The commander should first try to understand how people from different cultures think and what symbols, themes, messages, etiquette and practices are most likely to resonate with them. This should include systems of reciprocity, kinship, allegiances and social obligations."[56] The emphasis on respect for cultural difference is evident from British soldiers' harsh judgments of their American allies. High-ranking British officers complained about the Americans' inability to take on the appropriate mind-set for working in unfamiliar environments and aggravating the local people. Brigadier General Aylwin-Foster said of the US Army, "Despite its own multi-cultural nature, the Army was not culturally attuned to the environment,"[57] and "whilst they were almost unfailingly courteous and considerate, at times their cultural insensitivity, almost certainly inadvertent, arguably amounted to institutional racism."[58]

This attitude seems to have been fairly widespread throughout the ranks. John Newsinger argues that "as far as the British were concerned, the Americans made the situation worse by their excessive firepower, downright brutality and cultural insensitivity."[59] A British soldier, in his memoir of his time in Afghanistan, criticizes the American forward operating bases, which had "an incongruous parade of fast-food outlets—Burger King, Pizza Hut, Tim Hortons' coffee shop, plus a souvenir shop for fuck's sake—built by the Americans to create a home from home." He goes on to say, "Unsurprisingly this was not how we did things. New arrivals wouldn't find such a High Street at Bastion [the main

British forward operating base in Helmand Province, Afghanistan]."[60] He also describes an unnamed American general as being "contemptuous, arrogant" because of the things he said to British soldiers.[61] Again, this is evidence of the British military defining itself as moderate and culturally engaged against an image of American excess and naïveté.

Myth and Reality

The popular narrative of the British military conducting a more friendly and successful type of counterinsurgency helps to explain why the US Army relied so heavily on the British model when reformulating its own practices and why the British Army seems to have so much more confidence in its approach than the more overtly self-critical US Army or IDF. However, the myth of British counterinsurgency excellence has not always been borne out in practice, and one of my goals in analyzing the British performance is to call attention to the reasons why incidents of misconduct occur, despite the widespread belief that it is an exemplar of ethical warfare.

The Bloody Sunday attacks illustrate some of the unpleasant realities of British counterinsurgency in practice. On January 30, 1972, British paratroopers shot fourteen civilians during what was supposed to be a peaceful protest in Derry, Northern Ireland. Another twelve were injured by rubber bullets or beaten. Far from attempting to build trust through a show of restraint, the soldiers were quick to fire on crowds of protesters who were only throwing rocks and bottles. Such a dramatic escalation of force plainly contradicted the minimalism that the British military tries to cultivate, and reports from some of those involved suggest that the soldiers intended to provoke a gunfight that could draw out Irish Republican Army members attending the protest.[62] Investigations into the attack compounded the problem by clearing the soldiers of wrongdoing. It was not until a renewed inquiry in 1998 that the attacks were officially rebuked by the British government.[63] This failure to prosecute the soldiers compounded Catholic resentment of British forces in Northern Ireland and undermined confidence in the rule of law.[64] It was only in 2010 that the Saville Inquiry formally held some of the soldiers involved responsible.

Although it became the most famous example of excessive force in recent British military history, Bloody Sunday was not an isolated event. There was a pattern of brutal attacks against unarmed protesters throughout the early 1970s, including just a week before Bloody Sunday, when members of the Parachute Regiment shot unarmed protesters with rubber bullets at Magilligan Strand. Operations in other theaters were similarly marred by the internment of civilians and attacks against unarmed people. The tradition of counterinsurgency operations that the British military draws ethical guidance from is therefore a problematic source. It includes praiseworthy norms, but these are not consistently followed. Huw Bennett perfectly captures this inconsistency in implementation when he says of British soldiers suppressing the Mau Mau Uprising in Kenya that "soldiers were perfectly capable of offering one prisoner a friendly cigarette and another prisoner a slap with their rifle-butt."[65] This historical precedent provides ample evidence that the accumulated experience from past conflicts does not always promote moral excellence.

Although the British military has sought to learn from missteps, just as the US Army and IDF have, more recent instances of misconduct show that serious ethical problems persist. Soldiers fighting in Afghanistan and Iraq have been involved in wrongful killings, sexual assault, prisoner abuse, and misuses of force against civilians. They have even engaged in sexualized torture similar to what was done in Abu Ghraib.[66] British guards photographed prisoners wearing women's underwear on their heads or being restrained in stress positions.[67] British soldiers have even been linked to sexual assaults on Iraqi men and women.[68] In some cases the victims have been very young. One boy was only fourteen when he was forced to perform oral sex on other prisoners.[69] He was not even suspected of terrorism or political violence; he had been caught stealing milk.

The most prominent example of this came in 2011 when Alexander Blackman, a member of the Royal Marines, killed a wounded Taliban fighter. What made the incident especially shocking was the video recordings from a helmet camera that revealed him saying, "I've just broke the Geneva Convention," immediately after firing the shot, then instructing other marines not to report the incident.[70] This was shocking evidence that Blackman not only acted illegally but did so while cognizant of this, which suggests that simply teaching soldiers the laws of war may be insufficient for promoting compliance with them. Although he was initially sentenced to serve three life sentences in prison, this was later changed to seven months, leading to Blackman's release in April 2017. As in the case of Bloody Sunday, this resolution raised concerns about how serious the British military is about enforcing ethical standards and whether inquiries into soldiers' conduct could be fair. Also worrying is that these incidents have not promoted the same interest in reformulating, or at least formalizing, ethical codes as in the US Army and IDF.

Conclusion

The British military's continual participation in small wars shapes the identity of British soldiers who see themselves as heirs to a long tradition of success in small wars and derive confidence from that identity. The British prestige in counterinsurgency was generally known among the soldiers I spoke with, and it was evident in the level of confidence they expressed about their proficiency. The soldiers and marines tended to see themselves as members of a highly adaptable force that could transition easily between conventional and counterinsurgency operations. They also typically thought the British military was superior to the American military when it came to counterinsurgency, sometimes complaining of the US Army's cultural insensitivity or disproportionate violence.

The British military shows far less interest in formalizing its ethics than the American or Israeli militaries. British military ethics arises inductively. The guiding norms are those that have developed over the course of dozens of unconventional conflicts over the past half century and have even deeper roots in the country's colonial history. Ethics are rarely discussed explicitly. When they are, they are stated in broad terms and with frequent references to the importance of tradition and effective performance. There is a strong sense of mission demands dictating efficacious norms, with these taking on an ethical character because counterinsurgency demands efforts to win support from indigenous populations.

Although the British military incorporates elements of virtue-based and deontological reasoning in its hybrid system, its approach is generally pragmatic. Norms are grounded in practices that have proven effective in past conflicts, and that are often explicitly justified with appeals to their efficacy. Tactical minimalism, strategic minimalism, reliance on foreign support, and respect for other cultures display this pragmatic ethic. In principle, these ideals push British soldiers to comply with just war precepts, treat civilians with respect, and prioritize noninvasive methods of restoring security. These ideals were imperfectly realized during the wars in Iraq and Afghanistan, sometimes with disastrous results, yet they grounded soldiers' attempts to act ethically and helped to form their identities.

8

The British Military's Adaptive Struggle

Adjusting to New Challenges

The British military avoids casting its operations in moralistic language and is more reluctant to borrow insights from moral theory than the American or Israeli armed forces. Instead, it relies on established practices and techniques that have helped it achieve political objectives in the past and constructs norms of conduct around those techniques. As I discussed in chapter 7, the four most ethically important characteristics of the British counterinsurgency doctrine are tactical minimalism, strategic minimalism, reliance on foreign support, and respect for other cultures. This was reflected in the attitudes of the soldiers I spoke with. They took a more detached and pragmatic view of ethics and of the conflicts they were involved in than Americans and Israelis. They were not primarily concerned with acting ethically or embodying a particular warrior ideal. They were instead highly mission oriented and took on ethical attitudes that seemed to best promote the British mission of achieving the political goals at hand. This was evident in their comments on the wars in Afghanistan and Iraq and their own self-conception as military professionals.

When encountering ethical challenges, British military personnel usually followed the guidelines of minimalism, seeking the least destructive or invasive courses of action. At times they put themselves at heightened risk by doing this. The stories soldiers were most proud of were those in which they showed restraint during combat and avoided harming civilians. This was especially true of the interviewees from the British Army. The marines I interviewed tended to tell more stories of heroism in combat, which reflected their greater involvement in offensive operations. However, those from both branches seemed more attuned to the demands of cultivating good relations with indigenous civilians than were the Americans or Israelis, and they were more apt to cite instances of good conduct that did not fit warrior archetypes associated with conventional conflicts.

British soldiers and marines avoided some of the escalation of force situations that tested American and Israeli soldiers by relying on local security forces to perform some of the most ethically challenging tasks. Local fighters helped to protect convoys, provided some of the security for checkpoints, and sometimes even cleared buildings in advance of British forces. This did not stop dilemmas from arising but rather shifted the burden of decision-making and the blame for missteps onto others. In some instances it also created new challenges. Many interviewees recalled strained relations with Iraqi and Afghan militias, the Iraqi Army, the Afghan National Army (ANA), and the Afghan National Police (ANP), with these forces sometimes fighting among themselves or abusing their authority.

The British military fell short of its ideals of minimalism, reliance on foreign support, and respecting other cultures during the wars in Iraq and Afghanistan. Its small forces were overstretched, leading them to rely more heavily on indirect fire, reduce the manpower available for civil-military relations missions, and build stronger links with dubious allies. This indicates the limitations of the pragmatic approach to military ethics. With good conduct grounded in specific techniques, soldiers lose clear guidance as those techniques are abandoned or revised. Moreover, the heavy investment in established practices, overconfidence in their effectiveness, and aversion to self-reflection and reform put the British military at a disadvantage when navigating emerging challenges or reorienting itself following crises. Whereas the US Army's ethics (and its counterinsurgency doctrine) went through a series of reforms and alterations, the British approach to counterinsurgency and the norms embodied in it were largely unchanged and therefore not able to adapt as easily when the circumstances proved unsuitable for existing techniques.

The first section of this chapter discusses the attitudes British soldiers had to military ethics and their sense of the differences between the demands of counterinsurgency and conventional operations. In the second section I consider how they described their ethical reasoning processes. I also present several examples of how British soldiers made ethical decisions that they considered to be good. These examples show interviewees struggling to act with restraint whenever possible. They also illustrate efforts to learn more about and build relations with people in contested areas. In the fourth section I turn to how the British Army manipulates the structural conditions that give rise to ethical challenges to prevent them from occurring. I also discuss the costs of relying heavily on support from local forces and tell a few of the many stories soldiers had of difficult relationships with foreign soldiers and police. Finally, the last section is devoted to explaining why the British counterinsurgency doctrine and its pragmatic norms were imperfectly realized during the wars in Iraq and Afghanistan. Small force size, overconfidence, and uncooperative local personnel interfered with applying established norms or adapting to confront new obstacles.

Thinking about Ethics

The British soldiers and marines I interviewed tended to think about ethics as arising directly from operating procedures rather than from lists of rules or values, just as the official publications on ethics would suggest. Each of the soldiers had a great deal of confidence in the British style of counterinsurgency. Even those who were pessimistic about the prospects of victory in Afghanistan and Iraq felt the doctrine was sound and the problems of those wars were related to how that doctrine was applied. They were not eager to innovate, as their American allies were, because they were not inclined to see problems as the result of systemic mistakes. Rather, problems were rooted in specific concerns that emerged in a particular context and did not seem to require any fundamental reevaluation of operating procedures. This confidence made the soldiers enthusiastic about following established practices of countering insurgencies and conforming to the associated norms.

The British personnel had a strong awareness of the differences between conventional fighting and counterinsurgency and were committed to conducting these types of operations in much different ways. Whereas the Americans and Israelis described being bound to follow their codes of conduct in all types of conflicts, the British soldiers had a flexible way of thinking about ethics that led them to determine the right way of acting based on what seemed to be the most effective for achieving the objectives at hand. There was no perceived contradiction in following one set of norms for the conventional battles fought during their initial invasion of Iraq and a different set once Basra was captured. In particular, the soldiers lacked the same sense that a "warrior ethos" or strict rules should be stable over time and embody some kind of deep morality of the military profession reflected in aretaic or deontological theories. They emphasized a kind of intuitive ethic based on using minimal force and without any supporting ideas that evoke conventional war.

It was revealing that they often anchored the differences between conventional and counterinsurgency warfare in the material they used. The veterans of Iraq described changing their uniforms and weapons to signal the shift from the conventional fighting of the invasion to counterinsurgency. They thought that removing their Kevlar helmets and body armor, leaving their armored vehicles, and not carrying heavy weapons would prime them and the local people for more peaceful relations. Brigadier General Paul Gibson recalls that "we basked in the misguided praise for our decision to patrol in soft hats, enjoying the comparison with our heavily armed US colleagues."[1] This not only showed the easy transition between normative frameworks but also the extent to which ethical conduct was thought to be predetermined by operating procedures and equipment. Ethics was not merely about choices but also about structuring conditions to pave the way for the right kind of attitude.

British soldiers were sometimes scornful of the Americans, who tended to follow the same procedures whether they were launching an attack on Republican Guard tanks or patrolling through civilian neighborhoods. Accounts from British soldiers suggest they saw their American counterparts as being more liberal in the use of force. For example, Dan Mills says that "Americans need no encouragement to start shooting things."[2] Reflecting on an American marine's murder of an Iraqi, Quintin Wright says, "My training in the Paras [Parachute Regiment] instilled in me the need to use aggression coldly, without the need for anger. The kind of group revving-up that can often be observed in the US military always has the potential to allow anger to cause collateral damage."[3] Of course, this changed over the course of the occupations. As violence in Iraq and Afghanistan intensified, the British soldiers went through a remilitarization, returning to their armored vehicles, carrying their heavy weapons during patrols, and routinely wearing Kevlar.[4]

Most of the American and Israeli soldiers described feeling inadequately prepared for counterinsurgency and reported carrying out missions that they felt were not suitable for soldiers. Working at checkpoints and searching houses were especially objectionable. The British soldiers had a different conception of their roles. Those I interviewed were proud of their combat effectiveness and thought of themselves as soldiers rather than as peacekeepers or police officers. They generally did not think that their identities as soldiers were threatened by taking part in counterinsurgency operations or that this was beyond the scope of their training. On the contrary, many said they were happy for a deployment and eager to have the same adventures as the veterans of Northern Ireland. None of the interviewees objected to taking part in low-intensity military operations or described feeling like their work would be better given to police officers.

Some soldiers were frustrated by insurgents' tactics, especially the practice of hiding among civilians, but the soldiers unanimously thought that operations in Iraq and Afghanistan were within the scope of the British military's capacities and that the missions they were asked to accomplish were generally appropriate. The only reports of role strain came from two officers who were charged with helping in the reconstruction of the local infrastructure while they were deployed to Iraq.[5] They were present during the fall of Basra and were among those military personnel who had to restore power, sanitation, and other basic services even though they had no prior experience doing this. Thus, there were limits to what they felt competent doing, resulting in stress when the soldiers were pushed beyond their abilities, but the scope of roles that were perceived as being appropriate was fairly broad. Journalist Mike Rossiter corroborates in his research on how British forces attempted to take over work that went far beyond the scope not only of military operations but also law enforcement. He explains that "a power vacuum ensued, which the troops on the ground were unable to fill," leading to "intermittent power," "a public-health crisis," "water contaminated with sewage," and a lack of food.[6]

The British experience in small wars shaped soldiers' attitudes. More than half of the soldiers explicitly referenced historical examples when explaining British counterinsurgency operations. They described learning from past conflicts by emulating the operating procedures that were best suited for restoring peace in the past while also avoiding known mistakes. Northern Ireland was the most common model, followed by Bosnia and Malaya. Some units were even given explicit orders to "regroup in the formations they had used in Northern Ireland."[7] Five of the soldiers were veterans of Northern Ireland and Bosnia; they not only borrowed insights from those operations but also served as a link to them by relating their experiences to younger soldiers. They would draw explicit parallels between operations, instructing their more junior comrades in how to conduct patrols without offending the locals or how to search for improvised explosive devices (IEDs).

Applying the Norms of Counterinsurgency

Most of the British personnel were highly sensitive to how they appeared to local civilians. Whereas the American and Israeli soldiers tended to view civilians with suspicion—seeing them as potential insurgents or even as insurgents who happened to be momentarily unarmed—the British tended to see civilians more as an audience. This audience was capricious, carefully watching at all times and ready to shift allegiances at the slightest error. This was both an opportunity and a hazard. Civilians were potential allies as well as potential insurgents. Which side they supported depended on earning and keeping their trust, which in turn depended on how effectively the soldiers could act with restraint and work toward their political objectives. This required the soldiers to always be on show—to be constantly engaged in managing perceptions and to even think of decisions related to self-defense with that goal in mind.

Emile Simpson, who was an officer in the Ghurkas, perfectly captures this mentality and presents it as the best way of understanding the unique challenges of counterinsurgency. "Definition of the outcome of the Afghan conflict for the international coalition extends into the perceptions of audiences well beyond the insurgency. The Afghan people are deemed to be a central audience. Beyond Afghanistan the perception of the conflict's outcome within the Muslim world, and particularly in Pakistan, for instance, is a key factor."[8] He goes on to explain that shaping audience perceptions is a more important goal than any immediate military successes because the meaning of success and failure on the battlefield depend on the perspective of the audiences involved. Toby Harnden echoes this sentiment when he describes civilian casualties as being more of a concern for their potential strategic impact than for any directly moral reasons: "Civilian deaths could be disastrous in terms of relations with locals, but it depended on the area and whose family had been killed."[9] This is not to say that there was no concern with civilian welfare, only that this was closely mixed up with a sense of efficacy that makes the concepts difficult to extricate.

The attentiveness to earning civilians' trust and support was guided by the British counterinsurgency doctrine. It is an established part of the effort to divide insurgents from their base of support and from potential recruits. In some past conflicts, such as the Boer War, Malayan Emergency, and Mau Mau Uprising, the British physically separated insurgents through force resettlements or by constructing physical barriers to restrict movement. In Iraq and Afghanistan, this was impossible, so they instead gave greater weight to psychologically distancing the civilians from the insurgents. They attempted to provide effective security while still being polite and respectful.

Efforts to win support from the indigenous population took on an ethical character insofar as these informed soldiers' actions and promoted empathy. One infantry officer said, "I always tell my men that they have to remember how the Iraqis must feel. It cannot be easy going about your life with foreign troops stationed in your town."[10] He went on to say that it is critical for soldiers to remember how the world looks from the civilians' perspective and to be mindful of how civilians' fears can best be allayed. Other interviewees made similar comments about the importance of seeing through the eyes of the civilian audience. One noncommissioned officer even said he tried to understand the people he interacted with by imagining how his family and friends at home would appear to an occupying force and how he would want those relatives to be treated. "I ask myself. What if this lady was my mum? What would I say to her then? Or what if this guy was my brother? Thinking about it that way really changes things."[11]

The soldiers and marines engaged in many activities to understand the local people and build trust with them. Among the most common were "Find, Feel, and Understand" patrols, in which the primary goal was to meet people living near bases and give them a positive image of the British military.[12] The patrols were also seen as an opportunity to learn about the people in the area and to watch for suspicious behavior. These patrols were in themselves indicative of the British approach to counterinsurgency and its embedded norms. Foot patrolling is a core part of British counterinsurgency. It was an important technique in Northern Ireland and Bosnia, and the veterans of those conflicts said they initially modeled the patrols in Iraq and Afghanistan on those precedents. It was only when ambushes and IED attacks intensified that they abandoned this approach and began patrolling in larger, vehicle-mounted groups.

Interviewees were aware that the insurgents' strategy in Iraq and Afghanistan was to push the British soldiers to overreact so that public opinion could be turned against them, and they knew that even small mistakes could lead to disastrous setbacks in achieving a political resolution to the conflict. One of the soldiers told me that "returning fire when we don't have a target only makes us less safe. If we hit the wrong person we create more enemies."[13] He went on to say, "Even if we fire blindly and fail to hit anything, we put people at risk and make them feel threatened. That can have a disastrous effect on how the people feel about us." Lieutenant Colonel Ewen Southby-Tailyour recalls that he "had to explain to the young marines that just because their Rules of Engagement said they could open fire doesn't necessarily mean that they should open fire. 'If you open fire the ramifications could sometimes be far greater than those resulting from not opening fire'"[14]

British military involvement in Iraq and Afghanistan was unpopular at home, yet the interviewees generally did not express animosity toward the British public or the same feelings of detachment described by many of the US soldiers I spoke with.[15] At the same time, they did think their military service was not valued and were quiet about this aspect of their lives when they were at home. Soldiers were proud that they had been in the military and felt they had a special identity, but most said they were close to the civilian world and that they could easily shift identities.

The relatively low level of confidence in major objectives of the wars, such as nation building and democratization, coupled with the low level of support at home, gave the soldiers a fairly disinterested view of the strategic context. They were less concerned with winning the War on Terror and more concerned with surviving their tour and making incremental changes in the local quality of life. This led them away from the kind of idealistic attitudes of some American and

Israeli soldiers, for whom success was perceived as being essential for promoting democracy or protecting national security.

Minimizing Force

When asked to describe examples of good conduct, the British Army soldiers usually cited instances in which they came under fire from enemy fighters and refused to retaliate. As I discuss in chapter 4, decisions about when to respond to enemy fire and how to respond were heavily influenced by the level of threat the soldiers perceived. Across militaries, the soldiers were apt to use lethal force against their attackers—even at the risk of harming innocent bystanders—when they or other members of their unit were threatened. Soldiers were more restrained and more conscious of civilian security when they were relatively safe and could afford to act cautiously without endangering themselves. However, soldiers differed in the extent to which they perceived threats as being serious, and those from the British Army stood out as being the most outspoken in using their stories of restraint under fire to illustrate their highest ethical achievements. They were particularly proud of moments in which their commanding officers refused requests to open fire or when they personally refrained from firing even though they were being attacked.

One scenario that five of the interviewees described was defending a forward operating base (FOB) or an outpost against attack from unseen assailants. Although they were deployed at different times and with different units, the interviewees recounted almost identical experiences. The FOBs or outposts would suddenly come under small-arms or mortar fire. The soldiers then rushed to the walls or into their sangars (small bunkers, usually constructed with sandbags or hesco barriers) to return fire. The problem was that the insurgents could be difficult to locate. Those with rifles would open fire from inside of civilians' homes, and rather than engaging in protracted firefights, the attackers fired in short bursts and then shifted to alternative positions—often other homes. Mortar crews would launch a few rounds from an unseen location and then run away before a patrol could be organized to intercept them. By moving quickly and using civilian structures as firing positions, insurgents made it difficult for the overstretched British forces to organize counterattacks.

When facing these attacks, the soldiers were torn between a desire to return fire against any apparent threats and the imperative to avoid harming innocents. They invariably said they refrained from shooting unless they could visually identify the threats. When the enemies were using rifles and machine guns, a muzzle flash was usually the best evidence that they could engage a building. When the enemies fired mortars, the resulting cloud of dust could give away the location. Nevertheless, the soldiers stressed that their retaliatory fire was usually delivered in short bursts and that they had to patiently wait to reacquire targets each time the insurgents shifted to a new position. This made them largely reactive—a frustrating experience but one the soldiers were able to rationalize as being necessary for their overall effort to build relations with the local population and to reestablish working governmental institutions.

One soldier recalled a time when his FOB came under a particularly intense and accurate mortar bombardment. The location of the enemy mortar team was unclear, but a "dicker" (an unarmed person directing the fire using a mobile phone) could be seen on a nearby rooftop. Dickers were a persistent challenge for the British in Northern Ireland, which is also when the term came into the British military vernacular. They helped to improve the accuracy of indirect fire without clearly identifying themselves as hostiles. Worse still, many dickers are children, whom soldiers have an aversion to attacking. Soldiers requested permission to engage and readied a heavy machine gun, but the commanding officer intervened. The interviewee thought the Afghan man was obviously an insurgent, but his commander refused to authorize lethal force against someone who was unarmed and possibly innocent. The mere appearance of assisting the attack was insufficient grounds for shooting.[16]

Similar stories come up frequently in soldiers' memoirs and almost always reflect on the possibility of shooting before deciding against it. David Wiseman recalls of one dicker who was standing in the open during a gunfight, though not visibly armed, that "I could have killed him easily but I couldn't be totally sure that he was working for the enemy and this would have been against our rules of engagement, so I sent a warning shot into the ground next to him instead."[17] James Fergusson recounts several engagements in which British units had to endure mortar fire without being able to retaliate. They were tempted to deploy their own mortars to bombard the areas where the attacks seemed to be coming from, "but the risk to innocent civilians was great," so force could be used only when soldiers were able to visually identify armed insurgents.[18]

Interviewees told similar stories about coming under attack during patrols. In these instances they were more apt to return fire because they were more exposed. They also felt heightened pressure to quickly eliminate enemy threats when they were in exposed areas, such as irrigation ditches or city streets. It was common for insurgents to initiate ambushes with an IED and for wounded British soldiers to be cut off from medical evacuation until they could push the insurgents away from the attack site or reduce the volume of incoming gunfire. Nevertheless, the soldiers emphasized that they were restrained in their uses of force—only attacking buildings with a confirmed insurgent presence and calling in indirect fire as a last resort. They only relaxed these standards when they had to put down covering fire for evacuation aircraft or break contact. Again, the rationale interviewees gave was that the consequences of misdirected fire were potentially serious. They were concerned that the effects of inflicting civilian casualties would be felt immediately. Sometimes it was. Four of the interviewees recalled civilians coming to their FOBs the day after an engagement, requesting compensation for injured or dead family members or payment for damaged property. "We paid them when there was good cause," one said, "but who knows if it really did any good."[19]

Although soldiers regularly criticized insurgents for using civilian homes as fighting positions, they often felt it necessary to do the same thing. Whether in the dense urban areas of Basra or in the farmlands of Helmand Province, homes often provided the best cover. Soldiers would typically rush into nearby structures whenever they were in a protracted gunfight and unable to make a quick getaway. The soldiers put the civilians and their property at risk but emphasized that they tried to minimize the discomfort for civilians. "It was a matter of necessity for us," one soldier said. "It's not like we'd try to put people in the line of fire. We just had to get into cover to survive."[20]

A Royal Marines Commando said he felt sympathy for the civilians whose homes became embroiled in gunfights, and he would do whatever he could to offer assistance and ensure they were safe.[21] He recalled always traveling with chocolate or other sweets to give to the children when the incoming fire intensified. Another man who led an infantry company in Afghanistan said that, whenever possible, he would send ANA soldiers into the buildings first.[22] This would ensure that the ANA would have the sensitive task of searching for hidden enemies and moving those inside to the safety of basements or back rooms. If any misdirected gunfire struck civilians, then it would come from the Afghan soldiers who would be better prepared for dealing with the locals. "It was easier for them, culturally easier." This was not only an instance of the British soldiers attempting to minimize the appearance of harming civilians but also an example of how this could be done by acting through the local security forces. It was, in a sense, a way of outsourcing the ethical dilemmas and potentially the adverse consequences of misconduct. This approach not only defined British efforts but was later adopted by Americans.[23]

Of course, the British soldiers were not always operating with local security forces and sometimes had to clear buildings themselves—an extremely dangerous task of venturing into an unknown space that could be a family's shelter or setup for an ambush. One marine remembered coming under attack during a foot patrol in Basra and being the first man through the door of a nearby house as his squad sought cover. As he burst into the room, a man in baggy clothes rushed forward. "Everyone was screaming. The man was screaming. The guys behind me were screaming. We had gunfire coming in. I shouted at the guy—told him to get down. He probably didn't even hear me it was so loud."[24] In that moment the marine faced the decision of whether to shoot the assailant, who looked like he might be a suicide bomber with explosives hidden under his clothes. "He definitely looked threatening and he didn't listen to me. I didn't even have a chance to think about it really. I didn't want to shoot him, so I knocked him down." The marine struck the Iraqi man in the head, sending him to the ground. The man turned out to be innocent. He was only a father who was startled by the intrusion and trying to protect his family. "He looked very threatening, but he wasn't aware of it probably," the marine told me as he expressed his relief for not shooting.

Managing Conflict

Despite the many stories British soldiers told of exercising restraint during combat or avoiding uses of force that might inadvertently harm civilians, it is clear that compliance with civilian immunity is not absolute. The rules of engagement (ROE) varied across time and place. Moreover, interpretations of those rules could shift dramatically based on how they were presented. Dan Mills, a British sniper, recalls one of his commanders suggesting that it was acceptable to shoot dickers or other suspicious people without actually modifying the ROE or giving an explicit authorization. The colonel's instructions were "nowhere in the ROE does it say you can't shoot unarmed people." Mills observes that "Without actually openly saying so, the colonel had completely rewritten our Rules of Engagement. He had given us tacit permission to shoot unarmed civilians if and when we felt it necessary. That was proper war fighting ROE and it was unheard of for the sort of tour we were supposed to be on."[25] Such a broad understanding of the ROE illustrates their malleability in a military that generally takes a pragmatic approach to ethics. It was possible for the ROE to be applied differently merely by the colonel changing how they were framed and by implying that soldiers were free to shoot unarmed people when they felt there was good cause. As one British soldier told me, "The Rules of Engagement are vague, but that's a good thing. It gives you benefit of the doubt. It would have hurt to have really strict ROE. It's better to have some freedom to do what you have to do."[26]

The marines I spoke with tended to see themselves more as combatants than as peacekeepers; they were generally less enthusiastic about the kind of policing and civil-military affairs work that went along with counterinsurgency. While they were committed to protecting civilians and maintaining good relations with the local security forces, they also expressed a greater willingness to initiate contact or to escalate hostilities. One marine told me he regularly had to deliberately attack vehicles during patrols in Afghanistan. When he was driving, he might ram vehicles to knock them out of the road. When he was a passenger, he would fire warning shots past vehicles that strayed too close or would even kill their drivers. "If they got too close and didn't stop for a warning shot, then I'd have to put a round through the window."[27] When asked whether he was concerned that he might have shot an innocent person, he said "Look, I tried my best to not hit the wrong person, but I wouldn't lose sleep killing someone over their own stupidity." These incidents are almost identical to those reported by Americans, which is evidence that even when armed forces draw from different sources of ethical guidance and frame their operations differently, actions may turn out to be similar in practice.

Cooperation with local allies was another source of ethical troubles and was ethically questionable in itself. Almost every soldier and marine I spoke with had a story of local security forces fleeing in the midst of a gunfight or doing something dangerous and irresponsible. One enlisted infantryman who did two tours in Afghanistan described a typical scenario. He was on patrol with around a dozen other British soldiers and an equal number from the ANA. As the British soldiers moved through an irrigation ditch, they came under intense fire from a nearby compound. The plan was for the supporting ANA unit to provide covering fire to suppress enemy fighters, which would allow the British soldiers to maneuver into a better position. However, the interviewee was shocked to see that the ANA simply disappeared when the gunfire started. "I couldn't believe it. They just fucked off. They vanished, and we were stuck there on our own."[28] To make matters worse, reinforcements would take some time to reach them because they had to check for IEDs as they approached the ambush site.

The interviewee and his comrades survived the encounter but only at the expense of taking an ethical risk. They were unsure whether civilians were in the compound that the Taliban had occupied but trapped in the middle of an irrigation ditch without adequate cover. With their survival in jeopardy, they called for an air strike, which demolished the building and killed everyone inside. The heavy reliance on untrustworthy auxiliaries allowed the soldiers to get into a position of vulnerability that they might not have faced otherwise and led them to escalate the level of force in self-defense. To make matters worse, the ANA soldiers later reported that they had stayed in position throughout the encounter and had even killed several Taliban fighters.

Patrick Bishop reports an even more extreme case in which British paratroopers came under fire from the ANP. The soldiers did not return fire and were later told by the local police chief that the shots had come from Taliban fighters in disguise, though the lesson was clear enough to the soldiers: "the police were not only corrupt but potentially hostile."[29] This kind of friction between indigenous security forces and British personnel made cooperation difficult and hindered efforts to build trust.

One British officer said he had to intervene in several confrontations between groups of ANA soldiers or between members of the ANA and members of the ANP.[30] These groups were drawn from different regions (the ANA from across the country and the ANP from the local area) and from different tribal groups. Bringing them into close proximity risked activating deeply rooted prejudices. The officer said the tensions could even become violent and turn into gunfights. When he first arrived in Afghanistan, he was warned about the ANP setting ambushes for the ANA and killing several of them. Both sides had to be appeased in these encounters, although it was particularly important to maintain support from the ANA, which was generally more reliable. As the officer said, "We were lucky because we could let the ANA lead. When it came to dealing with civilians, the ANA would usually take care of it. It really helped."

In one encounter, the officer had to mediate a dispute between members of the ANP and Afghan civilians who accused the policemen of stealing from them. "They were all just screaming at each other, and I couldn't understand a word of it. I had to go through the interpreter, but it's hard to know if they're reliable." Lacking the means to determine whether the charges were true, the soldier said his squad focused on preventing the disagreement from escalating by separating the police from the civilians and watching the former more carefully on future joint patrols. The officer's solution—attempting to separate the two groups to avoid conflict—is one that characterizes the pragmatic type of ethical reasoning. The soldier's concern was not to determine whether the dispute was legitimate or to punish any wrongdoing but to simply end it in a way that seemed most likely to prevent the conflict between civilians and the ANP from diverting them from the mission at hand.

The same officer told another story of the local ANA unit threatening to mutiny when they found a burned copy of the Qur'an in an outpost recently vacated by the Danish military. "The locals insisted that the Danes had burnt it. The ANA and the locals were outside our base going crazy." The officer went on to complain that the interpreter, who had to serve as an intermediary when opening a dialogue with the angry crowd, "tried to inflame things." It turned out that the interpreter the British had hired "wanted to establish himself as some kind of anti-Western leader." Nevertheless, the officer managed to calm the crowd by insisting the burned Qur'an was left by the Taliban to incite misdirected anger. Although this officer spoke in more detail about difficulties with the ANA and ANP than others I interviewed, mistrust of the two organizations and strained relations with them comes up frequently in other firsthand accounts of the war in Afghanistan.[31]

The practice of relying extensively on local support helped the British soldiers displace some of their burdens, yet these stories are evidence that this reliance created new ethical challenges when it came to resolving disputes between security forces or between them and the civilians. Moreover, the practice was often employed in ways that made it ethically questionable in itself. Soldiers recalled instances of the local security forces stealing from, extorting, or abusing the civilians. Their actions took on a sense of legitimacy coming from British allies and were often impossible to investigate given the paucity of evidence and resources. Patrick Bishop says that "it seemed to the Paras that the population felt they had more to fear from the Afghan National Police who were supposed to protect them than they did from the insurgents."[32] The Chilcot Inquiry ultimately concluded that British reliance on militias was not only "humiliating" but that it was also one of the central reasons for the failed mission in Iraq.[33]

The Americans likewise relied on local assistance, with soldiers sometimes giving similar complaints of them being unreliable or victimizing innocent people. However, the British military was distinguished by the extent of reliance and by sometimes selecting local allies that were clearly untrustworthy. Nowhere is this clearer than from the deal struck with the Mahdi Army to turn over control of Basra in exchange for safe passage out of the city during the British withdrawal. With the British gone, the Mahdi Army killed at least forty-five women for un-Islamic behavior. One local told reporters, "I had to buy an AK-47 for personal protection. They started killing people who sell alcoholic drinks and barbers who shave beards."[34] Transferring authority to Iraqi militias also strained relations with the US military, which was increasing its presence in Iraq as part of the troop surge during the British withdrawal. It would ultimately be the American military's responsibility to restore security in Basra and expel the militias that the British had entrusted with controlling the city.

The Struggle to Adapt

The norms embodied in the British counterinsurgency doctrine are attractive. The minimalist approach seems to be preferable to more invasive or aggressive methods, both because it can permit greater local political autonomy and because it may restrict levels of violence. This approach also seems like it has the best record of success in practice. Commentators often praise British counterinsurgency techniques, and the counterinsurgency doctrine the US military released in 2006 relies heavily on lessons gleaned from British operations. Some studies of the new American counterinsurgency doctrine even maintain that it has an "embedded morality" akin to the norms embedded in the British military's practices.[35] However, the British counterinsurgency doctrine and the norms that arise from it depend on essential prerequisites that were missing in Afghanistan and Iraq. The result was a mismatch between the idealized British approach to counterinsurgency and what it could actually achieve in practice. British forces then found themselves unable to adapt or to develop new ethical guidelines as readily as the Americans could. As Gibson explains, "When the environment turned ugly, the shortcomings of our strategy were ruthlessly exposed. By contrast the Americans demonstrated a remarkable ability to learn from their mistakes mid-campaign, rewrite their doctrine and implement it with considerable success."[36]

In Iraq and Afghanistan, the British Army was unable to achieve the same level of local cooperation it had received in its more successful campaigns, such as those in Northern Ireland and Malaya. This had much to do with the Iraqi and Afghan people being unwilling to cooperate with the British or only helping to achieve some modest goals like providing local security while still undermining the coalition forces' overall political objectives. Whereas the US Army and IDF were able to employ their ethical systems in the contexts in which they were fighting, the British Army's ethics depended on the assumption it could rely on a level of cooperation with local people that was never actually realized in practice. This was shown by how the local allies, including interpreters, police, militia members, and army personnel, could be a source of dilemmas and strain relations with the local civilians.

Despite making much stronger claims about the importance of cultural sensitivity and their willingness to learn about and respect the Iraqi and Afghan cultures, British soldiers faced the same cultural barriers as the Americans. Language presented a significant obstacle, and while the soldiers generally learned basic greetings, they had to rely on interpreters to serve as intermediaries in most interactions with foreign civilians. Again, this was a shared problem. The Americans were just as much affected by the language barrier. However, they were prepared to keep the interpreters at a distance and to think about their norms without putting the same degree of faith in intermediaries to help them overcome ethical challenges. The Americans were, after all, apt to see a sharp line separating themselves from outsiders. Their virtue ethics encouraged suspicion that was healthy in small doses.

Five of the British soldiers I interviewed expressed concerns about how effectively the counterinsurgency doctrine could be applied in Iraq and Afghanistan because of the differences between the conflicts in those countries and the conflicts that have informed the development of the counterinsurgency doctrine. One of the veterans of Northern Ireland explained that although he attempted to emulate the tactics he had considered successful in that country, they became untenable over the course of his deployment in Iraq. He found the fighting in Iraq was much more like a conventional war than the fighting in Northern Ireland, and he could not rely on local police forces to be as effective as they had been there.[37]

The number of British soldiers in Iraq and Afghanistan was extremely small given the large territory it had to cover. The British military lost its usual flexibility and was forced to rely more on fixed defensive positions modeled on the American military's FOBs to compensate for its numerical weaknesses.[38] This proved to be a source of ethical troubles for two reasons. First, because most of interviewees' efforts were taken up with defending their bases, they had fewer opportunities to go on patrols and interact with the locals. This prevented the soldiers from establishing the level of rapport with the Iraqi and Afghan people that the ethics embedded in their counterinsurgency doctrine demands. Second, the overstretched British military was unable to engage in the same degree of self-examination and oversight as the other countries I discuss.

During the summer of 2003, the size of the British force in Iraq went from the forty-three thousand soldiers who took part in the invasion to around twelve thousand, then to eight thousand by the end of the year.[39] The number sunk further in the fall, reaching seven thousand by the time it began to withdraw in 2007.[40] The British Army's strength remained at this level for the rest of the war. Most of these soldiers were not part of combat units. They were support personnel needed for administrative purposes, to maintain equipment, and to manage civil affairs. Ledwidge reports that "of the force at [General Richard Shirreff's] command of about 7,000 soldiers, only 200 were available for patrolling Basra's streets."[41] Initially the British forces in Iraq were able to patrol on foot without carrying heavy weapons or wearing body armor. However, as the insurgency intensified, the British forces turned out to be too small to provide security.

Ledwidge argues that as they lost control of southern Iraq they became more cautious. In the absence of a military presence beyond the bases, the British Army had to rely on militias to police the city.[42] "There were insufficient forces to hold any area of Basra for more than a few hours, often even then under severe fire."[43] He goes on to say that the difficulties providing security led to a deterioration of the British Army's ethics. The strain of the mission led some to deviate from the minimal-use-of-force strategy and reduced oversight that could counteract violations. "Unfortunately, the atmosphere of growing lawlessness engendered by the lack of planning crept into the approach of a small minority of soldiers and some of their commanders, who took the view that there were some occasions when the usual, tightly enforced rules need not apply."[44] The British typically controlled use of force decisions with the help of rigorous after-action reports and investigations, but this became impossible. There was insufficient time to perform these oversight functions with the soldiers already overwhelmed by other duties. Soldiers interviewed did not describe this strain as causing an ethical decline as Ledwidge does, but several agreed with him in describing the oversight as being weaker than it normally would have been.

The British occupation of Afghanistan followed a similar course. At their peak, the British had only around ten thousand soldiers in the country.[45] Most of these were not combat arms specialists, and a majority of those who were needed to provide security for bases. As James Fergusson says, "It was clear to everyone that the 650-strong battle group wasn't nearly large enough to hold down an area that was roughly the size of Wales."[46] Most personnel were needed to protect bases and local infrastructure, so few performed tasks that led them to have regular contact with the Afghans. As in Iraq, soldiers and marines found it necessary to deviate from their standard operating procedures and to relax oversight because of the demands placed on the small force. "The Army normally tried to account for every bullet fired in operations. Commanders in the field were supposed to fill out forms called a PIP (post-incident pro-forma) or a SIR (shooting incident report) whenever anything happened. But the battle group had deployed so fast and the tempo of fighting was so intense that the standard systems of accountability were somehow forgotten."[47] They were also unable to conduct the frequent patrols necessary to control territory. Instead, the soldiers often had to either remain in their bases, waiting to be attacked, or conduct short-range patrols and react to ambushes set by Taliban fighters who were often able to roam freely.[48] Granting the enemy free movement further aggravated problems because it allowed them to hide IEDs, which could then be used in future attacks that might be able to provoke overreactions against any unfortunate civilians in the area.

Although the small force size would be a hindrance for any type of ethics, it is especially problematic for one that emphasizes interaction with noncombatants to build trust, restrain uses of force, and provide local security. Not only did accountability suffer but soldiers were sometimes driven to abandon their minimal-use-of-force guidelines. Stories of soldiers having to request indirect fire support or use heavy weapons when they were outnumbered were not only common in my interviews but also in soldiers' memoirs. For example, Toby Harnden says of one unit in the Welsh Guards: "The size of Corbet Burcher's force meant that he often had little choice but to resort to artillery and air power to prevent a patrol becoming surrounded. Inevitably, this increased the risk of civilian casualties. Early in May, three civilians were killed when Corbet Burcher ordered a mortar team to be fired on a 10-figure grid square from which rockets were being fired by a Taliban team."[49] The point here is clear: ethical conduct falls by the wayside when it is grounded in practices that are impossible for soldiers to perform.

Despite the British rejection of the idealistic program of nation building and their more pragmatic approach to counterinsurgency, the British military displays its own type of idealism: its confidence in past techniques and determination to continue using these even when they seem poorly suited for the context. Colonel Ian Rigden attempts to dispel myths associated with British counterinsurgency—including that it is the best approach and that its success in Malaya can serve as a model for operations elsewhere.[50] As he points out, attempting to reproduce the victory in Malaya overlooks the context-specific details that made it possible. The same can be said for Northern Ireland. Many of the soldiers I interviewed described borrowing patrolling tactics and methods of integrating with local security forces from that war only to find that these were usually not amenable to radically different contexts.

Christopher Elliott says of the campaign in Iraq that "the British Army had several generations of counter-insurgency experience to draw on, following the withdrawal from Empire and its critical role in quelling 'The Troubles' in Northern Ireland 1969–97. So it knew what it was required to do and how to do it, but it was to prove no better than the US at reading the situation correctly."[51] Rory Stewart points to similar faults in the Afghanistan campaign: "The ingredients of successful counter-insurgency campaigns in places like Malaya—control of the borders, large numbers of troops in relation to the population, strong support from the majority ethnic groups, a long-term commitment and a credible local government—are lacking in Afghanistan."[52] As it became increasingly difficult to follow the standard counterinsurgency model, the ethical system that arose from it also began to break down. This left the British military with tenuous ideal principles that could only be imperfectly realized.

Overconfidence in established techniques was evident in the inadequate formal cultural preparation that was provided. Most of the British soldiers I spoke with emphasized the importance of understanding the local culture. This was a precondition for building trust and maintaining the right appearances. However, most thought this ideal was poorly realized in practice because the cultural training they received was superficial. They were disoriented to find that some of their instructions were inaccurate or that they were only true for certain tribal groups and not for others. Some were also sent on accelerated deployments, which led to reduced cultural training of a week or less. Even a soldier who was deployed to Afghanistan in 2009—late enough in the war for preparation to be improved—said that the cultural training was poorly developed and gave little indication of the substantial differences between tribal groups. "Training was too uniform. There was more difference between groups and cultures than they told you about. People weren't quite as strict with the practices as they made them out to be."[53] Reflecting on similar comments in soldiers' memoirs, Elliott notes that "it makes chilling reading to witness the poverty of the cultural and language preparation conducted in accounts of British operations."[54] He goes on to say that "the British troops involved had poor interaction with the local population and very little understanding of their culture, largely because neither side could comprehend what the other side was saying."[55]

Finally, it is important to point out that problems arise when pragmatic norms blur the boundaries between what is moral and what is effective. Many of the techniques employed by British soldiers may be informed by the goal of reducing the risks to civilians and promoting local security, but these techniques also assume subservience to British authority and assume the rules may be flexible when they are not effective. One British soldier writes that when conducting searches, "more often than not we'd use the subtle approach"[56] This could mean "a gentle tap with the knuckles as if calling on a friend, weapons held non-threateningly, barrels pointed to the floor. In the politest of manners we'd ask people for their help, seek permission to search their premises."[57] This sounds like an admirable approach, yet the soldier admits that it was largely for show. "Of course we'd never take no for an answer, but it would appear as if we might. It was all about keeping friendly with the locals who weren't the enemy."[58] In other words, maintaining good appearances for the audience is what mattered; the underlying intent did not.

One could question whether pragmatic norms are truly ethical from the other perspectives I introduced in chapter 2. From a deontological viewpoint, pragmatism lacks the good intent that is the hallmark of moral conduct. Without the intent to do what is right for its own sake, the actions may not be truly good. Moreover, without good intent, it becomes all too easy to deviate from norms as the circumstances change. Consequentialists would find more to like in the pragmatic approach because of its emphasis on doing what works yet would probably object to the attempts to conform to established practices even when these are no longer useful. Moreover, consequentialism does not place the same value on tradition and maintaining institutionalized practices. From a virtue ethics perspective, good conduct may be context and actor relative but must still be embodied in some conception of good character and good values. It may be acceptable for good character to promote different kinds of actions under different circumstances, yet good character should be genuine and not primarily based on efforts to present good appearances for an audience.

Conclusion

The British approach to ethics rejects formalization. The counterinsurgency doctrine, along with the diverse assortment of techniques developed around it, serves as the primary guide for how soldiers should act. The British military correspondingly avoids developing any detailed explicit ethical guidelines, such as an elaborate set of institutional rules or a vision of some timeless warrior ideal. The British style of counterinsurgency embodies values and can provide guidance for resolving ethical challenges, yet it is designed with functionality, not ethical responsibility, in mind. The soldiers' attitudes toward military ethics reflected this, as soldiers conceptualized ethics as a collection of specific practices ranging from not wearing body armor during patrols to not engaging insurgents when there was a risk of inadvertently harming innocent bystanders. Their thoughts about the strengths and limitations of their tactics, especially when comparing these against American tactics, further emphasized the link between ethics and expediency.

The British military's esteem for minimalism was evident on the strategic and tactical levels from how interviewees described their goals and the examples of good conduct they provided. The soldiers generally emphasized that they only wanted to achieve modest objectives related to restoring security in the contested areas and were suspicious of nation building or democratization programs. During engagements, the pinnacle of good conduct was the selfless desire to avoid escalating confrontations even when doing so might provide short-term security. Thus, soldiers were proud of refusing to fire at unseen adversaries or unarmed dickers. Their stories further reflected the British effort to establish cooperative links with local forces, as many were deeply involved in joint operations and struggled with facilitating cooperation and cultural tolerance.

The guiding norms that underlie the British approach to counterinsurgency operations depend on ideal conditions that may not exist during all wars. They assume that the local population will generally be well disposed to British forces, that there will be institutions capable of being salvaged, that allies will follow similar norms, that local security forces will be reliable, and, most of all, that indigenous populations will be willing to submit to foreign administration. These are all dubious assumptions that may be borne out in Northern Ireland and former colonies but that were contradicted by the campaigns in Iraq and Afghanistan. Thus, the norms put forth by the British military were imperfectly realized. Soldiers were left to follow the guidelines of tactical and strategic minimalism, cooperation with local auxiliaries, and respect for other cultures even as contextual necessities sometimes compelled them to disregard those norms.

9

The Israel Defense Forces

On Guard against Existential Threats

The system of ethics of the Israel Defense Forces (IDF) can be best described as a hybrid that mixes deontological and consequentialist elements. These theories are contradictory in principle, as they evaluate the rightness or wrongness of actions based on much different grounds—the former by adherence to rules and the latter by outcomes. Nevertheless, these styles of reasoning are paired and jointly influence how personnel are supposed to make decisions. The deontological component of the IDF's norms have two primary sources. The first is *The Spirit of the IDF*, a document that was published in 1994 and reformulated in 2001. *The Spirit of the IDF* is a more unified and definitive code of ethics than is found in the American or British militaries. Unlike the US Army's ethics, which is composed of multiple interlocking pieces and lacks a single definitive statement, *The Spirit of the IDF* reflects an effort to develop a unified system. The second source of deontological thinking comes from the many specific rules Israeli soldiers are supposed to follow. These go beyond the rules of engagement (ROE) of the US and British militaries, as they are often very specific and are intended to provide a comprehensive framework that can guarantee good conduct.

Intense scrutiny of the IDF from domestic and international human rights organizations and the use of conscription push the IDF toward deontology. Strict rules provide evidence of ethical sensitivity that can be more easily put on display for third-party audiences than the ethereal virtue-based or pragmatic systems. Short-term service personnel can also be more easily trained to follow rules than they can be initiated into virtue ethics or pragmatic ethics, which both require a strong sense of group membership and exposure to informal enculturation processes that may take years to produce an identity shift or profoundly alter soldiers' character. However, rules invariably come into conflict or omit important considerations, thereby creating a demand for judgment skills or a decision procedure to overcome the resulting ambiguities.

Consequentialist reasoning is evident in IDF ethics on tactical and strategic levels. At the tactical level, it appears in soldiers' instructions to resolve contradictions between rules by doing what is best for the State of Israel. The demand of promoting national interest serves as a tool for arbitrating conflicts that may arise when employing deontological ethics. At the strategic level, consequentialist reasoning becomes even more important. The IDF affirms that it cannot afford to lose a war. Every war is an existential crisis that must be won at all costs. There is considerable disagreement over whether this narrative is realistic, and a large contingent of conscientious objectors and concerned veterans oppose it.[1] However, this perception of threats influences IDF doctrine and strategic discourse to provide a standing justification for extreme actions on a strategic level, including preemptive attacks and indiscriminate attacks in populated areas, when these are deemed necessary for national security. It is also a pervasive narrative in political discourse, especially from the Likud Party, which dominated the government during the period under investigation.[2] The reliance on consequentialist reasoning in response to existential crises even receives support from the just war tradition, as some theorists defend the view that these give rise to "supreme emergencies" in which states are justified in doing whatever they must to survive.[3]

The first section of this chapter discusses how the IDF's strategic position sets it apart from the American and British militaries and how this influences its ethics doctrine and training. The second section discusses the institutional structure and culture of the IDF as well as its relations with Israeli civil society. I argue that the IDF's structure makes it a poor candidate for any type of virtue-based or pragmatic ethics because those systems require a higher degree of institutional insularity. The third section analyzes the IDF's ethics, focusing on *The Spirit of the IDF*. The fourth section builds on this by considering the many other more specific rules that Israeli personnel must follow and how these differ from the American and British ROE. Finally, the last section explores the consequentialist dimensions of the IDF's ethical theory, including how these undermine the deontological elements and how they are potentially harmful in themselves because they are combined with a sense of persistent existential threat.

Israel's Strategic Position

Persistent security threats have had a profound influence on the IDF's development, leading to a much different culture and institutional structure than the militaries of the United States or United Kingdom. This has in turn produced a distinctive approach to military ethics. Geographical barriers and distance from powerful enemies prevent the US and UK from being seriously threatened by land invasion, allowing both countries to wage wars away from their home territories. With few threats of invasion, the British and American militaries can usually choose when and where they will fight. They are rarely compelled to pursue victory at any cost. This security shapes their strategic doctrines as well as the consciousness of the individual members. Most of the American and British soldiers I spoke with were aware that their successes and failures rarely have an immediate impact on national security. Americans wanted to win the War on Terror to avert future threats but were not concerned that terrorism could actually destroy the United States if it were left unchecked. The British soldiers were even more reticent about describing their wars as being essential for national security.

The IDF and its personnel face far more immediate challenges. The IDF came into existence on May 26, 1948, shortly after Israel's establishment, when the country came under attack from a coalition of Arab militaries. It was created in the midst of a war and has developed under the constant threat of renewed hostilities. Consequently, the IDF has not had the same freedom to remake its institutions or to recreate itself during peacetime as the American and British forces. It has faced serious threats over its entire history because of its close proximity to multiple hostile states and its continual struggle against Palestinian resistance. The sense of perpetual danger from internal and external sources has had a profound effect on the IDF and its soldiers, leading the organization and individual members to see themselves as permanently standing on the brink of a war that could determine the country's fate.

Israel confronts more immediate strategic challenges than the US and UK not only because of its proximity to enemies but also because the land itself puts Israeli forces at a disadvantage. Israel is a comparatively small country, and so narrow from east to west (ranging between ten and seventy-one miles) that it could be easily divided by invaders. This limits the IDF's prospects of mounting successful defensive operations, which require the depth to create multiple defensive lines, space to mount tactical retreats, and freedom of maneuver to launch counterattacks. Because Israel's geography is poorly suited for defense, the IDF consistently seeks to take the initiative in its wars, preemptively striking at enemies before they have a chance to launch invasions or quickly countering attacks before they penetrate deeply into Israel.

The value of preemption was clear from the Six-Day War of 1967. Israel won a resounding victory over the combined armies of Egypt, Syria, Jordan, Lebanon, and Iraq by striking first, while its enemies were still assembling and organizing themselves. It was reaffirmed during the Yom Kippur War in 1973 when Israel suffered humiliating initial defeats because it was caught off guard. These experiences weigh heavily on the Israeli military. They provide lessons about the importance of offense, preemption, and maneuver. The result is that the ethos of the IDF is heavily oriented toward quick, decisive engagements facilitated by overwhelming firepower, technological advantages, and superior organization. Like the American military, it favors conventional operations in which its technology can be used to greatest effect.[4] The IDF won a major conflict in each decade of the twentieth century following its founding, solidifying confidence in the organization and reinforcing the belief that its strategies were those best suited for national defense.[5]

Despite Israel's strategic vulnerabilities, some of the IDF's ethical tests are analogous to those of the American and British militaries. Starting in the mid-1980s the IDF's priorities shifted from fighting conventional wars to counterinsurgency. This was triggered by the extended low-intensity fighting of the First Lebanon War (1982–83) and, even more powerfully, by the First Intifada (1987–93).[6] Earlier conflicts with Arab states had been fought in the open terrain of the Sinai and the Golan Heights, which allowed Israel's superior air power and armor to prevail over poorly equipped and poorly organized conventional forces. The First Lebanon War and First Intifada changed the locus of conflict to urban areas, negating many of the IDF's advantages and introducing the dilemmas characteristic of counterinsurgency operations.

The changing mission from conventional fighting to counterinsurgency has brought soldiers into greater contact with civilians, politicized the military, and given junior leaders more freedom of action—processes associated with the devolution of responsibility to soldiers at the junior officer, noncommissioned officers, and enlisted ranks. Changing mission demands have also caused considerable strain among those same soldiers, forcing them to act in roles that are often much different from the ones they were trained for and that lie outside the scope of the IDF's conventional warfighting expertise. The devolution of ethical responsibilities and involvement in new types of operations might have been sufficient in themselves to generate greater demand for military ethics education. Further incentive was provided by the intense scrutiny of the IDF by human rights organizations, foreign governments, and international legal institutions.

The IDF's image has suffered during recent counterinsurgency operations because of reports that it employed disproportionate and indiscriminate violence.[7] As Martin van Creveld says, the IDF's past victories in conventional wars have transformed it "into an occupying force, complete with all the corrupting moral influences that this entails."[8] The Israeli government is persistently concerned that it is losing the propaganda war against nonstate adversaries and losing popularity internationally.[9] Charges of human rights abuses and international scrutiny have generated more pressure for the IDF to abide by strict ethical standards, or to at least give the appearance of doing so.

The IDF's institutions and culture, and its ethics in particular, must be seen in this strategic context of a persistent sense of threat, an ongoing effort to adapt from conventional to unconventional operations, and intense critical pressure. Past struggles inspire feelings of insecurity and a corresponding imperative to elevate national security above any competing ethical demands. As the threat of other attacks by states has subsided, this sense of threat has continued, albeit largely displaced onto violent nonstate actors like Hezbollah and Hamas.

The Institutional and Cultural Forces Shaping IDF Ethics

The IDF is distinctive not only in its strategic context but also in its culture and institutional structure. It is a unified organization that closely links land, air, and sea components and attempts to maintain shared norms across the branches. It also relies heavily on conscription and maintains close links to civil society. These characteristics help to shape the IDF's ethics doctrine and training procedures by limiting opportunities to employ aretaic and pragmatic ethical systems while encouraging the use of deontology and consequentialism.

Israeli air, naval, and ground forces are all branches of the IDF and not distinct services as they are in the US and Britain. This is primarily an operational decision, meant to unify command and to facilitate joint actions, but it is also important from a moral standpoint. Whereas the ethics doctrine and training for American and British military personnel can vary substantially depending on their branch of service (with each branch having its own code of values and ethics education programs), all members of the IDF are supposed to follow the same basic norms.[10] A unified system identifies a single common ideal to which all personnel are supposed to aspire, thereby elevating the status of that ethical code. A shared normative framework promotes consistency across different branches and within each. It facilitates moral absolutism of the type found in deontological and consequentialist theories. This is in sharp contrast to virtue ethics and pragmatism, which permit the existence of much different ethical guidelines for actors in different roles or within different institutional contexts.

The unified structure of the IDF and its unified code of ethics lead to a high level of agreement among soldiers when they define their values. During interviews with American and British soldiers, I discovered that Army personnel thought they followed different norms than those in other branches. Several of the US Army soldiers insisted they were far more judicious in the use of force than their marine counterparts. One even illustrated his good conduct by telling a story about how he reprimanded marines for endangering civilians when they decided to set up a target-practice range near homes during operations in Somalia in the early 1990s.[11] I also found disagreements between the British Army soldiers and Royal Marines Commandos. The former were more apt to express comfort with civil-military affairs work and to endorse a minimalist approach to counterinsurgency. The latter emphasized their skill in combat and their greater professionalism. The perceived differences gave rise to distinctive identities and ethical sensibilities.

I found a high level of agreement among Israeli soldiers when they were asked to define their ethical priorities and a strong sense that all members of the IDF were fundamentally the same when it came to their values. All said that *The Spirit of the IDF* was their primary source of guidance. There were, of course, differences between units. Some were more prestigious than others, and each cultivated its own esprit de corps. However, these differences did not seem to foster the same level of interservice rivalry as in the American and British armed forces. This allowed the rules to function as a shared reference point and mark of identity in the absence of the more insular British and American military cultures that tend to mark sharper distinctions between insiders and outsiders.

Absolute ethical rules also have a public relations benefit. James Eastwood argues that "ethics has become a crucial part of the way in which war-fighting and war-preparation are made to seem normal and desirable in Israel."[12] By this account, the IDF's concern with ethics allows it to present itself as a military with a conscience, which in turn contributes to the impression that any misconduct is accidental and contrary to the IDF's goals. Ethically sensitive warfare helps to make Israeli militarism more palatable to a civilian public that might otherwise shy away from violence. Eastwood contends that this also makes military service more attractive to potential recruits and gives those who join a sense of shared purpose—outcomes that contribute to the IDF's military effectiveness.

The IDF is primarily made up of conscripts. All Israeli citizens over eighteen, except for Arabs and those who qualify for physical, psychological, or religious exemptions, are required to perform military service. Conscription tends to be a denigrated practice in countries where military service is voluntary, yet it offers some advantages. Conscription can provide higher quality recruits than would be available otherwise.[13] Voluntary forces struggle to reach recruiting goals and must appeal to the altruism or patriotism of potential soldiers, many of whom have prospects of higher pay and a more comfortable life in civilian employment. During war, military service may become unpopular, forcing militaries to lower recruiting standards to fill the ranks or to revert to conscription. The US Army dropped its standards considerably during the wars in Iraq and Afghanistan, raising age limits, lowering educational minimums, and making more exemptions for criminals.[14] Worse still, it employed "stop loss" to prevent soldiers from leaving once they had done their required time.

With the power to pick its personnel from an entire country's population and to even bring in recruits of Jewish heritage who grew up abroad, the IDF can create a more skilled force than if it relied on voluntary service to fill all positions. During the 1990s, it was able to increase its standards and become more selective.[15] The high quality of recruits is one of the reasons the IDF has been so consistently successful in conventional warfare,[16] but it may also be advantageous from an ethical standpoint. Just as recruits can be screened for problems that may impede their combat effectiveness, they can also be checked for psychological and disciplinary problems—a critical advantage in light of research showing that psychological testing can help to predict misconduct.[17] Because the IDF can be more selective in recruitment, it does not have to rely on the same kind of character development programs in place in many all-volunteer militaries, which are epitomized by the US Army's virtue ethics training programs. The IDF can choose soldiers who already seem to have good character instead of facing the demand of inculcating it.

Conscription helps to bring soldiers and civilians together. Most Israelis, male or female, have served in the IDF at some point. During the late twentieth century, around a fifth of the country's workforce was engaged in a defense industry.[18] This has declined slightly, although it is anticipated that around 40 percent of Israelis will spend time in the IDF by 2020—a large share of the population compared to countries with voluntary military service.[19] In the US only around 2.5 million people are members of the military (active or reserve) out of a population of around 321 million.[20] And because most recruits are drawn from similar backgrounds, few US civilians have firsthand experience of the military or extensive contact with military personnel.[21] The same is true in the UK, where only around 320,000 out of 64 million British citizens are members of the military. Israel maintains a force of roughly 790,000 military personnel for a population of only 8 million. The result is a much narrower civil-military divide in Israel than in the United States or United Kingdom. Widespread participation in the military ensures that most Israeli civilians can understand the military's culture and soldiers' unique ethical challenges because they have either been soldiers or know people who have. This prevents soldiers from feeling alienated from the civilian population.

Conscription links civilian and military values. As Karen Guttieri says, "Israel is the archetype of a nation-in-arms, whose highly militarized culture permeates society as much as it indoctrinates the armed services."[22] Similarly,

Stuart Cohen claims that Israeli soldiers "have always been citizens temporarily in uniform,"[23] and Edwin Micewski says this "guarantees a constant exchange of values and permanent interdependence between the armed forces and society at large."[24] For many immigrants, service in the IDF is an initiation into Israeli citizenship. Around 70 percent of recruits have lived in the country for less than four years, and only 22 percent are born in Israel.[25] The IDF goes beyond teaching military skills to provide language training for those who do not know Hebrew, professional development, civic education, and access to universities.[26] Good performance in the military can even be a requisite for success in civilian life. As Samuel Katz explains, "Military service is such a focal point in Israel that for one who does not perform well or honourably in the IDF it is almost impossible to succeed in the civilian sector."[27] Many continue working with former military comrades when they go into civilian employment, thereby sustaining affiliations and unit subcultures

This is not to say that conscription is always advantageous. The UK and US armed forces have both abandoned this practice, the former since 1960 and the latter since 1973. There were multiple reasons for this choice, but among them were ethical concerns. Conscription never offered the same route to employment opportunities and social advancement in those countries as it did in Israel, and rather than being used as a mechanism for selecting the most suitable soldiers, it was more likely to bring in disadvantaged people who could not qualify for exemptions. The lesson here is that conscription cannot be classified as an unmitigated benefit or defect. Instead it is best seen as introducing certain opportunities that depend heavily on how it is implemented.

The differences between soldiers and civilians in countries with all-volunteer militaries were reflected in my interviews. A majority of the US Army soldiers, as well as a sizable minority of the British soldiers, expressed some feelings of alienation from their countries' civilian populations. This was especially pronounced among Americans who supported the wars in Iraq and Afghanistan, as they felt that the declining civilian support for those wars was a sign of betrayal or of the civilian population's weakness. None of the Israeli soldiers I talked to felt there were serious civil-military antagonisms, especially not any approaching a betrayal. Their opinions of Israeli civilians were overwhelmingly positive, and they sensed a high degree of mutual trust and support. This reflected the fact that "throughout Israel's history—in its experience of statehood and in its very ethos as a nation—the security establishment and particularly the military have wielded extensive influence over civil society and politics."[28]

The much different culture of the IDF compared to the American and British militaries and the barriers against virtue-based ethical thinking are evident in the IDF's conception of professionalism. Unlike the US and UK soldiers, IDF soldiers' understanding of professionalism has little to do with ethics and more to do with proficiency in military operations. Asa Kasher finds most IDF officers think about professionalism in nonmoral terms and said this was something he hoped to change.

> Most of the officers I have met held naive views of being a professional and of being a citizen in a democratic society. More often than not, officers (as well as members of other professional communities) take proficiency to be the core of being professional. They can easily be convinced that proficiency requires systematic knowledge and that both should be constantly updated. The idea that they are required to deeply understand the things that they do, such as their Rules of Engagement (ROEs) and other routine procedures, often comes as a surprise to them.[29]

Given the differences between the IDF and the British and American militaries as well as their different understandings of professionalism, it would be impossible for the IDF to base its ethics on the same type of professional identity.

The use of conscription makes the IDF a poor candidate for virtue-based or pragmatist systems of ethics for two reasons. First, given the epistemic and cultural links to the civilian population, there is little basis for defining membership in the military in terms of some exceptional status like participation in a profession or the embodiment of a unique type of virtue. Unlike those in the US and British militaries, who described their professional ethos as being partly the result of having chosen to become members of the military when so many other citizens did not, Israeli soldiers tended to see themselves as taking part in a civic duty that makes them like other Israeli citizens or Jewish people beyond Israel. This was especially clear from the foreigners who joined the IDF because of a sense of affinity with the country. Whereas American and British soldiers felt they had made a choice that set them apart from the civilian population, Israeli soldiers tended to see themselves as being very similar to their civilian counterparts, with roughly the same culture and experiences—attitudes at odds with ethical systems that foster a sense of exceptionalism. Many foreigner members even spend time living and working on a kibbutz before they join, which gives them a social network.[30]

Second, the steady turnover of personnel ensures that most members of the IDF will have short terms of service and will return to civilian life rather than making the military a career. The male soldiers I interviewed were required to serve only thirty-six months, while the women did twenty-four-month terms of service. Since I completed the interviews, the commitment from males was reduced by four months, with two months being taken away from training.[31] Because most members of the IDF join for brief periods, they may not have time to undergo the kind of personal transformation that would cause them to internalize a new set of values. Instead, it is easier to train these soldiers to follow a set of rules or a standardized decision-making procedure.

The same conditions that hinder the implementation of virtue ethics as a guide for the IDF facilitate the use of deontological and consequentialist ethics. Deontological and consequentialist theories do not presuppose the same kind of demanding educational programs as virtue ethics, nor do they require the feeling of participation in an enduring community or institution as pragmatism does. Deontology and consequentialism can be formulated as rules or decision procedures that soldiers can apply to make ethical decisions, without making any assumptions about the sociological conditions of those who follow them. These two ethics are neutral when it comes to the actors' identities and background conditions, issuing universal guidelines that apply for all people and in all circumstances.

Code of Ethics

In December 1994 the IDF adopted a formal code of ethics called *The Spirit of the IDF*, which became the basis for ethics training for all of the country's soldiers. The decision to make a single comprehensive philosophy was a radical departure from how military ethics are usually formulated. Rather than being created through a gradual process of accumulated experience, as in the British Army, or produced by numerous attempts to assemble and reformulate a heterogeneous system of ethics, as in the US Army, the IDF attempted to create a single definitive guide in one moment. The IDF's ethics doctrine was developed by a committee that reflected the close relationship between Israel's military and its civilian population. The committee was headed by Asa Kasher, a professor of philosophy at Tel Aviv University, who was joined by three IDF officers.[32]

The code the committee developed reflects the many challenges the IDF has faced while changing its mission from conventional war to counterinsurgency. Stuart Cohen says of its creation:

> In immediate terms, the process owes its origins to revelations of deviant and/or criminal Israeli troop conduct vis-a-vis Palestinian civilians during the course of the *intifadah*, which resulted in the instigation of over 200 judicial proceedings against individual soldiers and their immediate superiors. Probably just as important a stimulant, however, was a less tangible (but even more profound) sense that instances of IDF misconduct during the *intifadah* might constitute just an extreme expression of a fundamental change in values which had begun to affect numerous other areas of army life.[33]

Kasher agrees with Cohen's assessment, though he is more tentative in describing the ethical crisis that first demonstrated the need for reform. Kasher and Amos Yadlin say the code of ethics was designed to be a guide in the sensitive interactions between the IDF and Palestinian organizations.[34] It was influenced by the need to define how a democratic state could react to terrorism, suicide bombing in particular. Thus, as they present it, *The Spirit of the IDF* can be seen as a response to the moral predicaments that arose during the IDF's transition from being primarily involved in conventional military operations to fighting asymmetric conflicts against insurgents and terrorists.

The Spirit of the IDF's influence was evident from my interviews with Israeli soldiers. Everyone I talked to said the document was their primary source of ethical guidance. Each received a pocket-sized copy of *The Spirit of the IDF* in their native language soon after joining, and they were required to always carry it with them. This was enforced by military police, who would write violation reports for anyone caught without it. Ethics training focused on discussing the rules and values described in the book. Soldiers were also given discussion time with their commanders in which they were allowed to ask questions about the document and explore hypothetical scenarios in which its rules might be applied. This was supposed to give them the opportunity to clear up any ambiguities in the text and to gain a better appreciation of how to relate the text to their own actions. Interviewees also reported that their study of *The Spirit of the IDF* focused on the discipline section, which addresses how to formulate legal orders, how to judge the legality of an order that is received, and how to respond to illegal orders.

This was a much different response than what I heard in interviews with American and British soldiers. Almost none of the interviewees from those militaries mentioned a specific ethics text at any point during the interview. Around half of the Americans did discuss the Army values, but they had different views on how these should be defined and usually did not refer to a particular text. The lack of a clear referent for the Army values was significant, as they are defined differently in various training materials. The British personnel were even less clear about the exact reference point of their norms, describing them in terms of operating procedures and standards of conduct that lack a single decisive formulation. Thus, it is clear that the IDF's goal is consistency—a single code of conduct that spans its entire military and that is subject to fairly uniform interpretations.

The Spirit of the IDF

According to Kasher, *The Spirit of the IDF* was designed to defy classification according to the types of moral theories I employ in this book. As Kasher explains, military ethics should be a distinct subject that relies only indirectly on moral philosophy, thereby "circumventing philosophical debates between different schools of moral philosophy."[35] Kasher attempts to provide a solid foundation for ethics by relying on guidance from political and cultural values rather than on theoretical abstractions. He says that "officers do not have to take sides in philosophical debates, but have to apply the moral foundations of the democratic regime in which and for the sake of which they serve as officers."[36] The aim of *The Spirit of the IDF* is therefore to make explicit the moral foundations of the State of Israel and to develop those into a practical theory of military ethics that can be followed even by soldiers who are not aware of the underlying ideas.

Kasher's attempt to develop a code of ethics grounded in democratic values and national culture is one that may plausibly be both inclusive and legitimate among those who are supposed to follow it. However, constructing a theory of military ethics in this way does not circumvent the search for moral direction. Rather, it only raises the question of what kind of moral thinking those values embody and whether they are philosophically sound. Kasher may not derive the IDF's ethics directly from a moral philosophy, yet *The Spirit of the IDF* nevertheless bears deep similarities to those theories and can be traced back to specific styles of moral thought. *The Spirit of the IDF*'s language reflects Kasher's goal of philosophical neutrality, as it combines terms characteristic of various competing moral theories. The varied language suggests authorship by someone who is aware of the schools of moral thought I discuss in chapter 2 and who is struggling to avoid aligning too closely with any. Nevertheless, this effort to conceal the moral norms inherent in *The Spirit of the IDF* tends to be limited to its language. When the document's guidelines are analyzed carefully, they reveal the IDF's deontological and consequentialist ethical modalities.

Before analyzing *The Spirit of the IDF*'s philosophical themes, it is first important to point out that there are two different versions of the text. The first was made up of eleven values and thirty-four basic principles, while the updated document released in 2001 includes thirteen values with simpler descriptions. This revision of the document, which simplified it considerably, is instructive in itself. It shows that the rules set out in the original were too complex to be easily memorized and applied. Whereas the original document seems to be more directed at providing a theoretically convincing statement of ethics, the 2001 version is more carefully crafted to be applied in practice.

The 1994 version of *The Spirit of the IDF* describes the organization in terms of eleven values: tenacity, responsibility, integrity, personal example, human life, purity of arms, professionalism, discipline, loyalty, representation, and camaraderie. Each of the values is given a short definition and a long definition. The short definitions state the values as rules of individual conduct. Each of these definitions begins with the phrase "The IDF soldier will" and then goes on to explain exactly how the soldier is supposed to act in light of the stated value. For example, the short definition of the value of human life is "The soldier will do his utmost to preserve human life, with an awareness of its supreme importance, and will endanger himself and his colleagues only to the extent necessary for implementation of the mission."[37] The long definitions describe the values in more abstract terms and attempt to operationalize them at an organizational level. The long definition of the value of human life is "The sanctity of life in the eyes of IDF troops will be manifest in all of their actions, in thoughtful and precise planning, in astute and safely conducted exercises and in proper implementation, in accordance with the mission, with the appropriate level of risk and caution, and with continual effort to restrict the loss of human life to the extent required by the mission."[38] Each of the values stated in the original version of *The Spirit of the IDF* is stated in a similar manner, with individual and organizational formulations of the values and definitions that emphasize what the values mean in practice. The principles of the original *Spirit of the IDF* are revealing not only because they are evidence of deontological thinking but also because of what types of rules they are. They reflect the difficult transition of IDF ethics during the 1990s, as they say virtually nothing about the types of challenges pervasive in counterinsurgency contexts. They address the importance of obeying orders, exhort soldiers to act bravely when facing their enemies, and even provide instructions for addressing the media, but they fail to give clear recommendations for interacting with civilians or for dealing with escalation of force decisions. The absence of these considerations in the IDF's defining statement of its ethics indicates their marginalization in the IDF's ethical consciousness during the time *The Spirit of the IDF* was drafted.

The updated version of the text contains thirteen values and distinguishes between those that are basic or fundamental and additional values that are derived from the basic values. The former include the IDF's duty to defend Israel and its citizens, loyalty to the state and its citizens, and a duty to protect human dignity because "every human being is of value regardless of his or her origin, religion, nationality, gender, status or position."[39] The additional values are human life, purity of arms, personal example, responsibility, comradeship, professionalism, discipline, vocation, reliability, and dedication to mission and the pursuit of victory. Unlike the original *Spirit of the IDF*, the values in the revised version are defined in a single sentence. The definitions of the basic values are framed as organizational imperatives, while each additional value is stated as a rule of personal conduct. For example, the basic value of "Defense of the State, Its Citizens and Its Residents" says, "The IDF's goal is to defend the existence of the State of Israel, its independence and the security of the citizens and residents of the state."[40] The additional value of professionalism affirms that "the IDF servicemen and women will acquire the professional knowledge and skills required to perform their tasks, and will implement them while striving continuously to perfect their personal and collective achievements."[41]

The central difference between the two versions of *The Spirit of the IDF* is how values are operationalized. The revision draws a clearer distinction between organizational and personal directives, with completely different values regulating the conduct of the IDF as an organization and its individual members, albeit with the latter norms being described as derivable from the former. The definitions are also much shorter and simpler to more clearly express how the values are meant to be enacted. The newer version therefore reflects more concern with ensuring that the values are narrower and able to regulate soldiers' conduct in fairly predictable ways. It sacrifices philosophical abstraction with more specific claims about how to behave.

Although *The Spirit of the IDF* calls its guidelines "values," they are not stated as character traits. Instead, the values are expressed as rules. They set up inviolable imperatives, of the form characteristic of deontological moral theory. For example, "Purity of Arms" is defined as, "The IDF servicemen and women will use their weapons and force only for the purpose of their mission, only to the necessary extent and will maintain their humanity even during combat." It then goes on to elaborate on this rule with further requirements: "IDF soldiers will not use their weapons and force to harm human beings who are not combatants or prisoners of war, and will do all in their power to avoid causing harm to their lives, bodies, dignity and property."[42] Discipline affirms that "IDF soldiers will be meticulous in giving only lawful orders, and shall refrain from obeying blatantly illegal orders."[43] These values are better seen as rules and not values in the sense of being equivalent to virtues; values in the latter sense describe general character traits enacted according to the moral sensibilities of the actor and not according to a strict universal standard. These values also lack the same emphasis on individual judgment as one finds in virtue ethics.

As Kasher himself explains, the IDF deliberately avoids casting its ethics in terms of virtue because it considers these to be less suitable to a conscript military than rules:

> We prefer principle-guided behaviour as the subject matter of military ethics in the context of IDF not only because of our philosophical inclination to prefer principles over virtues as major elements of practical normative systems, but mainly because a military force of a democracy that includes people who are conscripts and people who are reserve officers or NCOs should educate them to follow the principles of military ethics necessary for the effective functioning of the military force, but avoid any attempt to change their character in a deep and broad way of long lasting effect.[44]

This intent is clarified by one of the major modifications to *The Spirit of the IDF* when it was updated. The original document includes thirty-four basic principles, which are absent in the revision. Like the values, the principles are rules, but they are distinct in their specificity. Whereas the values describe general rules, the principles address specific actions that soldiers should perform or avoid. As with the IDF's values, each of these principles is stated as an imperative for "the IDF serviceman." They are therefore constraints imposed from above, rather than personal attributes that are supposed to enable soldiers to use their own judgment.

Reflecting on the Rules

The primary architect of both versions of the document, Asa Kasher, claims that *The Spirit of the IDF* not only provides ethical guidance, but does so in such a comprehensive way that it eliminates the need for ethical reasoning. As he puts it, "The advantage of *The Spirit of the IDF* is that there aren't any dilemmas anymore. A soldier has to understand that even when he comes across certain dilemmas, he doesn't need to think or philosophize anymore. Someone else already sat down, did the thinking, and decided. There are no dilemmas."[45] This again reflects a rejection of aretaic and pragmatic theories that would require soldiers to take a more direct role as architects of their moral development. It instead sets the foundations for soldiers receiving rules from superior officers who are in a position to solve the dilemmas and issue directives.

Kasher's claim about the absence of dilemmas is also deeply problematic. No matter what requirements senior leaders establish, soldiers have a responsibility to determine which ones pertain when they face ethical dilemmas, whether the rules are fair, and how to manage conflicting ethical demands. The idea that any code would free soldiers from the burdens of moral thinking is seriously misleading and even potentially dangerous, as it amounts to a tacit encouragement for soldiers to uncritically follow orders without reflecting on whether they are truly moral. It is precisely this way of thinking that much of the work on military ethics education attempts to counteract. Beyond this, Kasher's comments are revealing because they illustrate the extent to which the IDF has confidence in establishing a constrictive system of ethics that can reliably produce uniform conduct. By this account, ethical precepts do not merely *inform* individual judgments but make them superfluous. Moral reasoning is reduced to the task of applying the right rule and rigidly adhering to higher authorities. This is an effort to reverse the decentralization of decision-making I discussed in the first chapter. It shows that whereas some armed forces (especially the US Army) respond to decentralization by increasing the ethical burden on individual soldiers, others may resist this tendency with norms designed to reassert control over personnel at lower levels of the chain of command.

In addition to learning the "Spirit of the IDF," Israeli soldiers are taught many specific rules about how they should conduct themselves in various types of operations. These are far more expansive than those contained in *The Spirit of the IDF* and provide exacting guidance for how soldiers should respond to every conceivable dilemma. The rules soldiers have to memorize go beyond the broad restrictions set out in the ROE used by American and British forces to provide extremely specific instructions for responding to different types of threats.

One soldier who thought the IDF's rules were sometimes too demanding cited the rules for responding to a person armed with a Molotov cocktail as evidence of their narrowness. As he explained, the rules state it is permissible to shoot at a person armed with a Molotov cocktail, but only once it has been lit. If it is unlit the person must be subdued with nonlethal force.[46] Moreover, once a person has thrown the Molotov cocktail, that person is no longer a combatant. The person who threw the explosive is now unarmed and therefore considered nonthreatening even if he still shows hostile intent. The interviewee who explained this seemed to think it was ridiculous to treat someone who had just carried out an attack as a civilian, yet it was another instance of a rule that had to be followed rigidly, despite its implications. Rules like this one go far beyond the ROE that soldiers in the American and British armies described in the sense of being more elaborate and narrowing the scope for individual judgment but were frequently recounted by the Israelis I spoke with.

ROE are rarely publicized, but a change to them in August 2015 provides some indication of how specific the rules can be and what impact this has. Among the new requirements was one that soldiers are forbidden from shooting at the lower extremities of suspected terrorists. Soldiers who were upset by the change posted comments about their displeasure online. In a comment that closely mirrors the one from the interviewee, one soldier said, "There are new rules and we are now studying them. If a Molotov cocktail is thrown at me, even from a distance of just 10 meters, I'm not allowed to shoot at the person throwing it." Another soldier commented that the procedure for stopping vehicles at checkpoints was becoming more strict: "In order to understand the significance [of the new rules], if a terror suspect rams his car through a checkpoint and the driver didn't run over anybody and didn't attack anybody, then the soldiers are not permitted to shoot at the car," the officer said. "They are only allowed to fire in the air."[47] These and other comments give some hints about how exhaustive and strict IDF ROE have become, suggesting they are far more specific than the broad restrictions issued to US and UK forces.

When taken together, the many IDF rules were also far more comprehensive, covering myriad potential dilemmas, which is evidence of a very strong desire on the part of IDF commanders to prevent soldiers from resolving ethical challenges by using their own judgment and to ensure that ethics are enacted consistently. This stands in sharp contrast to the freedom individual soldiers are granted by virtue-based systems that permit them to use their own judgment or pragmatic systems that allow them to flexibly employ loosely codified practices as the circumstances demand.

Consequentialism and Its Contradictions

The IDF's ethics are generally stated in deontological terms, from *The Spirit of the IDF* to the more mission-specific ROE. However, despite the reliance on rules, there are deep consequentialist currents running throughout the IDF's ethics at both the individual level and the organizational level. These threaten to undermine the deontological components of the IDF's ethics because of the underlying difficulties in fitting these two philosophies together. The rule-based affirmations of universal respect for human rights and the value of life are contradicted by consequentialist norms that urge the abandonment of rules in those moments of crisis when moral clarity is most important.

The individual-level tensions between deontological and consequentialist norms are evident in *The Spirit of the IDF*. It acknowledges that rules are prone to conflict with each other and that there must be some guidance for resolving them, thereby introducing grounds for resorting to consequentialism as an arbitrating device. The 1994 version of *The Spirit of the IDF* says: "The complex nature of military activity in general, and of combat in particular, is liable to produce conflicts among the values and basic principles of Spirit of the IDF, and to raise problems in judgment and decision making regarding the balance required among them in practice."[48] It goes on to say that soldiers should seek to take the course of action that ensures military victory. "The obligation to execute the mission and to win in the war will be the compass in every effort to arrive at a proper balance within the system of values and basic principles."[49] The assertion that soldiers should do whatever they must to achieve victory is not surprising in itself, especially because this is the overriding interest of any military. What makes this claim important is that it comes in the preface to a guide for ethics and that it is presented as an ethical precept. This positioning elevates a nationalistic imperative to the status of a moral principle—and not just any moral principle but the one that is capable of performing the sensitive task of resolving conflicts between competing ethical imperatives. In essence, employing this type of partisan consequentialist reasoning puts it in a position to override the many rules stated throughout other parts of *The Spirit of the IDF*.

At the organizational level, the IDF's consequentialism comes from its insistence that the country is in a permanent state of existential threat and that it must win every armed struggle it enters, regardless of the costs. This belief is reflected in the IDF's Main Doctrine, which affirms that "Israel cannot afford to lose a single war."[50] It emphasizes that threats to national security will directly affect vulnerable civilians. The IDF's mission is "to defend the existence, territorial integrity and sovereignty of the state of Israel. To protect the inhabitants of Israel and to combat all forms of terrorism which threaten the daily life."[51] Kobi Michael finds this is a common perception in the IDF, which is "the result of the persistent threats that Israel has faced, the numerous wars and violent conflicts it has fought, and the deep sense of existential anxiety that dwells in the consciousness of the Jewish people."[52] Moreover, he argues that the IDF is in a powerful position to shape civilians' threat perceptions because of its high status. The result is a narrative of threats reiterated by conservative politicians, threats that Israeli civilians are socialized into long before they enter military service.

The conviction that Israel faces enormous threats and could potentially be destroyed is understandable. Over the past half-century Israel has been continually attacked by its neighbors and threatened with total annihilation. However, the belief that no war can be lost is likely inaccurate. Israel has had mixed success in counterinsurgency over the past three decades, usually failing to achieve many of its objectives, yet it has not suffered any major long-term setbacks. Its enemies in counterinsurgency operations are also unlikely to pose an existential threat simply because they lack the military capacity for this. The belief that Israel cannot lose a war is based on past conflicts against conventional armed forces, not on a realistic assessment of the threat posed by Hezbollah and Hamas. This perception of threat is not shared by everyone. There are dissenters in Israel, including IDF veterans who speak out against aggressive counterterrorism and counterinsurgency practices.[53] What is important is that the sense of threat is pervasive and that it shapes strategic thinking at the highest levels. This is why opponents have had to seek support from human rights organizations in the first place.

Belief that Israel is threatened and cannot afford to lose is ethically disconcerting. Studies of state attacks against civilians show that one of the primary reasons for pursuing a strategy of intentionally harming civilians or of using tactics that may lead to high levels of civilian collateral damage is desperation to win.[54] When states decide that they face an existential threat or that they simply cannot allow themselves to be defeated, they become more willing to attack civilians or pursue other unethical strategies. The IDF's insistence that Israel cannot lose a war indicates it is in a perpetual state of desperation to win, and the prominence of this belief in the IDF's doctrine further suggests this is the primary motive for Israel's controversial strategies, which I discuss in more detail in the next chapter.[55]

The consequentialist elements of *The Spirit of the IDF* at the tactical and strategic level are analytically distinguishable, but they are manifestations of the same basic attitude. They reflect a willingness to suspend moral rules in the types of emergency situations when norms are most important. The endorsement of this reasoning at the strategic level and the decision to enshrine this reasoning in the IDF's code of ethics authorizes soldiers to go beyond the limits of their ethical rules, especially those that reflect general humanitarian concerns that may conflict with national interests.

The IDF's sense of facing existential threats leads it to morally questionable practices, such as targeted killings, preemptive attacks, lethal violence against protestors, cluster bombs, and destroying the homes of terrorists' family members.[56] B'Tselem, an Israeli human rights organization, reports many incidents of IDF soldiers assaulting unarmed Palestinians.[57] The nongovernmental organization Breaking the Silence has conducted dozens of interviews with IDF veterans who report witnessing or taking part in human rights abuses, such as attacks on peaceful protestors, insurgents' family members, and even children.[58] Worse still, the reports reveal that these practices are deliberately adopted by those at the highest levels of the chain of command—the same people who, according to Kasher, are responsible for solving ethical dilemmas so their subordinates do not have to. These organizations show that Israel and its military personnel are by no means unanimous in thinking that existential threats still exist or that these should provide license to deviate from moral ideals. The dozens of current and former soldiers who have spoken out against the aggressive counterinsurgency doctrine is evidence that alternative perspectives exist. There is, therefore, some hope of revising this dangerously permissive element of IDF strategic thinking if opposition voices succeed in pressuring policymakers and senior military personnel to reconsider the impact this narrative may have on promoting good conduct at lower levels of the chain of command.

Conclusion

The IDF's ethics arise from its struggle to transform a conventional military into an effective occupying force while still remaining within the boundaries of what is possible for a conscript military whose personnel serve for relatively short periods. *The Spirit of the IDF* provides a clear structure for this project, with explicit rules meant to guide soldiers so effectively that they do not have to make independent ethical decisions. This assertion of central authority deprives lower-ranking soldiers of the autonomy they would have in the American and British militaries, at least when it comes to ethical issues. The first edition of that document sought to clarify the theoretical groundwork of Israeli military ethics, while the revised version transforms it into a series of more practical directives that soldiers can deploy in the field. When *The Spirit of the IDF* is combined with the rules that apply to specific contingencies arising in combat, it establishes an elaborate deontological system that has the potential for circumventing expensive and time-consuming character formation processes, promoting consistency, reducing the ethical burden on individual soldiers, and presenting a better image of the IDF to audiences in Israel and around the world.

A potential for conflict arises from how the IDF's ethics doctrine combines deontological and consequentialist components. Soldiers are supposed to resolve conflicts between rules or ambiguities in them by acting in Israel's interest, and the rules may be overridden by the IDF's overall imperative of protecting the country against perceived existential threats. Soldiers can ordinarily follow their rules without sensing any conflict between these and the goal of promoting national security. The tension between deontology and consequentialism is latent during peacetime and may even fail to arise during counterinsurgency operations. The disagreement between the elements of the IDF's ethics is therefore best characterized as a serious potential disruption that may not be realized so long as Israel refrains from claiming that it faces an existential crisis. Nevertheless, such a threat is routinely declared, and as I show in chapter 10, this leads to disagreements between the deontological and consequentialist components of IDF ethics.

10

The Ethics of Israeli Counterinsurgency Operations

Navigating the Rules of War

The ethical system of the Israel Defense Forces (IDF) is based on an elaborate set of rules ranging from broad guidelines that reflect institutional values to specific instructions for resolving the countless dilemmas that might arise in various conflict scenarios. This promotes uniformity across the IDF and facilitates centralized control by senior commanders. The interviews I conducted with members of the IDF confirmed that their ethical reasoning is primarily deontological. When commenting on why they made a particular decision, soldiers almost always said that they applied rules they were given by senior officers. They likewise validated their decisions not with reference to a warrior archetype or to the demands of satisfying the civilian audience but rather by discussing how the actions were judged by superior officers.

My primary goal in this chapter is to describe how the IDF soldiers employ deontological thinking about ethics and to explore the costs and benefits associated with this. I argue that relying on explicit rules makes members of the IDF more aware of the ethical implications of their actions by marking the decisions that should be considered ethically significant (that is to say, distinguishing ethical dilemmas in a narrow sense from the broader ethical significance of actions informing individual character). The reliance on rules also promoted consistency and transparency. As I showed earlier, American soldiers follow a single system of ethics, yet they may have radically different interpretations of what qualifies as good character and how values should be enacted. Virtue ethics' emphasis on individual character and judgment hinders the creation of clear, uniform guidelines. By contrast, members of the IDF were more consistent in their attitudes because they had clear reference points. This characteristic of deontological reasoning is particularly important for Israeli soldiers because they are drawn from a diverse range of backgrounds and do not serve for the extended periods of time that are necessary for fundamentally reshaping identities and values.

I also explore three problems that arise when relying on a deontological system of military ethics. First, if rules are designed to provide a comprehensive framework for action, such that soldiers are given few opportunities for exercising independent judgment, then soldiers have little guidance for how to react to unexpected dilemmas. The IDF veterans I interviewed reported feeling frustrated when encountering decisions for which they were unprepared because they lacked the tools needed to act on their own initiative. Second, systems of ethical rules may become difficult to operationalize. Establishing rules for all potential moral challenges requires either framing these so broadly that it is difficult to determine what they require or increasing their number to the point that it is prohibitive for soldiers to memorize all of them and to recall them under stress. Finally, resolving the conflicting demands that may be imposed by different rules generates a need for some way of either determining which should take precedence or some decision procedure capable of resolving disagreements. This leads back to the problem I discussed earlier of a consequentialist style of thinking intruding into the IDF's deontological ethics. Consequentialism emerges when arbitrating between the competing rules and can provide a rationale for selectively following those that are most expedient.

In the first section of this chapter I discuss the Israeli soldiers' attitudes toward military ethics. I found that Israeli interviewees were more conscious of their decisions having an ethical character than American and British soldiers. This has much to do with the explicit focus on military ethics training, the elaborate rules of engagement (ROE), and a sense that the IDF is under intense scrutiny by international observers. In the second section I turn to interviewees' comments about escalation of force decisions. Soldiers generally made these types of decisions by considering which rule should apply to the problem at hand and acting accordingly. Rules were beneficial insofar as they offered clarity, yet interviewees were frequently unsure of exactly how they should act when encountering dilemmas that could not be clearly settled by the rules. The third section discusses some of the instances in which rules were superseded because of strategic considerations. Here I focus on moments when soldiers did things that seemed to contradict their ROE, usually at the behest of senior commanders, such as destroying civilian property or occupying civilian homes. The last two sections evaluate the problems associated with a primarily deontological system of military ethics, such as inattention to the role of individual judgment and the tendency of allowing moral norms to be superseded by strategic interests.

Training for Good Conduct

Israeli soldiers seemed far more used to discussing the ethical implications of their actions than the American or British interviewees. This does not mean that they were more ethical but rather that they seemed accustomed to reflecting on ethical decisions as a discrete part of their lives that could be detached from other professional obligations. Almost all quickly understood my request to discuss the ethical dilemmas they experienced without needing any explanation of what types of situations I had in mind. The Israelis also had a much better memory of ethics training. They were usually able to say exactly when they first received it, how it was presented, and how it related to *The Spirit of the IDF*. Most were even able to cite specific examples of issues and case studies they discussed. This easy recall of training contrasted with what I heard from American and British personnel, most of whom reported that they had little formal ethics education or that they could not recall many details about what they had learned.

The IDF soldiers' ability to identify ethical challenges, as well as their recall of training, was symptomatic of the IDF's attention to ethics training and the extent to which it seeks to make ethical issues explicit. Ethics training in the American and British militaries often takes place indirectly, through socialization into the values of a particular role or by learning established institutional practices. It also operates through intermediary concepts like professionalism, the warrior ethos, and tradition. Good conduct may therefore be more familiar if it is characterized as professionalism or adherence to tradition. The Israeli soldiers found that ethics training was usually clearly identified as such and that ethics was sharply distinguished from other activities. As I discuss in the previous chapter, this was out of necessity. It would be difficult to link the norms of conscript soldiers, most of whom are serving for three years or less, to notions of professionalism or a warrior status that depend on an enduring commitment to the military.

Israelis were also far more consistent in how they described their sense of ethics and how they made decisions than members of the other armed forces. American and British soldiers had shared ethical reference points but tended to interpret these in various ways. The Americans sometimes had divergent conceptions of exactly what actions were required to exemplify virtue or what actions showed good judgment. British interviewees likewise sometimes had divergent conceptions of how to employ the lessons of the past and how they should adapt to new challenges. By contrast, Israeli soldiers gave nearly identical responses when asked to describe how they would respond to specific types of ethical decisions, which reflected the uniformity of their ethics training.

Every IDF veteran I interviewed reported undergoing extensive ethical instruction during basic training. Those from different units and occupational specializations described almost identical experiences learning about *The Spirit of the IDF* and discussing the dilemmas they might face. They received lectures on how to interact with civilians, listened to reports about past incidents (such as the Sabra and Shatila massacre), discussed ethical dilemmas, and conducted simulations about common problems they might encounter. Moreover, they received additional ethics training each time they were deployed to a new location. This additional training was itself standardized to ensure consistency across units deployed in the area. During this training, the soldiers also received lessons from their commanders and other veterans of operations in the region to further ensure that soldiers were prepared for the challenges they would encounter and would follow established rules of conduct.

Many of the interviewees thought that the IDF's attention to ethics is among its greatest strengths—something that sets it apart from other militaries. One said that "the IDF prides herself on being the most human/moral army in the world."[1] This point is often repeated with almost identical wording by many current and former soldiers, and it has been central to its public relations efforts directed at discrediting critics like the organization Breaking the Silence, indicating that it is a sentiment that has been instilled through training.[2] Others also said they thought the IDF made a more consistent attempt to follow its code of ethics than other armed forces. They were especially proud of how rigidly they would follow the absolute rules governing their conduct. It was a mark of pride that the soldiers would obey even the most demanding and inflexible requirements simply because it was the right thing to do. There was a sense that this kind of uncompromising moral absolutism guaranteed faultless conduct in practice. The soldiers provided examples of how strict their rules could be to emphasize that these were beyond what many people would be able to follow. James Eastwood finds a similar pride in IDF ethics and sense of moral exceptionalism and traces it back to earlier conceptions of self-restraint when Zionist settlers fought against Palestinians—evidence that my interviews reflect a general sentiment and that this feeling is an enduring aspect of Israel's military culture.[3]

One of the strict rules that soldiers cited is that it was never acceptable to take any property from a Palestinian, regardless of the circumstances. Two of the interviewees said one example they were given during training was that this could not be violated even in as simple a case as a soldier taking water from a Palestinian. Even if an Israeli soldier were badly dehydrated and desperately needed the water, they were told, it would still be unacceptable to violate the rule. Both soldiers who cited this example proudly said they would follow the rule in such a scenario, although the act of taking water seemed relatively trivial, especially when compared to the harm they might suffer from dehydration. Following the rule was an end in itself and a mark of professionalism. Some units employed peer monitoring and encouraged soldiers to anonymously report each other for theft to ensure compliance.[4]

Although soldiers underwent recurrent ethics training in the formal rules and values written in *The Spirit of the IDF*, this was poorly connected to other aspects of training. Interviewees described their ethics education as consisting almost exclusively in classroom activities. Little of the training took place in the field or in conjunction with practice for combat. Ethics was a distinct subject, presented apart from applied military skills like tactics or marksmanship. Several of the soldiers said they did not carry weapons at all during the early periods of their initial training, which is when they received most of their ethics instruction. For example, one interviewee said, "Immediately after lunch we were given a lesson on the basic values of the IDF (a week before I even touched a rifle)."[5]

The classroom training that IDF veterans described was presented in many different ways to appeal to various learning styles. Activities ranged from passive forms of instruction, such as listening to lectures and watching movies, to more active learning, like group discussions of dilemmas. However, even the most active lessons still took place in the classroom. The soldiers reported that live training of any sort is rare in the IDF and that, when it is conducted, it is not used to teach ethics. One said: "I did not participate in any live training exercises in which I was forced to demonstrate my understandings of these laws. I figure that participating in training scenarios would of course benefit the understanding and application of these rules, however the IDF continuously tries to maximize time and money."[6] This experience was common among the soldiers I interviewed. None reported engaging in ethics training in conjunction with field exercises.

The IDF's focus on classroom ethics training may seem strange when the rules are meant to be followed in nonclassroom settings. However, this method of instruction is consistent with and reinforced by the deontological character of the IDF's ethics. Because the IDF expects absolute adherence to rules, there should, at least in principle, be no difference between how the rules are applied in classroom abstractions and how they are applied in the real world. The practical training that is essential from a virtue ethics perspective or for a pragmatic ethic may not appear to be as important when good conduct is supposed to arise from rigid adherence to precepts that can be memorized in any setting. Field training could even be seen as counterproductive insofar as it might suggest that the content of rules may change based on the context or on soldiers' judgment.

Contending with Ambiguity

The Israeli soldiers I interviewed were generally at much lower risk of being attacked than the American or British interviewees. Most were veterans of Operation Cast Lead or the Second Intifada, so they described the ethical challenges that they encountered during those conflicts. Although the IDF sustained casualties in both operations, these were much lower than those of American and British forces in Iraq and Afghanistan. Only 10 members of the IDF were killed or wounded during Operation Cast Lead (4 to friendly fire[7]) and around 301 during the Second Intifada.[8] The length of these conflicts was also shorter, with the former lasting three weeks and the latter lasting four and a half years. The comparatively low casualty numbers suggest that members of the IDF were not exposed to the same degree of risk as American and British personnel. The length of the conflicts and their location within Israel also indicates that the soldiers were probably under less stress than the Americans and British, who had to endure longer periods of deployment far from their homes. This was borne out by interviewees' comments. Only half had experience in gunfights against enemy fighters, and those who did were in contact for relatively short periods—usually just a few minutes.

Given these differences, it is unlikely that Israeli soldiers faced the same contexts of ethical decision-making as American and British personnel. The lower level of threat meant that it would have been easier for them to follow strict ROE without endangering themselves. The shorter length of these conflicts, especially Operation Cast Lead, probably mitigated the effects of chronic stress. Moreover, because they were stationed close to home, the soldiers I spoke with did not have the feeling of interacting with an alien population, which was fairly common among American and British soldiers. This tended to give members of the IDF greater confidence when judging the intent of those around them and how much danger they were in. These characteristics, along with the rule-based style of thinking that characterize the IDF's ethical system, shaped IDF members' reactions to dilemmas.

The Israeli soldiers frequently encountered potential threats that required them to decide what level of force was justified. These challenges were structurally similar to those faced by the Americans and British. They involved unknown vehicles approaching checkpoints without following orders to stop, seeing nonuniformed people who appeared to be armed, or searching the homes of suspected militants. Whereas the Americans and British often had a reasonable fear that a vehicle might be hostile and that it could contain an immediate threat, such as a suicide bomber or a group of gunmen, the danger to the Israelis was generally less urgent. Rather than being concerned that they might be personally attacked, the Israeli soldiers tended to think that the greatest threat posed by unknown vehicles was that it could bypass a checkpoint to transport weapons and explosives to militants who would use them in a future attack. Rather than worrying that a nonuniformed person was hiding a rifle or a bomb beneath their clothes, the Israeli interviewees tended to worry more about nonuniformed people stealing military equipment or collecting intelligence.

Given the vastly different types of conflicts they were involved in, it is impossible to draw conclusions about whether the IDF acted more or less ethically than American and British armed forces or whether its personnel were inclined to use more or less force. The lower level of risk to the Israeli soldiers made it easier for them to act with restraint and often gave them more time for making difficult decisions. This relative safety also facilitated the predominantly rule-based IDF ethics by making it possible for soldiers to follow strict guidelines that might be dangerously inflexible during more intense conflicts.

Instead of being permitted to use their judgment to assess and respond to each threat, soldiers were supposed to follow their rules to the letter and typically avoided making any judgment calls that would take them beyond what was addressed in those rules. The IDF personnel attempted to follow the rules even when these failed to provide adequate guidance—and failures were common. Almost every interviewee described moments when they were unable to identify a relevant rule to help them during a moment of decision. These situations offer some of the best examples of the limitations of deontological military ethics because they show an unwillingness to go beyond or outside of the explicit instructions—a resistance against importing any moral standards that might undermine the rules' absolute status. When the rules were unclear or did not cover a particular eventuality, the Israeli soldiers tended to be reluctant to take the initiative. They described feeling frustrated and conflicted because they were inadequately prepared for the situation or were unsure whether they could act independently.

One soldier reported being on patrol in the Golan Heights when his squad was told to establish a roadblock and prevent any vehicles from moving past it.[9] The local residents were upset by this. The roadblock was unexpected, preventing some people from returning to their homes and others from going to work. The interviewee and the members of his squad struggled to calm the angry crowd as it grew larger. One of the civilian vehicles left the road, bypassing the checkpoint and heading in the direction the soldiers were supposed to keep free of traffic. It was able to drive easily across the flat, dry ground and then cut back onto the road once it had passed the obstruction. The soldier was frustrated at having no means of stopping the vehicle and no clear instructions about what to do if a vehicle went around the roadblock. He and the members of his squad were all armed and could have easily disabled the vehicle, but it was not clear whether they were authorized to shoot. They also doubted that force was warranted because the driver was probably a civilian and showed no signs of hostility. The soldier and the members of his unit decided to let the vehicle pass. The situation deteriorated as other cars circumvented the checkpoint, yet he and his comrades felt that they were powerless to do anything but watch idly and attempt to prevent other cars from leaving the road.

Adam Harmon describes a similar experience while working at a checkpoint. He was under orders to not allow any vehicles to cross because of fears that a high-ranking Palestinian fighter in the area was fleeing capture. He detained dozens of cars, including one with a woman who needed to go to the hospital. After hours of waiting, the people at the checkpoint left their cars and tried to walk around through the desert. "Sometimes this works, though not with me," he says.[10] He explains that other soldiers at the checkpoint remain in their places and fail to prevent the exodus, despite fears that enemies could be hiding among them. In the end Harmon was the only one who attempted to control the crowd or find a way for the woman needing the hospital to pass through. He emphasizes the complacency of the other members of his unit, and he gives the impression that they would only stop traffic without doing anything else because that was all that was covered by their ROE.

Another IDF veteran reported an incident in which he saw three unidentified men inside of an IDF base near the shooting range while he was on patrol.[11] The guard chased the three men, shouting at them to stop, first in Hebrew, then in Arabic. As they continued, he loaded his rifle, seeing this as a more serious warning for them to stop. This progression of warnings followed the escalation of force procedures that IDF soldiers are supposed to employ. However, after proceeding through these steps, the interviewee was unsure about whether to actually open fire. He chose to avoid shooting, allowing the men to escape. He reasoned that the intruders were probably searching for weapons or ammunition left near the range. They dropped shell casings as they ran away, which could have made them legitimate targets. The soldier refused to fire because he was not directly threatened and the exhaustive rules he had learned did not cover the situation. Not shooting at the three intruders was recognized as the right course of action by the soldier's superiors, who commended him for this. Nevertheless, the soldier did not seem to have a good sense of how his commanders would react until afterward. It is also telling that his decision was finally vindicated with reference to how it was judged by those authority figures. They were the primary arbiters of what qualified as good conduct.

This sense that commanders are the source of moral guidance is supported by other interviews with soldiers that reveal a tendency to emphasize commanders' judgment as the highest moral authority. For example, one soldier interviewed by Breaking the Silence said, "In a state of war, the rules of engagement are that people on the ground must exercise their own judgment, the commander's judgment at the moment."[12] Here the language of exercising judgment calls to mind the comments from US soldiers, but it is immediately qualified to indicate that this means obedience to the commander. Another soldier confirms this by saying, "My impression about rules of engagement was that, at least at our level, they were not clear. There were no clear red lines. In urban areas it's very much at the commanders' own discretion."[13] Again, the language suggests that the IDF soldiers were apt to rely on commanders' instructions over their own judgment.

A third interviewee experienced a similar situation while his unit was participating in combat operations in Gaza. He described not only facing the difficult decision of whether to shoot but also having good reason to believe that the prospective targets were enemy fighters.

> Whilst in Gaza I saw what was extremely suspicious activity by four men that kept running in and out of a building down the road (This was a known Hamas stronghold). We weren't sure what they were doing exactly. I saw them carrying equipment inside the building but I couldn't be sure of what it was. We decided to wait and not shoot. It was very nerve-racking. I'm not sure if we did the right thing, many rockets were launched from that block a few days after.[14]

As in the other scenarios, this one involved a situation in which it was unclear whether to shoot. It was made particularly serious because of the possibility that the four men could be militants preparing for an attack. The soldier and his comrades were not directly threatened, yet they were confident that they were looking at hostiles who could attack them later.

Each of these stories involves soldiers deciding whether to escalate force when they were unsure of whether their potential targets were insurgents or civilians. As I discuss in chapter 4, this is one of the most common ethical challenges of counterinsurgency operations—a difficulty that plagues soldiers from each of the militaries. Like the British personnel, Israelis tend to illustrate their good conduct with these kinds of examples of acting with restraint even when there are grounds for using force. However, the underlying motives are different. The British soldiers generally explain their reasoning with reference to the imperative of maintaining a good appearance and building relationships with the local people. Restraint was expedient; it helped to accomplish the mission. By contrast, the Israeli soldiers emphasized their uncertainty in these situations. They found themselves navigating ethical challenges without clear guidance from their extensive ROE and showed restraint because this seemed to be the safest option.

There is also a difference in the source of moral valuations. Whereas the British soldiers see themselves as being accountable to an audience of foreign civilians whose good opinion had to be sustained for operational success, the Israeli interviewees see themselves as being accountable to superiors in the IDF. British soldiers generally substantiate their claims to have done the right thing by telling stories about how the local people responded. Overreacting to provocations led to civilian casualties, complaints from civilians, strained negotiations with local leaders, and even an intensification of violence over the following weeks. The benefits of restraint were less tangible but could be ascertained by the return to normal following an engagement. The Israeli soldiers validate their decisions by recounting their commanders' reactions. They were commended for not using lethal force and were in several instances held up as models for their comrades. This kind of enforcement suggests that the IDF personnel had less concern about how they were seen by the civilian audience and that they felt a powerful need to meet the standards set by those higher up the chain of command. Divergence in the perceived source of ethical oversight reflects the extent to which the rules are supposed to free soldiers from the burdens of independent ethical decision-making and the effort to centralize control under leaders who are responsible for resolving ethical dilemmas.

Superseding the Rules

Almost all the Israeli soldiers I spoke with told me that they were forbidden from taking property from Palestinians and that even the most trivial items—a bottle of soda or an apple—could not be seized no matter how thirsty or hungry a soldier might be. Absolute respect for property was cited as evidence of the IDF's high ethical standards but was routinely discarded in practice. Several interviewees described conducting aggressive patrols through Palestinian areas. They drove heavy vehicles through the streets in a show of force, displaying their weapons prominently and firing warning shots. The gunfire was directed at inanimate objects, such as walls, garbage cans, water tanks, and cars. There was no theft in these instances, yet the gunfire could inflict a heavy toll on civilian property. Shooting in dense urban areas also raised the possibility of inadvertently injuring or killing innocent bystanders. A burst of gunfire directed at a water tank or a flimsy wall could easily pass through the target and hit something else. At times tanks and other armored vehicles would participate in the patrols, crushing streets and sidewalks. The shows of force therefore inflicted considerable property damage, raised the chances of accidental deaths, and degraded the local infrastructure.

Other reports from IDF veterans substantiate these stories. One soldier describes causing extensive property destruction while searching the homes of people who were suspected of being affiliated with Hamas. "You go in with live fire after breaking in the door, the soldiers are looking to smash television and computer screens, looking for interesting stuff in drawers."[15] Another soldier recalls the destruction of an innocent family's home in South Hebron. "And their house was destroyed. Burning tires were thrown at it. It was an innocent house, just picked off the map. . . . And those people's home was ruined. Windows were broken, stones thrown in. That's it. Their house was ruined."[16]

Most of the soldiers I interviewed also described participating in or witnessing aggressive searches of Palestinian homes. Usually they would enter the houses by breaking down the doors and rushing inside, though two interviewees described making entries by blasting holes through the walls of adjoining buildings. Breaking the Silence has also published testimonies of soldiers using sledgehammers to smash through walls.[17] Going through the walls made it possible to move without being exposed to the dangers of passing through doorways or moving through the open streets. It helps to protect soldiers but comes at the expense of seriously damaging civilian homes.

Regardless of the entry procedures, storming houses was traumatic for those inside. Soldiers would enter the houses without warning and move quickly to prevent anyone from leaving or hiding weapons. The soldiers generally thought that searching houses was a necessary and justified tactic, though many also expressed remorse at how this terrorized families—especially children. In this respect they were like the American interviewees who took part in similar searches. "It was hard to watch. They were scared and crying," one recalled of a family. "Usually we'd try to move them all to one room in the house and leave them there. That would get them out of the way and let them calm down."[18] This resulted in civilians being detained for hours or even days inside their homes. Even if a search yielded no sign of weapons or military equipment, the soldiers often remained in place to use the home as an observation position. They could discretely watch a neighborhood without indicating their presence in the hopes of catching insurgents moving in the open.

Breaking the Silence, an Israeli nongovernmental organization that opposes the country's treatment of Palestinians and advocates on behalf of veterans who share this view, has collected dozens of firsthand accounts that describe similar incidents. One report notes that "nearly every night, IDF forces invade homes of Palestinian families, often taking post in the house for days or even weeks."[19] The goal is "to improve the IDF's control of territory by capturing and controlling positions and creating hidden lookout points."[20] Thus, despite enacting rules designed to prevent theft, the IDF routinely finds strategic grounds for violating Palestinians' property rights. The rules do not consistently protect civilian property but rather block certain reasons for violating property rights and disempower enlisted soldiers from making decisions about when and how property should be protected.

American and British soldiers likewise used civilian homes as observation and fighting positions, but this was more consistent with their ethics. Soldiers in those armed forces are not supposed to wantonly destroy civilian property, yet they had fairly broad authorizations to use their own judgment about when property rights could be breached. This was especially true during combat, when the right of self-defense superseded other considerations. Using civilian homes as observation points and deliberately destroying items for intimidation more clearly contradicts the IDF's ethics. It goes against the logic of protecting civilian property, which soldiers described as being a centerpiece of their rules. Yet it was rationalized by the soldiers' commanders and many of the soldiers themselves as being essential for catching terrorists before they could attack. In other words, deviating from the rules was described as being essential on the consequentialist grounds of protecting Israel's security.

Perhaps the most famous and controversial assault on civilian property is the practice of demolishing the houses that belong to suspected terrorists in order to deprive enemy fighters of defensive positions. Around three thousand Palestinian homes were destroyed during Operation Defensive Shield alone, leaving at least thirteen thousand people homeless and inflicting $350 million in property damage.[21] None of the soldiers I interviewed helped to demolish Palestinian homes, but several did witness this happening. Opinions were mixed about whether this was justified. One soldier who ardently defended the practice said it was the only way for the IDF to punish terrorists and discourage future attacks. "Sometimes they are family homes," he said, "but the people are not innocent. They know what is happening. They know if their brother or father or husband is a terrorist. They have a responsibility to do something when they know there's going to be an attack."[22] It was, he explained, vital for Israel's national security and an expression of its right of self-defense to destroy terrorists' homes. Another soldier who was opposed to the practice said that the evidence linking a building to terrorism could be weak and mentioned once seeing a house destroyed for storing too much fertilizer. The material could be used in a bomb, but with so many legitimate uses, destroying someone's home seemed disproportionate.[23]

Breaking the Silence interviewed one soldier who was involved in tearing down Palestinian houses; he described the destruction going far beyond what was necessary and proportionate. According to him, the bored soldiers would pretend they were driving monster trucks, using the bulldozers to smash or lift cars. He recalls, "We ran wild with that thing. We moved boulders, blocked access to homes, tore out gates. Just simply went ahead and played around with that shovel."[24] This comment reveals just how easily destruction could escalate to exceed what was reasonable for national security.

When I asked soldiers to explain the contradiction between rules aimed at protecting civilians' property and tactics that involved the destruction or temporary appropriation of civilian property, they returned either to the consequentialist thinking embodied in the IDF's doctrine or to the importance of following commanders' instructions. Occupying homes and destroying property were described as being essential for maintaining security. The soldiers recognized that home demolition and aggressive patrols were destructive, yet most thought these were warranted because they were essential for preventing attacks that could inflict more severe harm. Using homes as observation points was less objectionable still. Although this was upsetting to the families, soldiers generally saw this as the least invasive way of establishing a strong presence in an area and policing the local population. In other words, there was a sense of proportionality guiding this tactic. It inflicted some harm, although interviewees usually felt that this was outweighed by the benefit of catching insurgents.

The decision to conduct aggressive patrols or occupy civilian homes did not come from the enlisted soldiers and junior officers that I spoke with. They had a rationale for these decisions and usually agreed with them, but they were not the ones making them. The orders typically came from the brigade level or higher—from those who had the authority to revise the ROE. This was in sharp contrast to what I heard from the American and British soldiers. When American and British interviewees reported witnessing morally questionable actions, they typically described fellow soldiers at roughly their own level of the chain of command acting wrongly. Commanding officers were sometimes the facilitators of immoral action by being too permissive in their instructions or failing to punish transgressors, yet it was rare for interviewees to cite instances of their officers doing things that they felt were clearly wrong. Instead they criticized superiors for either framing excessively strict ROE or too readily shifting responsibility for mistakes onto subordinates. The Israeli soldiers were far more inclined to say they did something they felt was morally dubious because of directives they received from senior officers.

Members of the IDF were also in a weaker position to contest objectionable orders. Because most of the soldiers I spoke with only served their required three years, there were few veterans among the lower-ranking soldiers and no equivalent to the American and British sergeants who had over a decade of experience and the clout needed to question superiors. This shows the other side of a problem I discussed earlier with reference to the US Army. Veterans can have a harmful influence on unit subcultures, even acting as "ethical insurgents,"[25] yet they can also serve as a positive check on superiors because it may be more difficult to compel these independent-minded soldiers to go along with orders they disagree with.

It is also evident that the rules themselves could be problematic, even when they were not superseded by consequentialist reasoning. The general rules embodied in *The Spirit of the IDF* are consistent over time, but the more complex ROE governing use of force decisions could be altered depending on the circumstances. One of the soldiers I spoke with said his unit was given orders to change its targeting procedures at night, when civilians were forbidden from going outside. Whereas he was ordinarily only authorized to attack enemies who were clearly armed and threatening, he was told to presume that anyone outside after curfew was a potential threat and could be attacked. From this it became clear that rules, like values or pragmatic norms, are not inherently good. The authorization to attack anyone after curfew was a rule of conduct that was as much designed to guarantee consistent behavior as the rules urging restraint. It was, however, a questionable requirement that would likely result in civilian casualties if followed consistently.

Framing the Rules

The stories from IDF veterans illustrate how difficult it is to consistently apply deontological reasoning during war. No matter how elaborate they are, rules may be incomplete and inadequate for resolving unexpected dilemmas. Uncertainty, especially about the identity of nonuniformed people who may be civilians or insurgents, can impede rule following even when the rules are clearly formulated. Soldiers who have been trained to follow strict rules may be left without guidance when the context for applying them is unclear. Around half of the soldiers I talked to were acutely aware that rules were sometimes inadequate to address unexpected ethical challenges or unsuitable for the kinds of ambiguous threats they encountered during counterinsurgency operations. One soldiers said of the IDF's extensive training in rules that "the weaknesses of this training is that no matter how much they train you and no matter how hard they enforce them, a soldier will almost always find himself in an dilemma that he hasn't heard about before and he will have question marks about his required reaction."[26] Moreover, most of the soldiers who did not explicitly say this gave examples of encountering dilemmas that the IDF rules could not help them resolve.

The IDF's efforts to promote obedience to rules comes at the expense of discouraging soldiers from making independent decisions except in the most limited ways. Any encouragement to use personal judgment is potentially dangerous, as it could provide a rationale for dissent. The ethics training IDF soldiers receive seems to be designed with this in mind, given the IDF's emphasis on absolute obedience. The interviewees' comments confirm this. The soldiers generally echo Kasher, *The Spirit of the IDF*'s primary architect, in saying that their rules were meant to not only supersede individual judgment but to eliminate the need for subjective ethical decision-making entirely. One even told me that "soldiers make most of their ethical decisions by asking higher ranking officers and following their instructions."[27] The rules were meant to be followed even when soldiers' ethical intuitions might direct them to act differently.

Attempting to provide detailed rules governing how a person should act in various situations while substantially reducing the scope of individual judgment is problematic, as rules cannot account for every dilemma that might arise. This is clear from the examples I discuss earlier in the chapter. The soldiers who were unsure of how to react to vehicles bypassing a roadblock and who did not know whether to shoot at suspicious but not clearly armed adversaries each encountered the problem of determining how to act in the absence of clear rules. With little or no instruction on how to engage in ethical reasoning on their own, and with no rules to tell them what level of force to use against the potential threats they faced, the soldiers chose to refrain from attacking.

The interviewees reached these decisions by relying on their own judgment, but this took them beyond the IDF's deontological framework, leading them to contravene Kasher's claim that soldiers should not have to resolve dilemmas. The three interviewees acted with restraint in each instance, making it tempting to regard these situations as evidence of the effectiveness of IDF ethics. However, good choices resulted from these soldiers having strong personal conceptions of morality and being able to quickly revert to these when they encountered unexpected problems. Even though they acted well, they had to do so by thinking beyond the IDF's exhaustive rules. The risk that this raises is that the IDF's effort to create a consistent and high standard of ethics based on rules may ultimately be untenable because of the tendency for ethical challenges to force soldiers to revert to their own judgment. Without training in making independent ethical decisions, soldiers may be inadequately prepared for acting independently when this is required.

Challenges for Deontological Military Ethics

There are two ways that the IDF might attempt to make its rules more practically applicable while staying within the confines of a deontological framework: (1) by expanding the number of rules or (2) by making them broader so that they can encompass a greater range of potential ethical dilemmas. These strategies introduce their own set of costs and benefits.

Solving rule incompleteness by expanding the number of rules threatens to make rules too numerous for soldiers to learn or to recall under stress. Solving the incompleteness problem by constructing broader rules may only render them too vague to be applied consistently. Although the IDF members I spoke with seemed to have a strong understanding of their rules and when these should be applied, most said that the number could become overwhelming, especially when they had to be recalled under pressure. Around half of the soldiers also thought that the rules were too strict and inflexible, and thought that this actually became worse as rules proliferated. The more rules that were made, the more they could extend into every facet of every activity. Dissatisfaction was particularly strong among the soldiers who had spent longer in uniform or who had combat experience. For them, extremely specific rules like the one regarding when a person with a Molotov cocktail qualifies as a combatant were dangerously restrictive. Such rules can also be dangerous for civilians, especially if the rules change frequently. Comments from an IDF soldier who was interviewed in 2002 encapsulate this problem: "No one knows what is going on; the rules change every minute. Palestinians get shot because no one knows what they're supposed to be doing and everyone is scared. That's why an innocent man died last week."[28]

Increasing the generality of rules and allowing them to cover a wider range of actions holds the advantages of preventing rules from multiplying beyond what soldiers can remember and preventing them from becoming so specific that they leave soldiers feeling they have no freedom to adapt to new challenges. However, as rules become vaguer, they also become harder to operationalize. Rather than imposing too many restrictions, vague rules may impose too few. This can be just as cognitively demanding as an elaborate set of rules for every situation. Although vague rules may be easier to memorize, the more abstract they are, the more effort may be required to determine exactly how the rules should apply in specific situations.

In theory, it is possible to find a way out of this problem of rule vagueness. Part of Immanuel Kant's genius was framing a deontological moral system on a single fairly simple and intuitively clear categorical imperative that could be stated in several different ways. Kant's effort to do this was made easier because his moral theory was meant to account for universally binding duties. The IDF would struggle to follow his example because its norms have to apply to a specific group and to the actions that are unique to that group. Subordinating the rules to the country's strategic interests further hinders the creation of norms that can apply broadly and consistently. Strategic interests are apt to change, as are the tactics soldiers employ to pursue those interests. When used to create an institutional ethic, especially one for those who have exceptional responsibilities and authorizations, deontological thinking is persistently caught in the intractable struggle for rules to cover every situation while still being operationalizable.

Deontological ethical systems must also include some method of arbitrating between rules when they come into conflict. Rules can rarely be truly absolute; they must have some circumstances under which they can be suspended or when other rights or duties prevent them from being obeyed. There are three approaches to overcoming this challenge. First, rules may be weighted differently. Second, some decision procedure could be used for determining how precedence should be determined in a particular situation. Third, disagreements can be resolved by importing some external criteria. The IDF favors the last approach, with Israel's strategic interests serving as the final authority that informs how rules are interpreted and applied.

The priority of strategic goals is evident in how the rules are framed and interpreted. Interviewees described their rules as inviolable guidelines to be followed in all circumstances without exceptions. The absolutism not only prevents soldiers from satisfying personal wishes, such as by stealing property, but also proscribes actions that might seem militarily important. For example, one soldier reported learning during training that the rule to respect Palestinians' property is so important that soldiers are not even allowed to seize money that is being used to finance terrorism. He was instructed that he never had the authority to confiscate or destroy property, even when it was militarily valuable. This absolutism and universality reflects the status of rules in deontological moral thinking compared to the more permissive ROE used by the American and British armed forces. For the IDF, rules are not simply constraints that establish general limits of conduct, nor are they meant to always ensure the best outcome. Instead, they are supposed to provide an exhaustive account of how soldiers should act. Following the rules is considered good in itself, at least from the perspective of those soldiers at the enlisted and noncommissioned officer ranks.

For most of the soldiers I spoke with, the fact that the rules were those of the IDF and were meant to serve Israel's interests was sufficient reason for adherence. The soldiers did not see the need to find deeper moral justifications and therefore did not attempt to discover whether the rules were based on underlying moral principles that they might use for making independent judgments. The rules were not meant to be followed because they encapsulated a perfectly rational account of universal moral obligations but rather because they were framed to promote the interests of the IDF and of Israel. Therefore, to the extent that there was an underlying logic to the rules, it was one of national interest and not a universal sense of good conduct. This makes deontological thinking in a military context much different from deontological theories advanced by philosophers, which typically emphasize the universality of norms.[29]

Soldiers described their ethical responsibilities as being essential to the IDF's identity and to the identities of the soldiers themselves. However, they also understood the underlying strategic reasons for maintaining high ethical standards. Almost every one of the Israeli soldiers I interviewed said that the IDF's focus on ethics had much to do with the international scrutiny of Israeli military operations, which created an imperative to always act ethically, without exception. As one soldier put it, "There is a mentality within the IDF that the eyes of the world are upon us. It is well understood that despite our actions any event no matter how minuscule can turn into an international outrage."[30] Another told me that "Israel suffers immensely because of double standards and the media's portrayal of her."[31] Ethical conduct is a way of showing that the IDF is a force for good and that reports of misconduct are largely false. Moreover, unlike the British soldiers, who are concerned with how their actions were judged by indigenous civilians, the Israeli soldiers seem to think that the attitudes of Palestinians were unalterable. Their struggle for legitimacy took an international orientation, with a desire to show third-party observers around the world that the IDF's counterinsurgency operations are defensive and restrained.

As chapter 6 discusses, *The Spirit of the IDF* says that soldiers are supposed to make decisions based on what is in the country's best interest. When rules come into conflict, or when the state faces existential threats, rules are meant to be suspended without being altered or eliminated. This raises the possibility that however strict or comprehensive these rules are, they may be ignored in the situations when they are most needed. Whatever the merits of the individual rules of conduct, a system of rules can be effective only to the extent that rules can actually be used to regulate the activity they are meant to regulate. The fact that the IDF's mission statement defines every conflict as an existential threat means that any conflict can provide justification for circumventing the rules. In other words, because the IDF's mission statement and *The Spirit of the IDF* include clear provisions for suspending rules, they are under constant threat of being superseded by the more permissive consequentialist reasoning.

Deciding which rules should apply and when there were grounds for superseding them was left to senior commanders. The soldiers I interviewed, among the enlisted, noncommissioned officer, and junior officer ranks, did not have the authority to permit exceptions. At these levels, soldiers are supposed to be bound by ethical restraints and to have little if any power to revise them.

Conclusion

As I argue in this chapter, the IDF's ethics are primarily deontological in form. The IDF relies on an elaborate set of rules, ranging from the broad regulations contained in *The Spirit of the IDF* to narrower rules addressed to specific challenges that soldiers might encounter. These are meant to guide soldiers through ethical challenges and inform their overall outlook on what it means to be a member of the IDF. My interviews reveal that IDF personnel are generally strongly committed to strictly following their rules whenever they encounter dilemmas and that the rules are usually effective in helping soldiers identify ethical challenges. The rules themselves are generally laudable, showing a willingness to protect civilian lives and property. Nevertheless, the IDF's deontology is far from perfect, as the rules soldiers are trained to follow sometimes come into conflict or become confused when they are operationalized. They could also be superseded by commanders issuing countervailing orders. Thus, the rules are not absolute guidelines for what soldiers could do but rather prohibitions on what they could do in the absence of explicit orders from superiors.

Over the course of my interviews I also found that operationalizing deontological military ethics can become extremely demanding, especially under the difficult conditions of counterinsurgency warfare. First, rules and the situations to which they were meant to apply are often unclear, leaving soldiers to use their own judgment to overcome moral dilemmas. This pushes soldiers beyond the boundaries of their deontological ethics, leaving them to rely on personal judgment with little guidance. The IDF's attempt to limit ordinary soldiers' abilities to make independent judgments, which is both a consequence of rule-based thinking and a way of protecting it, contributes to this problem by precluding the establishment of an institutionalized method for going beyond the rules. Second, the IDF's deontological ethical system relies heavily on underlying consequentialist standards. The specter of existential threat and the corresponding imperative to win every conflict loom behind the IDF's ethics. This consequentialism based on national interest provides the groundwork for reconciling rules or suspending them entirely, which ultimately threatens to reduce the IDF's deontology to a stylized form of consequentialism.

Conclusion

Soldiers' choices profoundly shape the course of events during wars, fueling or destroying insurgencies, harming or protecting civilians, undermining or building local governmental institutions, and disrupting or advancing their countries' foreign policy objectives. Military ethics is a way of attempting to ensure that soldiers will act in fairly predictable and morally upright ways by establishing shared standards of conduct. The soldiers I interviewed generally said that when they were actively fighting, they made moral choices by evaluating the extent to which they were personally threatened. Those from each military said they placed a high value on protecting noncombatants and fighting according to the laws of war. However, those who perceived an immediate danger usually responded by doing whatever they thought was necessary to defend themselves, even if they had to put civilians at risk. This is consistent with the militaries' ethical codes, which affirm the right to self-defense. The high level of agreement between soldiers regarding the appropriate use of force in combat indicates the importance of international law in establishing norms that are shared cross-nationally. Soldiers uniformly expressed a commitment to following the laws of war and were generally aware of legal obligations. The laws of war were therefore able to establish basic guidelines for acceptable behavior that could be used by each military, regardless of the differences in their ethical philosophies. It was when the laws of war were either unclear or gave no instructions that soldiers from different countries were apt to disagree. If there were no established transnational norms for certain aspects of warfare or for counterinsurgency operations specifically, then it was up to individual militaries to decide for themselves what norms they would impose.

The American, Israeli, and British militaries each train their soldiers to make decisions based on systems of military ethics that reflect some of the dominant traditions of Western moral thought. These systems are rarely *explicitly* based on moral philosophies but rather show the same styles of thinking and appropriate certain elements of moral philosophies to create hybrid systems. The US Army employs rule-bounded virtue ethics. Guidance comes from a warrior ethos and values that are meant to be embodied in the character of individual soldiers. British military ethics incorporates rules and some of the language associated with virtue ethics but is generally pragmatic because it emphasizes the importance of norms that have proven most effective in reaching good political outcomes in past counterinsurgency operations. The Israel Defense Forces (IDF) mixes deontological and consequentialist reasoning. Soldiers are taught to obey strict rules that are meant to guarantee consistency and transparency, yet they must follow consequentialist reasoning under exceptional circumstances or when the rules are inadequate. The IDF also encourages consequentialist evaluations by casting enemies as existential threats that must be defeated at any cost.

The challenges that soldiers considered the most difficult were usually about when to initiate hostilities, how to interpret threats, and how to interact with people in occupied areas. This includes a broad array of different dilemmas, such as whether to attack unidentified vehicles at checkpoints, how to treat uncooperative or hostile civilians, how to conduct searches, and how to show cultural sensitivity. These types of decisions can best be described as ethical decisions about the escalation of force and the treatment of civilians, as opposed to ethical decisions in combat. The three armies' distinct ethical systems had a strong influence on how soldiers perceived these challenges and how they overcame them. There was no clear better or worse military with respect to decision-making. Each had strengths and limitations that were closely linked to how the ethical systems were structured and what degree of freedom soldiers had for acting independently.

US soldiers tended to think about ethical challenges in terms of their warrior ethos and a unique set of military values that separate members of the profession of arms from civilian outsiders. This system of virtue ethics has the advantage of being a comprehensive normative framework that encourages supererogatory actions and individual initiative. The Americans were generally good at improvising solutions to unexpected ethical problems, provided these were not radically different from the roles they were trained for. For example, members of combat arms units found it difficult to adapt to the challenges of interacting with civilians during searches but were quick to respond to unexpected dilemmas that occurred when fighting. The US Army's virtue ethics comes at the cost of strained civil-military relations—both at home and in contested areas. Of all the soldiers interviewed, the Americans generally expressed the most trouble understanding foreign cultures and empathizing with civilians. They were also prone to feeling resentful or mistrustful about American civilians because of their perceived lack of support and lower moral standards.

In principle, the British military's pragmatism appears to be the most conducive to good civil-military relations during counterinsurgency operations. It values tradition and encourages soldiers to feel they are part of a profession, yet it is not premised on a sharp division between soldiers and civilians. The pursuit of political objectives and tendency to see foreign civilians as an audience that must be won over promotes restraint and collaboration with local government and security forces. The weakness of the British system of ethics is that its grounding in tradition and accumulated experience made it unreflective and resistant to change. When the unsuitability of the British counterinsurgency doctrine for the conflicts in Iraq and Afghanistan became clear, the British military was slow to reassess its ethics, but then returned to a more conventional war posture without rethinking its guiding norms. The soldiers' efforts to follow this doctrine led to recurrent problems when interacting with local security forces, a questionable tendency to outsource morally challenging activities to dubious allies, and moments when they felt compelled to deviate from their minimalist norms—usually by relying on superior firepower to offset personnel shortages.

Soldiers in the IDF had a strong sense of their ethical obligations and were consistent in defining them. They showed a high degree of uniformity in how they identified and overcame ethical challenges. This reflects the IDF's effort to establish a clear and consistent system of ethics that is encapsulated in *The Spirit of the IDF* and the exhaustive rules that are supposed to routinize soldiers' actions to the extent that they do not even require ethical judgment. The greatest limitation of their rule-based ethics was determining how to act when the soldiers encountered unexpected dilemmas. This is not to say that these soldiers acted wrongly in these situations, only that they seemed unsure of what to do when their rules were vague or did not specify a precise course of action. Almost without exception, the decision was to not escalate the level of violence. This was a safe approach, but it seemed to be based on uncertainty about how to act rather than on personal moral deliberation. Commanders were able to take advantage of low-ranking soldiers' lack of autonomy when ordering them to engage in morally questionable practices, such as occupying civilian homes and conducting aggressive patrols, and were able to rationalize this by appealing to the necessities of national security.

My goal in calling attention to the strengths and weaknesses of various systems of military ethics is not to show that military ethics is a lost cause or that all approaches are defective. Rather, I have sought to show that the implications of competing approaches need to be carefully considered, especially in light of the future conflicts that armed forces anticipate and train for. Many of their challenges are linked to how they are operationalized, with the US Army relying on norms that are better suited for conventional wars, the British military relying too heavily on tradition and poorly formulated norms, and the IDF waging counterinsurgencies with a sense of existential crisis that it has inherited from decades of fighting against opposing states. The persistence of misconduct even when systems of military ethics are in place should be taken as a reminder that ethics are a vital means of improving soldiers' conduct but that perfectly moral warfare is illusory.

Improving Military Ethics

Military ethics may fail to guarantee flawless conduct, but it is possible to make incremental improvements that can reduce war's destructiveness. My findings suggest there are some ways each military could promote greater ethical compliance. One of the most important steps toward improving systems of military ethics and protecting civilians living in contested areas is continually revisiting the laws of war and updating or expanding them to cover the challenges that arise in different types of operations. Laws cannot ensure compliance, especially if the laws are not enforced. However, establishing a more comprehensive legal framework to cover the broad range of dilemmas that occur in counterinsurgency operations would compel those countries that do wish to comply with international law to rethink their counterinsurgency doctrines and ethics training programs. Above all else, this could help to achieve greater cross-national agreement about how to act.

Of course, the expansion of international law takes time, and some states may not accept new legal obligations when this would reduce the scope of their own unique norms. With this in mind, short-term improvements should be pursued by identifying problems with existing systems of military ethics and improving implementation. Despite their divergent norms, each of the militaries I discuss face some shared challenges that should inform their efforts to promote good conduct in the future: more clearly determining what roles soldiers have in counterinsurgency operations, providing more effective guidance for enlisted soldiers, and attempting to restructure the contextual factors that shape dilemmas and the range of available choices.

Distinguishing military from police roles and conducting mission-specific training is essential for giving soldiers routine actions they can fall back on when they encounter ethical challenges. Modern militaries tend to be rigidly segmented according to specializations. Soldiers are trained to carry out specific operations in specific environments. When the missions they are ordered to complete differ significantly from what they have been trained for, they may be less competent in performing new roles and making ethical decisions. This increases stress and may lead them to trust routinized behaviors modeled on conventional operations. A recurrent complaint among interviewees from each country was that military and police functions were not clearly distinguished. Many of the soldiers who took part in the interviews expressed frustration with being used in roles they considered to be inappropriate for military forces. They described being police rather than soldiers. In a study of American, British, and Israeli strategic thinking, Eitan Shamir reports that members of each force think their training in cultural sensitivity and civil-military relations has become excessive. "Many officers believe that the time allotted to sensitivity training would be better spent preparing for combat—indeed, that the military had been infiltrated by civilians emphasizing compassion, understanding, and friendship rather than courage, honor, sacrifice, and skill at arms."[1] This feeling is understandable given the different roles soldiers must take on, yet my research shows that the level of training in cultural sensitivity, civil-military affairs, and other noncombat aspects of counterinsurgency operations is inadequate.

Ideally, counterinsurgency and conventional fighting should be performed by different groups because they require different operating procedures and skills. Drawing such a distinction between unit specializations could prepare militaries for counterinsurgency while still preserving their conventional warfighting capacities. Failing this, armed forces need to think more carefully about what future security threats have priority and reconfigure training accordingly. Given the pervasiveness of asymmetric wars, it seems misguided for the American, British, and Israeli militaries to continue investing so heavily in ethical preparations for conventional wars against states.

The American, British, and Israeli militaries recognize that enlisted soldiers make important strategic decisions and that they must build local support through their daily interaction with the local people, yet they have been slow to enact institutional reforms that acknowledge this. Enlisted soldiers across the three militaries generally said they were given inadequate ethics training and were poorly prepared for navigating foreign cultural landscapes, and other studies have likewise found a lack of education at these levels.[2] Many felt their commanders filtered information as it went down the chain of command, removing vital details about how small-unit actions contributed to overall strategic goals. Without adequate information, soldiers found it difficult to use their own judgment and to understand the contexts in which they were acting. This is especially problematic for noncommissioned officers and senior noncommissioned officers who, although not officers, are in leadership positions and often tasked with key civil-military affairs work. Thus, the noncommissioned officers and the strategic privates and corporals may not be aware of how their objectives fit into their units' missions or the overall counterinsurgency strategy. Sensitive information must be guarded to prevent leaks, but enlisted soldiers sometimes feel that so much is withheld that they cannot make meaningful contributions.

This follows from institutional decisions each military has made—decisions to prioritize ethics training for officers and to limit moral autonomy for those lower in the chain of command. The extent to which enlisted soldiers are free to make independent moral decisions varies cross-nationally, yet even in the US Army, which puts the most emphasis on allowing these soldiers to make their own judgments, autonomy is often limited. This is evidence of a lingering desire to subordinate lower-ranking soldiers to centralized control—another relic of conventional warfare that creates problems in counterinsurgency. I agree with Jessica Wolfendale in thinking that "it is patronizing to treat enlisted personnel as less capable of moral development than officers, particularly since they are required to carry out acts of extreme violence that require a substantive moral justification."[3] Moreover, some of the most innovative proposals for improving counterinsurgency effectiveness involve rethinking the military hierarchy along the lines of the jurisdictions used by police forces rather than in terms of traditional top-down command.[4]

Ethical decisions in war are structured by the context in which ethical challenges arise. Each time soldiers face a moment of decision in which they must choose the right course of action, they do so in a context that is created by countless other actors. Their ethical challenges as well as the norms that they are supposed to apply are shaped by a range of decisions by their civilian and military leaders. The importance of context in structuring dilemmas and predisposing them to one outcome or another means that soldiers often find themselves making critical decisions in situations they did not choose. The result is that soldiers may be unprepared for the ethical challenges they face and may even resent those who make strategic decisions or frame the rules of engagement.

Although soldiers usually felt that they were able to effectively resolve the ethical challenges they encountered, some dilemmas were so heavily shaped by situational constraints that it was virtually impossible for soldiers to reliably employ ethical reasoning procedures, rules, or values. This was especially true when soldiers lacked adequate information to determine what variables were involved in a dilemma. For example, soldiers who guarded checkpoints and convoys, who conducted patrols in dense urban areas, or who searched civilian homes were routinely unsure of whether they were threatened, who they were interacting with, and what effects their actions would have. At times soldiers encountered ethically insoluble dilemmas—instances in which they were so mired in uncertainty that they felt they were at the whims of luck. In these types of situations, the context of ethical decision-making threatens to reduce ethical reasoning to a matter of chance.

Context can also be controlled, at least to an extent, and efforts should be made to either avoid those situations in which ethically insoluble dilemmas are most likely to occur or to give soldiers more options for resolving these. Those in leadership positions therefore have a responsibility to carefully consider the ways in which their strategic and operational decisions create contexts and prime soldiers for certain kinds of behavior. The persistent use of checkpoints in Iraq, Afghanistan, the West Bank, and other contested areas, even when these seem to be one of the most ethically problematic settings in counterinsurgency operations, indicates that leaders in each of the militaries have not given enough attention to their responsibility for creating ethical contexts in which soldiers can be reasonably expected to make the right decision. Improvements may be made by not employing the surprise traffic control points that are apt to catch civilians by surprise and cause them to act in apparently threatening ways. Similarly, roads used by convoys can be cordoned off and monitored by guard posts, as the US military did during the latter years of the occupation of Iraq, to reduce the overall threat to soldiers and make them feel more secure around civilian vehicles.

Soldiers and those they interact with can also be primed for good conduct. One of the most significant differences between the American soldiers and the British soldiers was that the former were often primed in ways that intensified their sense of threat while the latter were primed in ways that lowered it (at least initially). The default posture for US soldiers was one more suited to conventional war, as soldiers routinely wore body armor, carried heavy weapons, and rode in armed vehicles. By contrast, early during the operations in Iraq and Afghanistan the British soldiers attempted to appear as nonconfrontational as possible. Of course, this decision does involve a tradeoff. Priming soldiers for combat has the advantage of keeping them better protected if they are attacked. The intensification of violence caused the British military to return to a conventional war posture, to the detriment of the relationship they tried to establish with civilians. The challenge is avoiding excessively militarized approaches that can escalate violence and committing to a strong enough military presence to maintain peace without recourse to heavy weapons.

Of course, attempts to eliminate situations that are apt to produce ethical challenges with structural changes may raise new dilemmas. There is an important difference between eliminating or avoiding certain ethically challenging situations and simply shifting the burden of confronting them onto others. This is clear when comparing the US and Israeli operations with those of the British military. Interviewees from the British military, as well as other reports from British soldiers, show that the British were less involved in protecting checkpoints and convoys, often giving these jobs to local allies. This helped to minimize the British soldiers' exposure to danger and the resulting ethical challenges, but this structural decision was an ethically questionable choice in its own right because it required greater reliance on local forces. In other words, the ethical challenges inherent in establishing checkpoints and protecting convoys were outsourced, but their basic form as well as the danger to civilians passing through them remained much the same. It is vital to restructure ethical challenges without simply shifting the burden of making them onto others.

Nonlethal weapons offer another potential solution to use of force decisions.[5] There are risks associated with soldiers relying too heavily on these or deliberately targeting civilians. Any decision to intentionally attack a civilian violates the principle of discrimination and is therefore illegal. Nevertheless, nonlethal weapons may be justifiably employed when soldiers face ambiguous threats, as they so often do. When it is impossible to determine whether an apparent threat inside of a car or building is genuine, nonlethal weapons may permit soldiers to protect themselves without killing.

More research on operationalizing ethics is essential as militaries continue to grapple with the innumerable moral conundrums that arise during conflicts. And it will only become more important as soldiers are continually thrust into counterinsurgency operations in which the fate of civilians and entire countries rest on how effectively and responsibly soldiers are able to provide security. I hope this study takes another step toward reorienting research to give greater attention to the often-overlooked soldiers at the lower levels of the military hierarchy and that some of the potential routes for improvement that I have offered may be beneficial. Going forward, it is crucial to continue developing our understanding of what forces affect soldiers' choices and to explore the normative frameworks that may help to promote responsible uses of force.

Appendix

List of Interview Questions

What was your age while you were in the military?

What was your motivation for joining?

What was your occupational specialization?

What led you to choose that specialization?

Where were you deployed? What were the time periods of your deployment?

What was your rank while you were deployed?

What unit(s) were you a part of / attached to during your deployment(s)?

How would you describe your moral values before joining the military? Could you tell me how you tended to resolve ethical challenges you encountered before joining the military? What reasoning processes or values did you apply?

What is your religion? Did it have a significant effect on your moral thinking before training? Did your religious values influence the decisions you made when you were deployed? If so, how did it affect them?

What kind of ethics training did you receive prior to deployment? How useful was it? What went well? What went poorly? Was this training conducted in conjunction with other kinds of training (e.g., field exercises) or was it done in the classroom?

Did any of the training you received conflict with your values or cause you to change the way you made ethical decisions?

What legal instructions were you given prior to deployment?

Did any part of your training conflict with the ethical and legal instructions that you were given? If so, how?

Could you tell me about some of the ethical challenges you encountered when you were deployed? Which ethical challenges were the most common, and why? Which ethical challenges were the most difficult, and why? Could you tell me about your reasoning when you encountered ethical challenges, especially how you were able to resolve them? How did you feel about these challenges and your decisions afterward? (The follow-up questions to clarify the scenarios discussed and the reasoning that soldiers employed varied.)

Did your training provide useful guidance for resolving the ethical challenges you encountered during your deployment(s)? Why or why not?

What is your perception of the way other soldiers behaved, in your unit and outside of it? What kinds of ethical challenges did they encounter, and how did they tend to resolve them?

Notes

Introduction

1. Charles C. Krulak, "The Strategic Corporal, Leadership in the Three Block War," *Marines Magazine* 28 (1999), http://www.au.af.mil/au/awc/awcgate/usmc/strategic_corporal.htm.
2. Rebecca J. Johnson, "Moral Formation of the Strategic Corporal," in *New Wars and New Soldiers: Military Ethics in the Contemporary World*, ed. Jessica Wolfendale and Paolo Tripodi, 239–56 (Burlington, VT: Ashgate, 2011).
3. Glenn J. Gray, *The Warriors: Reflections on Men in Battle* (New York: Harper & Row, 1967), 188.
4. For example, Henri Hude says the French military borrowed heavily from US military ethics when formalizing its own system. See Henri Hude, "Reshaping the Ethical Training of Future French Commissioned Officers," in *Ethics Education in the Military*, ed. Paul Robinson, Nigel De Lee, and Don Carrick, 109–18 (Burlington, VT: Ashgate, 2008).
5. *FM 3-24/MCWP 3-33/5: Insurgencies and Countering Insurgencies* (Washington, DC: Department of the Army, 2014), 1–11.
6. Ibid., 2.
7. See *FM 3-24/MCWP 3-33.5 Counterinsurgency* (Washington, DC: Headquarters Department of the Army, 2006); and *British Army Field Manual*, vol. 1, pt. 10: *Countering Insurgency*, October (London: Ministry of Defense, 2009), 3-2, http://news.bbc.co.uk/2/shared/bsp/hi/pdfs/16_11_09_army_manual.pdf.
8. *US Marine Corps, Small Wars Manual* (Washington, DC: Department of the Navy, 1940), 1.
9. David Whetham, ed., *Ethics, Law and Military Operations* (London: Palgrave, 2011), 10.
10. Just to be clear, soldiers did not divulge classified information when discussing the ROE. Rather, they provided a general sense of how the ROE were structured, how

broadly the rules were defined, how many rules they were typically given, and how useful the rules were.

11. Among the many examples are Craig M. Mullaney, *The Unforgiving Minute: A Soldier's Education* (New York: Penguin, 2010); David Bellavia and John R. Bruning, *House to House: An Epic of Urban Warfare* (New York: Simon & Schuster, 2007); Benjamin Tupper, *Greetings from Afghanistan, Send More Ammo: Dispatches from Taliban Country* (New York: NAL Caliber, 2010); Stuart Tootal, *Danger Close: Commanding 3 Para in Afghanistan* (London: John Murray, 2009); Mark Townsend, *Point Man* (London: Faber & Faber, 2013); and Tyler E. Boudreau, *Packing Inferno: The Unmaking of a Marine* (Port Townsend, WA: Feral House, 2008).
12. On military ethics education, see Paul Robinson, Nigel De Lee, and Don Carrick, eds., *Ethics Education in the Military* (Burlington, VT: Ashgate, 2008); Don Carrick, James Connelly, and Paul Robinson, eds., *Ethics Education for Irregular Warfare* (Burlington, VT: Ashgate, 2009); Carl J. Ficarrotta, *Kantian Thinking about Military Ethics* (Burlington, VT: Ashgate, 2010); and Jessica Wolfendale and Paolo Tripodi, eds., *New Wars and New Soldiers: Military Ethics in the Contemporary World* (Burlington, VT: Ashgate, 2011). For educational materials to assist in training, see Stephen Coleman, *Military Ethics: An Introduction with Case Studies* (New York: Oxford University Press, 2012); Deane-Peter Baker, *Key Concepts in Military Ethics* (Sydney: University of New South Wales Press, 2015); and George Lucas, *Military Ethics: What Everyone Needs to Know* (Oxford: Oxford University Press, 2016).
13. For examples of the orthodox or traditionalist perspective, see Michael Walzer, *Just and Unjust Wars: A Moral Argument with Historical Illustrations* (New York: Basic Books, 1977); and Brian Orend, *The Morality of War* (Orchard Park, NY: Broadview Press, 2006). For examples of the revisionist perspective, see David Rodin, *War and Self-Defense* (New York: Oxford University Press, 2003); and Jeff McMahan, *Killing in War* (New York: Oxford University Press, 2009).
14. Jeff McMahan, "The Just Distribution of Harm between Combatants and Noncombatants," *Philosophy & Public Affairs* 38, no. 4 (2010): 342–79; and David Rodin, "Morality and Law in War," in *The Changing Character of War*, ed. Sibylle Scheipers and Hew Strachan, 446–63 (Oxford: Oxford University Press, 2011).

Chapter 1: The Emergence of Military Ethics

1. Hugo Slim, *Killing Civilians: Method, Madness, and Morality in War* (New York: Columbia University Press, 2010), 12.
2. Ibid.
3. Alex J. Bellamy, *Just War: From Cicero to Iraq* (Malden, MA: Polity, 2006).
4. Paul Robinson, "Introduction: Ethics Education in the Military," in *Ethics Education in the Military*, ed. Paul Robinson, Nigel De Lee, and Don Carrick, 1–12 (Burlington, VT: Ashgate, 2008).

5. Martin van Creveld, *Command in War* (Cambridge, MA: Harvard University Press, 1985); John Keegan, *The Mask of Command: A Study of Generalship* (New York: Penguin, 1987); and Barry Strauss, *Masters of Command: Alexander, Hannibal, Caesar, and the Genius of Leadership* (New York: Simon & Schuster, 2012).
6. Edward Hagerman, *The American Civil War and the Origins of Modern Warfare* (Bloomington: Indiana University Press, 1988), 62; and Mark Grimsley, *The Hard Hand of War: Union Military Policy toward Southern Civilians, 1861–1865* (New York: Cambridge University Press, 1995), 102–7.
7. Theodore Ropp, *War in the Modern World* (Baltimore, MD: Johns Hopkins University Press, 2000), 56; and Claus Telp, *The Evolution of Operational Art, 1740–1813: From Frederick the Great to Napoleon* (New York: Routledge, 2005), 135.
8. Hans Delbruck, *The Dawn of Modern Warfare*, trans. Walter J. Renfroe Jr. (Westport, CT: Greenwood Press, 1990); and Max Boot, *War Made New: Technology, Warfare, and the Course of History, 1500 to Today* (New York: Gotham Books, 2006).
9. Michel Foucault, *Discipline and Punish: The Birth of the Prison* (New York: Vintage, 1979), 164.
10. Alan I. Forrest, *The Soldiers of the French Revolution* (Durham, NC: Duke University Press, 1990), 44.
11. Richard Shelly Hartigan, *Lieber's Code and the Law of War* (Chicago: Transaction, 1983); and Henry Shue, "Civilian Protection and Force Protection," in *Ethics, Law and Military Operations*, ed. David Whetham, 135–47 (London: Palgrave, 2011).
12. Van Creveld, *Command in War*, 2.
13. Military bureaucratization was epitomized by the development of the German General Staff in 1814, which soon after became a model for bureaucratization for armies around the world. See Larry H. Addington, *The Patterns of War since the Eighteenth Century* (Bloomington: Indiana University Press, 1994); and Geoffrey Wawro, *Warfare and Society in Europe, 1792–1914* (New York: Routledge, 2000).
14. Jonathan Shay, *Achilles in Vietnam* (New York: Scribner, 1994), 14.
15. Christian Wolmar, *Engines of War: How Wars Were Won and Lost on the Railways* (London: Atlantic Books, 2010); and William G. Thomas, *The Iron Way: Railroads, the Civil War, and the Making of Modern America* (New Haven, CT: Yale University Press, 2011).
16. Paul T. Mitchell, *Network Centric Warfare: Coalition Operations in the Age of US Military Primacy* (New York: Routledge, 2006); and Manabrata Guha, *Reimagining War in the 21st Century: From Clausewitz to Network-Centric Warfare* (New York: Routledge, 2011).
17. Jeremy Black, *War in the Nineteenth Century: 1800–1914* (Hoboken, NJ: John Wiley & Sons, 2009); and Azar Gat, *The Development of Military Thought: The Nineteenth Century* (New York: Oxford University Press, 1992).
18. Gwynne Dyer, *War: The Lethal Custom* (New York: Carroll & Graf, 1984), 37.

19. Martin Kitchen, *The German Offensives of 1918* (Stroud, UK: Tempus, 2005); and David T. Zabecki, *The German 1918 Offensives: A Case Study in the Operational Level of War* (New York: Routledge, 2006).
20. Asa Kasher, "Teaching and Training Military Ethics: An Israeli Experience," in *Ethics Education in the Military*, ed. Paul Robinson, Nigel De Lee, and Don Carrick (Burlington, VT: Ashgate, 2008), 138.
21. On premodern armies, see John France, *Western Warfare in the Age of the Crusades, 1000–1300* (Ithaca, NY: Cornell University Press, 1999). On armies of the early modern period, see Thomas Arnold, *The Renaissance at War* (London: Cassell, 2001); and Michael Mallett, *Mercenaries and Their Masters: Warfare in Renaissance Italy* (Barnsley, UK: Pen & Sword, 2009).
22. Samuel P. Huntington, *The Soldier and the State: The Theory and Politics of Civil-Military Relations* (Cambridge, MA: Harvard University Press, 1959); and Morris Janowitz, *The Professional Soldier: A Social and Political Portrait* (New York: Free Press, 1960).
23. Huntington, *Soldier and the State*, 19.
24. Janowitz, *Professional Soldier*.
25. P. W. Singer, *Corporate Warriors: The Rise of the Privatized Military Industry* (Ithaca, NY: Cornell University Press, 2008); Steve Fainaru, *Big Boy Rules: America's Mercenaries Fighting in Iraq* (Philadelphia: Da Capo Press, 2008); and James Jay Carafano, *Private Sector, Public Wars: Contractors in Combat—Afghanistan, Iraq, and Future Conflicts* (Santa Barbara, CA: Praeger, 2008).
26. Fainaru, *Big Boy Rules*.
27. April 17, 2011, Albany, New York.
28. March 18, 2011, Albany, New York.
29. Tyler E. Boudreau, *Packing Inferno: The Unmaking of a Marine* (Port Townsend, WA: Feral House, 2008), 63.
30. Graham Lee, *Fighting Season* (London: Duckworth Overlook, 2012), 107.
31. George Lucas, *Military Ethics: What Everyone Needs to Know* (Oxford: Oxford University Press, 2016), 136.
32. Erik Prince, *Civilian Warriors: The Inside Story of Blackwater and the Unsung Heroes of the War on Terror* (New York: Penguin, 2013).

Chapter 2: Moral Theory and Ethics at War

1. David Whetham, ed., *Ethics, Law and Military Operations* (London: Palgrave, 2011); and Stephen Coleman, *Military Ethics: An Introduction with Case Studies* (New York: Oxford University Press, 2012).
2. William K. Frankena, *Ethics* (Englewood Cliffs, NJ: Prentice-Hall, 1973); and R. Hursthouse, "Normative Virtue Ethics," in *How Should One Live? Essays on the Virtues*, ed. R. Crisp and M. Slote (Oxford: Clarendon Press, 1996).

3. It is worth noting that other virtue ethicists have made major contributions to theorizing the morality of war. For example, Grady Scott Davis explores war in terms of the virtue of justice and argues that pacifism may be as great a test of virtue as fighting. See Grady Scott Davis, *Warcraft and the Fragility of Virtue: An Essay in Aristotelian Ethics* (Boise: University of Idaho Press, 1992).
4. Aristotle, *Nicomachean Ethics* (Upper Saddle River, NJ: Prentice Hall, 1999), 85.
5. Ibid., 45.
6. Myra MacPherson, *Long Time Passing: Vietnam and the Haunted Generation*, new ed. (Bloomington: Indiana University Press, 2009), 494.
7. Aristotle, *Nicomachean Ethics*, 22.
8. Ibid., 33–34.
9. Ibid., 66.
10. Richard Holmes, *Acts of War: The Behavior of Men in Battle* (New York: Free Press, 1985); and Nancy Sherman, *Stoic Warriors: The Ancient Philosophy behind the Military Mind* (New York: Oxford University Press, 2005).
11. Mark J. Osiel, *Obeying Orders: Atrocity, Military Discipline and Law of War* (New Brunswick, NJ: Transaction, 1999), 234.
12. Timothy L. Challans, *Awakening Warrior: Revolution in the Ethics of Warfare* (Albany: State University of New York Press, 2007), 80–81.
13. Immanuel Kant, "Critique of Practical Reason," in *Practical Philosophy*, ed. Mary J. Gregor (New York: Cambridge University Press, 1996); and Immanuel Kant, "Groundwork on the Metaphysics of Morals," in *Practical Philosophy*, ed. Mary Gregor (Cambridge: Cambridge University Press, 1999).
14. Kant is the prime example here, as his categorical imperative is an extremely broad rule that can be applied to many different types of moral dilemmas.
15. See Marcus Schulzke, "Kant's Categorical Imperative and the Value of Respect," *Journal of Military Ethics* 11, no. 1 (2012): 26–41.
16. James Hugh Toner, "Military OR Ethics," *Air & Space Power Journal* 17, no. 2 (2003); and Robert D. Kaplan, *Warrior Politics: Why Leadership Demands a Pagan Ethos* (New York: Vintage, 2002), 113.
17. Walzer's supreme emergency and Primoratz's moral disaster are examples of this. See Michael Walzer, *Just and Unjust Wars: A Moral Argument with Historical Illustrations* (New York: Basic Books, 1977); and Igor Primoratz, "Civilian Immunity, Supreme Emergency, and Moral Disaster," *Journal of Ethics* 15 (2011): 371–86.
18. Brian Imiola and Danny Cazier, "On the Road to Articulating Our Professional Ethic," *Military Review* (2010): 15.
19. J. Peter Bradley, "Psychological Foundations of Unethical Actions in Military Operations," in *New Wars and New Soldiers: Military Ethics in the Contemporary World*, ed. Jessica Wolfendale and Paolo Tripodi (Burlington, VT: Ashgate, 2011), 230.
20. Michael Golembesky and John R. Bruning, *Level Zero Heroes: The Story of U.S. Marine Special Operations in Bala Murghab, Afghanistan* (New York: St. Martin's, 2014), 164.

21. Jeremy Bentham, *The Principles of Morals and Legislation* (New York: Hafner, 1948); and John Stuart Mill, *Utilitarianism* (New York: Bantam Books, 1993).
22. David Miller, "The Ethical Significance of Nationality," *Ethics* 98, no. 4 (1988): 647–62; and David Miller, *On Nationality* (Oxford: Clarendon Press, 1995).
23. For examples of the utilitarian disagreements with just war theory, see Thomas Nagel, "War and Massacre," *Philosophy and Public Affairs* 1, no. 2 (1972): 123–44; R. B. Brandt, "Utilitarianism and the Rules of War," *Philosophy and Public Affairs* 1, no. 2 (1972): 145–65; and Stephen Nathanson, *Terrorism and the Ethics of War* (New York: Cambridge University Press, 2010).
24. Sam Harris, *The End of Faith: Religion, Terror, and the Future of Reason* (New York: W. W. Norton, 2005), 193; and Fritz Allhoff, "A Defense of Torture: Separation of Cases, Ticking Time-Bombs, and Moral Justification," *International Journal of Applied Philosophy* 19, no. 2 (2005): 243–64.
25. Brandt, "Utilitarianism and the Rules of War," 145–65.
26. See A. C. Grayling, *Among the Dead Cities: The History and Moral Legacy of the WWII Bombing of Civilians in Germany and Japan* (New York: Walker Books, 2006); and Hugo Slim, *Killing Civilians: Method, Madness, and Morality in War* (New York: Columbia University Press, 2010): 151–52.
27. Michael Sandel, *Justice: What's the Right Thing to Do?* (New York: D & M, 2009), 24; and Michael Sandel, *Public Philosophy: Essays on Morality in Politics* (Cambridge, MA: Harvard University Press, 2005), 164.
28. Hilary Putnam, *Ethics without Ontology* (Cambridge, MA: Harvard University Press, 2004).
29. John Dewey, *The Moral Writings of John Dewey*, ed. J. Gouinlock (Buffalo, NY: Prometheus Books, 1994), 104.
30. Ibid.; Putnam, *Ethics without Ontology*; and Richard Rorty, *Contingency, Irony, and Solidarity* (New York: Cambridge University Press, 1989).
31. Rorty, *Contingency, Irony, and Solidarity*, 198.
32. David Fisher, *Morality and War: Can War Be Just in the Twenty-First Century?* (New York: Oxford University Press, 2011).
33. Ibid.

Chapter 3: Constraints on Ethical Reasoning in Combat

1. Paolo Tripodi, "Understanding Atrocities," in *Ethics, Law and Military Operations*, ed. David Whetham (New York: Palgrave, 2011), 173–88.
2. Far more could be said about the extent to which external forces that shape our actions operate deterministically or leave some scope for free will. This intractable puzzle is beyond the scope of this book. I distinguish between actions that are determined and those that are free based on soldiers' own reports. That is to say,

I assumed soldiers had control over their actions whenever they described themselves as having free will and choosing what to do.

3. November 10, 2010, Albuquerque, New Mexico.
4. October 15, 2010, Lubbock, Texas.
5. June 12, 2014, London, United Kingdom.
6. Jonathan Shay, *Achilles in Vietnam* (New York: Scribner, 1994), 137.
7. Anthony Kellett, "The Soldier in Battle: Motivational and Behavioral Aspects of the Combat Experience," in *Psychological Dimensions of War*, ed. B. Glad (Thousand Oaks, CA: Sage, 1990).
8. S.L.A. Marshall, *Men against Fire: The Problem of Battle Command* (Norman: University of Oklahoma Press, 2000).
9. Daryl S. Paulson and Stanley Krippner, *Haunted by Combat: Understanding PTSD in War Veterans including Women* (Westport, CT: Praeger, 2007).
10. Erin P. Finley, *Fields of Combat: Understanding PTSD among Veterans of Iraq and Afghanistan* (Ithaca, NY: Cornell University Press, 2011); and Edgar Jones and Simon Wessely, *Shell Shock to PTSD: Military Psychiatry from 1900 to the Gulf War* (New York: Psychology Press, 2005).
11. Tyler Boudreau, *Packing Inferno: The Unmaking of a Marine* (Port Townsend, WA: Feral House, 2008); Rita Nakashima Brock and Gabriella Lettini, *Soul Repair: Recovering from Moral Injury after War* (Boston: Beacon Press, 2013); Tom Frame, *Moral Injury: Unseen Wounds in an Age of Barbarism* (Sydney: University of New South Wales Press, 2015); and David Wood, *What Have We Done: The Moral Injury of Our Longest Wars* (New York: Little, Brown, 2016).
12. Dave Grossman, "Human Factors in War: The Psychology and Physiology of Close Combat," in *The Human Face of Warfare: Killing, Fear, and Chaos in Battle*, ed. M. Evans and Alan Ryan (St. Leonards, NSW: Allen & Unwin, 2000); Dave Grossman and Loren W. Christensen, *On Combat, The Psychology and Physiology of Deadly Conflict in War and in Peace* (Mascoutah, IL: Warrior Science Publications, 2008); Uzi Ben-Shalom and Shaul Fox, "Military Psychology in the Israel Defense Forces: A Perspective of Continuity and Change," *Armed Forces & Society* 36, no. 1 (2009): 103–19; and Nita Lewis Miller, Panagiotis Matsangas, and Aileen Kenny, "The Role of Sleep in the Military: Implications for Training and Operational Effectiveness," in *The Oxford Handbook of Military Psychology*, ed. J. H. Laurence and Michael D. Matthews (New York: Oxford University Press, 2012).
13. Michael Evans, "Close Combat: Lessons from the Cases of Albert Jacka and Audie Murphy," in *The Human Face of Warfare: Killing, Fear, and Chaos in Battle*, ed. M. Evans and Alan Ryan (St. Leonards, NSW: Allen & Unwin, 2000).
14. Quoted from Peter Maslowski and Don Winslow, *Looking for a Hero: Staff Sergeant Joe Ronnie Hooper and the Vietnam War* (Lincoln: University of Nebraska Press, 2004), 201.

15. For examples of this, see Anthony Swofford, *Jarhead: A Marine's Chronicle of the Gulf War and Other Battles* (New York: Scribner, 2003).
16. David Bellavia and John R. Bruning, *House to House: An Epic of Urban Warfare* (New York: Simon & Schuster, 2007).
17. Ibid., 246.
18. Andrew Steadman, "Neuroscience for Combat Leaders: A Brain-Based Approach to Leading on the Modern Battlefield," *Military Review* 91, no. 3 (2011): 50–61; and Grossman, "Human Factors in War."
19. Steadman, "Neuroscience for Combat Leaders," 52.
20. Ibid., 56.
21. Grossman, "Human Factors in War," 14.
22. Ibid., 15.
23. Sebastian Junger, *War* (New York: Twelve, 2011), 73.
24. Steadman, "Neuroscience for Combat Leaders," 53.
25. Gordon C. Rhea, *Cold Harbor: Grant and Lee, May 26–June 3, 1864* (Baton Rouge: Louisiana State University Press, 2007).
26. Kenneth R. Williams, 2010. "An Assessment of Moral and Character Education in Initial Entry Training (IET)," *Journal of Military Ethics* 9, no. 1 (2010): 46–56; and Jeremy Manton, Carlene Wilson, and Helen Braithwaite, "Human Factors in Field Training for Battle: Realistically Reproducing Chaos," in *The Human Face of Warfare: Killing, Fear, and Chaos in Battle*, ed. M. Evans and Alan Ryan (St. Leonards, NSW: Allen & Unwin, 2000), 190.
27. Marshall, *Men against Fire*; and John Whiteclay Chambers II, "S.L.A. Marshall's Men against Fire: New Evidence regarding Fire Ratios," *Parameters* (Autumn 2003): 113–21.
28. For some poignant examples of the effects of anticipating combat and dealing with its consequences, see Boudreau, *Packing Inferno*.
29. Jaz Azari, Christopher Dandeker, and Neil Greenberg, "Cultural Stress: How Interactions with and among Foreign Populations Affect Military Personnel," *Armed Forces & Society* 36, no. 4 (2010): 585–603; and H. R. McMaster, "Preserving Soldiers' Moral Character in Counter-Insurgency Operations," in *Ethics Education for Irregular Warfare*, ed. Don Carrick, James Connelly, and Paul Robinson (Burlington, VT: Ashgate, 2009), 19.
30. Samuel A. Stouffer and the Social Science Research Council, *The American Soldier: Combat and Its Aftermath* (Princeton, NJ: Princeton University Press, 1949).
31. Benjamin Tupper, *Greetings from Afghanistan, Send More Ammo: Dispatches from Taliban Country* (New York: NAL Caliber, 2010).
32. Paddy Griffith, "Fighting Spirit: Leadership and Morale on the 'Empty Battlefield' of the Future," in *The Human Face of Warfare: Killing, Fear, and Chaos in Battle*, ed. M. Evans and Alan Ryan (St. Leonards, NSW: Allen & Unwin, 2000).
33. McMaster, "Preserving Soldiers' Moral Character."

34. Charles W. Hoge, Carl A. Castro, Stephen C. Messer, Dennis McGurk, Dave I. Cotting, and Robert L. Koffman, "Combat Duty in Iraq and Afghanistan, Mental Health Problems, and Barriers to Care," *New England Journal of Medicine* 351 (2004): 13–22.
35. Manton, Wilson, and Braithwaite, "Human Factors in Field Training for Battle," 190.
36. John B. Babcock, *Taught to Kill: An American Boy's War from the Ardennes to Berlin* (Washington, DC: Potomac Books, 2005), 139.
37. Ibid., 193.
38. Paolo Tripodi, "Deconstructing the Evil Zone," in *New Wars and New Soldiers*, ed. Jessica Wolfendale and Paolo Tripodi (Burlington, VT: Ashgate, 2011), 205.
39. J. A. Shaw, "Unmasking the Illusion of Safety," in *Military Psychiatry: Learning from Experience*, ed. W. W. Menninger (Topeka, KS: Menninger Foundation, 1987); M. Steiner and M. Neumann, "Traumatic Neurosis and Social Support in the Yom Kippur War Returnees," *Military Medicine* 143 (1978): 866–68; and Devorah Manekin, "Violence against Civilians in the Second Intifada: The Moderating Effect of Armed Group Structure on Opportunistic Violence," *Comparative Political Studies* 46, no. 10 (2013): 1273–1300.
40. Zahava Solomon, *Combat Stress Reaction: The Enduring Toll of War* (New York: Springer, 1993).
41. Amy W. Wagner and Matthew Jakupcak, "Combat-Related Stress Reactions among U.S. Veterans of Wartime Service," in *The Oxford Handbook of Military Psychology*, ed. Janice H. Laurence and Michael D. Matthews, 15–28 (New York: Oxford University Press, 2012); and Neal A. Puckett and Marcelyn Atwood, "Crime on the Battlefield: Military Fate or Individual Choice?," in *The Oxford Handbook of Military Psychology*, ed. Janice H. Laurence and Michael D. Matthews, 51–62 (New York: Oxford University Press, 2012).
42. Boudreau, *Packing Inferno*.
43. Miller, Matsangas, and Kenny, "Role of Sleep in the Military"; and Olav Kjellevold Olsen, Stale Pallesen, and Jarle Eid, "The Impact of Partial Sleep Deprivation on Moral Reasoning in Military Officers," *Sleep* 33, no. 8 (2010): 1086–90.
44. Junger, *War*.
45. Shay, *Achilles in Vietnam*, 73.
46. K. J. Wescott, "Modafinil, Sleep Deprivation, and Cognitive Function in Military and Medical Settings," *Military Medicine* 170 (2005): 333–35; and Rick L. Campise, Schuyler K. Geller, and Mary E. Campise, "Combat Stress," in *Military Psychology: Clinical and Operational Applications*, ed. C. H. Kennedy and Eric Zillmer (New York: Guilford Press, 2006).
47. Manton, Wilson, and Braithwaite, "Human Factors in Field Training for Battle," 188–89.
48. Campise, Geller, and Campise, "Combat Stress," 227.
49. Dante Picchioni, Oscar A. Cabrera, Dennis McGurk, Jeffrey L. Thomas, Carl A. Castro, Thomas J. Balkin, Paul D. Bliese, and Charles W. Hoge, "Sleep Symptoms as a

Partial Mediator between Combat Stressors and Other Mental Health Symptoms in Iraq War Veterans," *Military Psychology* 22, no. 3 (2010): 340–55.

50. Aaron Cohen and Douglas Century, *Brotherhood of Warriors: Behind Enemy Lines with a Commando in One of the World's Most Elite Counterterrorism Units* (Ecco: New York, 2008), 103.

Chapter 4: Ethical Decisions in Counterinsurgency Operations

1. Rita Nakashima Brock and Gabriella Lettini, *Soul Repair: Recovering from Moral Injury after War* (Boston: Beacon Press, 2012), xvii.
2. *FM 3-24/MCWP 3-33/5: Insurgencies and Countering Insurgencies* (Washington, DC: Department of the Army, 2014).
3. Stephen Coleman, *Military Ethics: An Introduction with Case Studies* (Oxford: Oxford University Press, 2012), 213.
4. Robert M. Citino, *Blitzkrieg to Desert Storm: The Evolution of Operational Warfare* (Lawrence: University Press of Kansas, 2004); and Eitan Shamir, *Transforming Command: The Pursuit of Mission Command in the U.S., British, and Israeli Armies* (Stanford, CA: Stanford University Press, 2011).
5. David Kilcullen, *Blood Year: Islamic State and the Failures of the War on Terror* (Oxford: Oxford University Press, 2016).
6. Carl Schmitt, *Theory of the Partisan: Intermediate Commentary on the Concept of the Political* (New York: Telos Press, 2007), 49.
7. John A. Nagl, *Learning to Eat Soup with a Knife: Counterinsurgency Lessons from Malaya to Vietnam* (Chicago: University of Chicago Press, 2002); Robert Cassidy, *Counterinsurgency and the Global War on Terror: Military Culture and Irregular War* (Stanford, CA: Stanford University Press, 2008); David Kilcullen, *The Accidental Guerrilla: Fighting Small Wars in the Midst of a Big One* (New York: Oxford University Press, 2009); David Kilcullen, *Counterinsurgency* (New York: Oxford University Press, 2010); and Alexander B. Downes, *Targeting Civilians in War* (Ithaca, NY: Cornell University Press, 2008).
8. Hugo Slim, *Killing Civilians: Method, Madness, and Morality in War* (New York: Columbia University Press, 2010).
9. Ivan Arreguín-Toft, *How the Weak Win Wars: A Theory of Asymmetric Conflict* (New York: Cambridge University Press, 2005).
10. Gil Merom, *How Democracies Lose Small Wars: State, Society, and the Failures of France in Algeria, Israel in Lebanon, and the United States in Vietnam* (New York: Cambridge University Press, 2003); Alexander B. Downes, "Desperate Times, Desperate Measures: The Causes of Civilian Victimization in War," *International Security* 30, no. 4 (2006): 152–95; Alexander B. Downes, "Restraint or Propellant? Democracy

and Civilian Fatalities in Interstate Wars," *Journal of Conflict Resolution* 51, no. 6 (2007): 872–904; and John Tirman, *The Deaths of Others: The Fate of Civilians in America's Wars* (New York: Oxford University Press, 2011).

11. For a detailed discussion of why violence against civilians is counterproductive, see Arreguín-Toft, *How the Weak Win Wars.*
12. Lester Grau, *The Bear Went over the Mountain: Soviet Combat Tactics in Afghanistan* (Washington, DC: National Defense University Press, 1996); Ian Becket, ed., *Modern Insurgencies and Counterinsurgencies* (Abingdon, UK: Routledge, 2001); and Gregory Feifer, *The Great Gamble: The Soviet War in Afghanistan* (New York: HarperCollins, 2009).
13. Tony Geraghty, *The Irish War: The Hidden Conflict between the IRA and British Intelligence* (Baltimore: Johns Hopkins University Press, 1998); and Rogelio Alonso, *The IRA and Armed Struggle* (New York: Routledge, 2003).
14. Lewis Sorley, *A Better War: The Unexamined Victories and Final Tragedy of America's Last Years in Vietnam* (New York: Harcourt Brace, 1999); and Nick Turs, *Kill Anything That Moves: The Real American War in Vietnam* (New York: Macmillan, 2013).
15. Laetitia Bucaille, *Growing Up Palestinian: Israeli Occupation and the Intifada Generation* (Princeton, NJ: Princeton University Press, 2004); and Sergio Catignani, *Israeli Counter-Insurgency and the Intifadas: Dilemmas of a Conventional Army* (New York: Routledge, 2008).
16. Nagl, *Learning to Eat Soup with a Knife.*
17. Sorley, *Better War.*
18. April 7, 2011, Fort Bragg, North Carolina.
19. Mark Bowden, *Black Hawk Down: A Story of Modern War* (New York: Atlantic Monthly Press, 1999), 19; and Matt Eversmann and Dan Schilling, *The Battle of Mogadishu: Firsthand Accounts from the Men of Task Force Ranger* (Novato, CA: Presidio Press, 2006).
20. Bowden, *Black Hawk Down*; and Eversmann and Schilling, *Battle of Mogadishu.*
21. Bowden, *Black Hawk Down*; and Eversmann and Schilling, *Battle of Mogadishu.*
22. Ben Anderson, *No Worse Enemy* (Oxford: Oneworld, 2011), 135.
23. Ibid., 5.
24. Frank Ledwidge, *Investment in Blood: The True Cost of Britain's Afghan War* (New Haven, CT: Yale University Press, 2014), 75.
25. April 18, 2014, Leeds, United Kingdom.
26. Ron E. Hassner, "Fighting Insurgency on Sacred Ground," *Washington Quarterly* 29, no. 2 (2006): 149–66.
27. Jon Sumida, "On Defence as the Stronger Form of War," in *Clausewitz in the Twenty-First Century*, ed. H. Strachan and Andreas Herberg-Rothe (New York: Oxford University Press, 2007), 178.
28. November 10, 2010, Albuquerque, New Mexico.

29. Center for Army Lessons Learned, *Traffic Control Point Operations (GTA 90-01-005)*, 2010. https://info.publicintelligence.net/CALL-TrafficControlPoints.pdf.
30. May 15, 2014, Colchester, United Kingdom.
31. Sebastian Junger, *War* (New York: Hachette, 2010), 45.
32. Tyler E. Boudreau, *Packing Inferno: The Unmaking of a Marine* (Port Townsend, WA: Feral House, 2008), 168.
33. Ibid.
34. Ledwidge, *Investment in Blood*, 77.
35. Ibid., 76.
36. April 9, 2011, Fort Bragg, North Carolina.
37. Chris Hedges and Laila Al-Arian, *Collateral Damage: America's War against Iraqi Civilians* (New York: Nation Books, 2008), 13.
38. Ibid., 16.
39. October 15, 2010, Lubbock, Texas.
40. Ledwidge, *Investment in Blood*, 76.
41. Stephen Coleman, "The Child Soldier: Teaching Points," *Journal of Military Ethics* 10, no. 4 (2011): 317–19.
42. April 6, 2011, Fort Bragg, North Carolina.
43. Bernard Williams, *Moral Luck* (New York: Cambridge University Press, 1981).
44. Brock and Lettini, *Soul Repair*, xv.
45. Aaron Cohen, *Brotherhood of Warriors: Behind Enemy Lines with One of the World's Most Elite Counterterrorism Commandos* (New York: ECCO Press, 2008), 209.
46. Steve Fainaru, *Big Boy Rules: America's Mercenaries Fighting in Iraq* (Philadelphia: Da Capo Press, 2008), 2–3.
47. April 7, 2011, Fort Bragg, North Carolina
48. June 21, 2011, Albany, New York.
49. Mark A. Bodrog, *Second Platoon: Call Sign Hades: A Memoir of the Marines of the Combined Action Company* (Bloomington, IN: iUniverse, 2013).
50. *FM 3-24/MCWP 3-33/5*, 2–3.
51. March 14, 2012, email correspondence.
52. April 8, 2011, Fort Bragg, North Carolina.
53. Ahron Bregman, *Israel's Wars, 1947–93* (New York: Routledge, 2000), 126.
54. Coleman, *Military Ethics*, 54.
55. Peter Warfe, "Post-Traumatic Stress and the Australian Defence Force: Lessons from Peace Operations in Rwanda and Lebanon," in *The Human Face of Warfare: Killing, Fear, and Chaos in Battle*, ed. M. Evans and Alan Ryan (St. Leonards, NSW: Allen & Unwin, 2000), 85.
56. David Horner, "Stress on Higher Commanders in Future Warfare," in *The Human Face of Warfare: Killing, Fear, and Chaos in Battle*, ed. M. Evans and Alan Ryan (St. Leonards, NSW: Allen & Unwin, 2000), 136.

Chapter 5: The US Army and Virtue Ethics

1. Chris Case, Bob Underwood, and Sean T. Hannah, "Owning Our Army Ethic," *Military Review* (2010): 3–10.
2. Paul Robinson, "Introduction: Ethics Education in the Military," in *Ethics Education in the Military*, ed. Paul Robinson, Nigel De Lee, and Don Carrick (Burlington, VT: Ashgate, 2008); and Henri Hude, "Reshaping the Ethical Training of Future French Commissioned Officers," in *Ethics Education in the Military*, ed. P. Robinson, Nigel De Lee, and Don Carrick (Burlington, VT: Ashgate, 2008).
3. Hude, "Reshaping the Ethical Training."
4. Stephen Skowronek, *Building a New American State: The Expansion of National Administrative Capacities, 1877–1920* (New York: Cambridge University Press, 1982), 91–97; and Thomas S. Langston, *Uneasy Balance: Civil-Military Relations in Peacetime America since 1783* (Baltimore: Johns Hopkins University Press, 2003), 55.
5. David Halberstam, *The Coldest Winter: America and the Korean War: America and the Korean War* (New York: Hyperion, 2007), 138; and Brian McAllister Linn, *The Echo of Battle: The Army's Way of War* (Cambridge, MA: Harvard University Press, 2009), 163.
6. Daniel Byman, *A High Price: The Triumphs and Failures of Israeli Counterterrorism* (New York: Oxford University Press, 2011), 186.
7. Jeffrey Wilson, "An Ethics Curriculum for an Evolving Army," in *Ethics Education in the Military*, ed. P. Robinson, Nigel De Lee, and Don Carrick (Burlington, VT: Ashgate, 2008); and Robinson, De Lee and Carrick, *Ethics Education in the Military*, 33.
8. Ibid.
9. Gregory Daddis, *No Sure Victory: Measuring U.S. Army Effectiveness and Progress in the Vietnam War* (New York: Oxford University Press, 2011).
10. Phillip Cole, *The Myth of Evil: Demonizing the Enemy* (Westport, CT: Praeger, 2006), 186; and Richard Winship Stewart, *American Military History*, vol. 2, *The United States Army in a Global Era, 1917–2003* (Washington, DC: Center for Military History, 2005), 350.
11. Douglas Porch, "Strategy Formulation and National Defense: Peace, War, and the Past as Prologue," in *Who Guards the Guardians and How?*, ed. T. C. Bruneau and Scott D. Tollefson (Austin: University of Texas Press, 2006), 107–8.
12. David Cortright, *Soldiers in Revolt: GI Resistance during the Vietnam War* (Chicago: Haymarket Books, 2005); and Marilyn B. Young, *The Vietnam Wars, 1945–1990* (New York: HarperCollins, 1991), 256.
13. Nancy Sherman, *Stoic Warriors: The Ancient Philosophy behind the Military Mind* (New York: Oxford University Press, 2005), 37.
14. Jay Austin and Carl E. Bruch, *The Environmental Consequences of War: Legal, Economic, and Scientific Perspectives* (New York: Cambridge University Press, 2000); and

Deborah Nelson, *The War behind Me: Vietnam Veterans Confront the Truth about U.S. War Crimes* (New York: Basic Books, 2008).

15. Kendrick Oliver, *The My Lai Massacre in American History and Memory* (Manchester, UK: Manchester University Press, 2006); and Philippe Sands, *Torture Team: Uncovering War Crimes in the Land of the Free* (New York: Penguin, 2009), 580.
16. John W. Brinsfield, "Army Values and Ethics: A Search for Consistency and Relevance," *Parameters* 28, no. 3 (1998): 69–84; and Lawrence P. Rockwood, "The Lesson Avoided: The Official Legacy of the My Lai Massacre," in *The Moral Dimension of Asymmetrical Warfare: Counter-Terrorism, Democratic*, ed. D.E.M. Verweij and T. A. Van Baarda (Danvers, MA: Martinus Nijhoff, 2009).
17. William J. Wattendorf, *The Ethical Development of the Professional U.S. Army Officer*. CAL3899c/May86 (1986), 1, http://isme.tamu.edu/JSCOPE87/Wattendorf87.pdf.
18. Wilson, "Ethics Curriculum for an Evolving Army."
19. Cited in Walter L. Hixson, *Military Aspects of the Vietnam Conflict* (New York: Routledge, 2000), 157.
20. Wattendorf, *Ethical Development*, 2.
21. Jared Tracy, "Ethical Challenges in Stability Operations," *Military Review* (January–February 2009): 92.
22. Ibid., 92–93.
23. John Wickham, *Guideposts for a Proud and Ready Army* (Washington, DC: Department of the Army, 1985).
24. Ibid.
25. John Wickham, *Values: The Bedrock of Our Profession* (Washington, DC: Department of the Army, 1986); and John Wickham, *Values: A Handbook for Soldiers* (Washington, DC: Department of the Army, 1987).
26. *Study on Military Professionalism* (Carlisle Barracks, PA: US Army War College, 1973).
27. Richard Lock-Pullan, *US Intervention Policy and Army Innovation: From Vietnam to Iraq* (New York: Routledge, 2006), 38.
28. H. R. McMaster, "Preserving Soldiers' Moral Character in Counterinsurgency Operations," in *Ethics Education for Irregular Warfare*, ed. Don Carrick, James Connelly, and Paul Robinson (Surrey, UK: Ashgate, 2009).
29. Lawrence A. Yates, *The US Military's Experience in Stability Operations, 1789–2005* (Fort Leavenworth, KS: Combat Studies Institute Press, 2006).
30. Wilbur J. Scott, David R. McCone, and George R. Mastroianni, "The Deployment Experiences of Ft. Carson's Soldiers in Iraq: Thinking about and Training for Full-Spectrum Warfare," *Armed Forces & Society* 35, no. 3 (2009): 461.
31. Gordon R. Sullivan and Michael V. Harper, *Hope Is Not a Method* (New York: Broadway Books, 1996).
32. McMaster, "Preserving Soldiers' Moral Character."
33. April 8, 2011, Fort Bragg, North Carolina.

34. Mark A. Viney, *United States Cavalry Peacekeepers in Bosnia: An Inside Account of Operation Joint Endeavor, 1996* (Jefferson, NC: McFarland, 1996), 220.
35. February 20, 2011, Albany, New York.
36. *FM 22-100* (The US Army Leadership Field Manual) (Washington, DC: Headquarters, Department of the Army, 2006).
37. "The Army Values," Army.mil, http://www.army.mil/values/.
38. Ibid.
39. Ibid.
40. *FM 22-100*, 4-57, 4-64.
41. Ibid., 4-62.
42. Benedict S. Cohen, *Ethics Training* (Washington, DC: General Council of the Department of the Army, 2007).
43. Tony Lagouranis and Allen Mikaelian, *Fear up Harsh: An Army Interrogator's Dark Journey through Iraq* (New York: Penguin, 2007), 233.
44. Paul Robinson, "Introduction," 9–10.
45. US Department of the Army, Foundations of Leadership (Boston: Pearson Custom, 2006), 146.
46. Ibid., 139.
47. Walter J. Jackson, "Appendix E: The Soldier's Creed," in *Soldier's Study Guide: A Guide to Prepare for Promotion Boards and Advancement*, 7th ed. (Mechanicsburg, PA: Stackpole Books, 2013), 213.
48. "Soldier's Creed," Army Values, http://www.army.mil/values/soldiers.html.
49. Gary Riccio, Randall Sullivan, Gerald Klein, Margaret Salter, and Henry Kinnison, *Warrior Ethos: Analysis of the Concepts and Initial Development of Applications* (Arlington, VA: U.S. Army Research Institute for the Behavioral and Social Sciences, 2004), 5.
50. US Department of the Army, *Foundations of Leadership*, 145.
51. Riccio et al., *Warrior Ethos*, 13.
52. See Lawrence J. Morris, *Military Justice: A Guide to the Issues* (Denver, CO: Praeger, 2011); and Joshua E. Kastenberg, *Shaping US Military Law: Governing a Constitutional Military* (Burlington, VT: Ashgate, 2014).
53. US Army Training and Doctrine Command, *The Soldier's Blue Book: The Guide for Initial Entry Training Soldiers* (Fort Monroe, VA: US Army Training and Doctrine Command, 2010), 4.
54. Richard Swain, "Reflection of an Ethic of Officership," *Parameters* (2007): 8–9.
55. Joe Doty and Walter Sowden, "Competency vs. Character? It Must Be Both!," *Military Review* (2010): 39.
56. April 9, 2011, Fort Bragg, North Carolina.
57. April 9, 2011, Fort Bragg, North Carolina.
58. December 9, 2010, Albany, New York.
59. Richard Holmes, *Acts of War: The Behavior of Men in Battle* (New York: Free Press, 1985), 68.

60. For more on the gap between civilians and the military, see Thomas Ricks, *Making the Corps* (New York: Touchstone, 1998); and Frank Hoffman, "Bridging the Civil-Military Gap," *Armed Forces Journal* 145 (2007): 18–20.
61. Alasdair MacIntyre, *After Virtue: A Study in Moral Theory* (Notre Dame, IN: University of Notre Dame Press, 2007), 132.

Chapter 6: The US Army in Afghanistan and Iraq

1. April 9, 2011, Fort Bragg, North Carolina.
2. May 27, 2011, Latham, New York.
3. Ben Anderson, *No Worse Enemy* (Oxford: Oneworld, 2011); and Frank Ledwidge, *Losing Small Wars: British Military Failure in Iraq and Afghanistan* (New Haven, CT: Yale University Press, 2011).
4. Ariel Ahram, *Proxy Warriors: The Rise and Fall of State-Sponsored Militias* (Stanford, CA: Stanford University Press, 2011), 90.
5. Martin L. Cook, "Teaching Military Ethics in the United States Air Force: Challenges Posed by Service Culture," in *Ethics Education for Irregular Warfare*, ed. Don Carrick, James Connelly, and Paul Robinson (Burlington, VT: Ashgate, 2009).
6. Human Rights Watch, *Off Target: The Conduct of the War and Civilian Casualties in Iraq* (New York: Human Rights Watch, 2003), 138.
7. August 4, 2011, Colorado Spring, Colorado.
8. April 9, 2011, Fort Bragg, North Carolina.
9. April 7, 2011, Fort Bragg, North Carolina.
10. Mark J. Osiel, *Obeying Orders: Atrocity, Military Discipline and Law of War* (New Brunswick, NJ: Transaction, 1999).
11. August 5, 2011, Colorado Spring, Colorado.
12. April 21, 2011, Albany, New York.
13. April 8, 2011, Fort Bragg, North Carolina.
14. April 8, 2011, Fort Bragg, North Carolina.
15. May 27, 2011, Latham, New York.
16. February 20, Albany, New York.
17. Nathan Sassaman and Joe Layden, *Warrior King: The Triumph and Betrayal of an American Commander in Iraq* (New York: St. Martin's Griffin Press, 2008), 290.
18. Paul Robinson, "The Fall of the Warrior King: Situational Ethics in Iraq," in *Ethics Education for Irregular Warfare*, ed. Don Carrick, James Connelly, and Paul Robinson (Burlington, VT: Ashgate, 2009).
19. Jim Frederick, *Black Hearts: One Platoon's Descent into Madness in Iraq's Triangle of Death* (New York: Harmony, 2010).
20. April 8, 2011, Fort Bragg, North Carolina.

21. Quoted in Raffi Khatchadourian, “The Kill Company,” *New Yorker*, July 6, 2009, http://www.newyorker.com/magazine/2009/07/06/the-kill-company.
22. April 8, 2011, Fort Bragg, North Carolina.
23. Chris Hedges and Laila Al-Arian, *Collateral Damage: America's War against Iraqi Civilians* (New York: Nation Books, 2008).
24. American Civil Liberties Union, “Documents Received from the Department of the Army in Response to ACLU Freedom of Information Act Request,” released on October 31, 2007, http://www.aclu.org/natsec/foia/log.html.
25. Michael Schwartz, *War without End: The Iraq War in Context* (Chicago: Haymarket, 2008), 79.
26. US Department of Defense, “News Transcript,” May 4, 2007, http://archive.defense.gov/Transcripts/Transcript.aspx?TranscriptID=3958.
27. Timothy L. Challans, *Awakening Warrior: Revolution in the Ethics of Warfare* (Albany: State University of New York Press, 2007), 24.
28. Joe Doty and Walter Sowden, “Competency vs. Character? It Must Be Both!,” *Military Review* (2010): 40.
29. Timothy L. Challans, “Leading Our Leader,” *Military Review* (2009): 81. See also Challans, *Awakening Warrior*.
30. Brian Imiola and Danny Cazier, “On the Road to Articulating Our Professional Ethic,” *Military Review* (2010): 15.
31. Doty and Sowden, “Competency vs. Character?,” 40.
32. Dick Couch, *A Tactical Ethic: Moral Conduct in the Insurgent Battlespace* (Annapolis, MD: Naval Institute Press, 2010).
33. Douglas A. Pryer, *The Fight for the High Ground: The U.S. Army and Interrogation during Operation Iraqi Freedom May 2003–April 2004* (Fort Leavenworth, KS: CGSC Foundation Press, 2009), 8.
34. Dexter Filkins, “The Fall of the Warrior King,” *New York Times Magazine*, October 23, 2005, http://www.nytimes.com/2005/10/23/magazine/the-fall-of-the-warrior-king.html.
35. Gary D. Solis, *The Law of Armed Conflict: International Humanitarian Law in War* (Cambridge: Cambridge University Press, 2016), 636.
36. Sassaman and Layden, *Warrior King*.
37. David E. Johnson, *Preparing Potential Senior Army Leaders for the Future: An Assessment of Leader Development Efforts in the Post–Cold War Era* (Santa Monica, CA: Rand, 2002).
38. David H. Ucko, *The New Counterinsurgency Era: Transforming the US Military for Modern Wars* (Washington, DC: Georgetown University Press, 2009); and Thomas Ricks, *Fiasco: The American Military Adventure in Iraq, 2003 to 2005* (New York: Penguin, 2007).
39. *FM 3-24/MCWP 3-33.5: Insurgencies and Countering Insurgencies* (Washington, DC: Department of the Army, 2014).

40. Tyler E. Boudreau, *Packing Inferno: The Unmaking of a Marine* (Port Townsend, WA: Feral House, 2008), 24.
41. Khatchadourian, "Kill Company."
42. Paul von Zielbauer, "Army Says Improper Orders by Colonel Led to 4 Deaths," *New York Times*, January 21, 2007, http://www.nytimes.com/2007/01/21/world/middleeast/21abuse.html?_r=1.
43. Filkins, "Fall of the Warrior King."
44. Ibid.
45. Robinson, "Fall of the Warrior King: Situational Ethics in Iraq."
46. February 10, 2011, Albany, New York.
47. April 17, 2011, Albany, New York.
48. October 15, 2010, Lubbock, Texas.
49. Johnny Rico, *Blood Makes the Grass Grow Green: A Year in the Desert with Team America* (New York: Ballantine Books, 2007), 160.
50. Daniel A. Sjursen, *Ghost Riders of Baghdad: Soldiers, Civilians, and the Myth of the Surge* (Lebanon, NH: University Press of New England, 2015), 56–57.
51. Hedges and Al-Arian, *Collateral Damage*, xxiv.
52. April 9, 2011, Fort Bragg, North Carolina.
53. Robert M. Cassidy, *Counterinsurgency and the Global War on Terror: Military Culture and Irregular War* (London: Praeger, 2006).
54. Joseph J. Collins and Ole R. Holsti, "Civil-Military Relations: How Wide Is the Gap?," *International Security* 24, no. 2 (1999): 199–207; Gregory D. Foster, "Civil-Military Gap: What Are the Ethics?," US Naval Institute *Proceedings* 126, no. 4 (2000): 82–87; Matthew J. Morgan, "Army Recruiting and the Civil-Military Gap," *Parameters* 31, no. 2 (2001): 101–17; Eliot A. Cohen, "Why the Gap Matters," *National Interest* 61 (2000): 38–49; Frank Hoffman, "Bridging the Civil-Military Gap," *Armed Forces Journal* 145 (2007): 18–20; David L. Leal, "Students in Uniform: ROTC, the Citizen-Soldier, and the Civil-Military Gap," *PS: Political Science & Politics* 40, no. 3 (2007): 479–83; Jason K. Dempsy, *Our Army: Soldiers, Politics, and American Civil-Military Relations* (Princeton, NJ: Princeton University Press, 2009); and Janine Davidson, *Lifting the Fog of Peace: How Americans Learned to Fight Modern War* (Ann Arbor: University of Michigan Press, 2010).
55. James Fallows, "The Tragedy of the American Military," *Atlantic*, January–February, 2015, http://www.theatlantic.com/magazine/archive/2015/01/the-tragedy-of-the-american-military/383516/.
56. Richard H. Kohn, "The Erosion of Civilian Control of the Military in the United States Today," *Naval War College Review* 55, no. 3 (2002): 29.
57. Challans, *Awakening Warrior*, 12.
58. Nancy Sherman, *The Untold War: Inside the Hearts, Minds, and Souls of Our Soldiers* (New York: W. W. Norton, 2010); and Shannon E. French and John McCain, *The Code of the Warrior: Exploring Warrior Values Past and Present* (Lanham, MD: Rowman and Littlefield, 2005).

Chapter 7: British Military Ethics

1. Although I do not discuss the US Marines, Challans characterizes them as having an approach to ethics similar to that of the British Marines. "As for the Marines, they do not have a leadership manual; they transmit their norms solely by recounting their own history." See Timothy L. Challans, *Awakening Warrior: Revolution in the Ethics of Warfare* (Albany: State University of New York Press, 2007). This is an interesting insight, as it suggests that different branches of a military may have substantially different systems of ethics.
2. Patrick Mileham, "Teaching Military Ethics in the British Armed Forces," in *Ethics Education in the Military*, ed. Paul Robinson, Nigel De Lee, and Don Carrick (Burlington, VT: Ashgate, 2008); Stephen Deakin, "Education in an Ethos at the Royal Military Academy Sandhurst," in *Ethics Education in the Military*, ed. Paul Robinson, Nigel De Lee, and Don Carrick (Burlington, VT: Ashgate, 2008); and Stephen Deakin, "Counter-Insurgency Ethics at the Royal Military Academy Sandhurst," in *Ethics Education in the Military*, ed. Paul Robinson, Nigel De Lee, Don Carrick (Burlington, VT: Ashgate, 2008).
3. *Security and Stabilisation: The Military Contribution*, Joint Doctrine Publication 3-40, Development, Concepts and Doctrine Centre, November 2009, 51. https://assets.publishing.service.gov.uk/government/uploads/system/uploads/attachment_data/file/43330/jdp340prom18novweb.pdf.
4. Mileham, "Teaching Military Ethics in the British Armed Forces," 45.
5. David Benest, "Aden to Northern Ireland, 1966–76," in *Big Wars and Small Wars: The British Army and the Lessons of War in the 20th Century*, ed. Hew Strachan (New York: Routledge, 2006), 115.
6. Anthony Clayton, *The British Officer: Leading the Army from 1660 to the Present* (New York: Pearson, 2006); Allan Mallinson, *The Making of the British Army: From the English Civil War to the War on Terror* (New York: Bantam, 2011); and Paddy Griffith, "The Extent of Tactical Reform in the British Army," in *British Fighting Methods in the Great War*, ed. Paddy Griffith (Portland, OR: Frank Cass Publishers, 1996).
7. Hew Strachan, Introduction to *Big Wars and Small Wars: The British Army and the Lessons of War in the 20th Century*, ed. Hew Strachan (New York: Routledge, 2006), 3.
8. Land Warfare Development Centre, *Land Operations*, Army Doctrine Publication AC 71940 (London: British Ministry of Defence Crown, 2010), 2–14, https://www.gov.uk/government/uploads/system/uploads/attachment_data/file/33695/ADPOperationsDec10.pdf.
9. Daniel Branch, "Footprints in the Sand: British Colonial Counterinsurgency and the War in Iraq," *Politics & Society* 38, no. 1 (2010): 15–34; and Theo Farrell and Stuart Gordon, "Coin Machine: The British Military in Afghanistan," *Orbis* 53, no. 4 (2009): 665–83.

10. Branch, "Footprints in the Sand," 15–34; and Warren China, "Examining the Application of British Counterinsurgency Doctrine by the US Army in Iraq," *Small Wars & Insurgencies* 18, no. 1 (2007): 1–26.
11. Mileham, "Teaching Military Ethics in the British Armed Forces."
12. British Army, *Values and Standards of the British Army*, January 2008, available at http://ethics.iit.edu/ecodes/node/5512.
13. Clayton, *British Officer*, 301.
14. Mileham, "Teaching Military Ethics in the British Armed Forces," 51.
15. Iain Torrance, "The Moral Component," in *The British Army, Manpower, and Society into the Twenty-First Century*, ed. Hew Strachan (New York: Frank Cass, 2000).
16. Clayton, *British Officer*, 300.
17. Paul Robinson, "Ethics Training and Development in the Military," *Parameters*, Spring (2007): 23–36.
18. British Army, *Values and Standards of the British Army*.
19. Land Warfare Development Centre, *Land Operations*, 2–11.
20. Ibid., 1.
21. Ibid., 11.
22. Ibid., 10.
23. British Army, *Values and Standards of the British Army*, 12.
24. Ibid., 15.
25. June 12, 2014, London, United Kingdom.
26. June 12, 2014, London, United Kingdom.
27. May 22, 2014, Leeds, United Kingdom.
28. Royal Navy, *The Royal Marines Vision: Think Commando* (Royal Navy, October 2011), 7. https://www.royalnavy.mod.uk/About-the-Royal-Navy/~/media/Files/Navy-PDFs/About-the-Royal-Navy/Royal%20Marines%20Vision.pdf.
29. Wade Markel, "Draining the Swamp: The British Strategy of Population Control," *Parameters*, Spring (2006): 35–48; Paul Dixon, "'Hearts and Minds'? British Counter-Insurgency Strategy in Northern Ireland," *Journal of Strategic Studies* 32, no. 3 (2009): 445–74; Paul Dixon, "'Hearts and Minds'? British Counter-Insurgency from Malaya to Iraq," *Journal of Strategic Studies* 32, no. 3 (2009): 353–81; and David French, *The British Way in Counter-Insurgency, 1945–1967* (New York: Oxford University Press, 2011).
30. Robert M. Cassidy, *Counterinsurgency and the Global War on Terror* (Stanford, CA: Stanford University Press, 2008), 93.
31. Eitan Shamir, *Transforming Command: The Pursuit of Mission Command in the US, British, and Israeli Armies* (Stanford, CA: Stanford University Press, 2011), 171.
32. Frank Ledwidge, *Losing Small Wars: British Military Failure in Iraq and Afghanistan* (New Haven, CT: Yale University Press, 2011), 174.
33. Glen Rangwala, "Counter-Insurgency Amid Fragmentation: The British in Southern Iraq," *Journal of Strategic Studies* 32, no. 3 (2009): 495–513.

34. John Keegan, *The Iraq War* (New York: Vintage Books, 2005), 182.
35. June 12, 2014, London, United Kingdom.
36. Patrick Cockburn, *The Occupation: War and Resistance in Iraq* (New York: Verso 2006), 102.
37. Nigel Aylwin-Foster, "Changing the Army for Counterinsurgency Operations," *Military Review*, November/December 2005, 2–15.
38. James Pritchard and M.L.R. Smith, "Thompson in Helmand: Comparing Theory to Practice in British Counter-Insurgency Operations in Afghanistan," *Civil Wars* 12, nos. 1–2 (2010): 65–90; Philip McEvoy, "Law at the Operational Level," in *Ethics, Law and Military Operations*, ed. David Whetham (London: Palgrave, 2011), 108–13.
39. James Fergusson, *A Million Bullets: The Real Story of the British Army in Afghanistan* (New York: Bantam Books, 2008), 124–25.
40. Ian Rigden, *The British Approach to Counter-Insurgency: Myths, Realities, and Strategic Challenges* (Carlisle Barracks, PA: US Army War College, 2008), 12.
41. Eric Carlton, *Occupation: The Policies and Practice of Military Conquerors* (London: Routledge, 1992); Rob Johnson, *British Imperialism* (New York: Palgrave Macmillan, 2003); Niall Ferguson, *Empire: How Britain Made the Modern World* (New York: Penguin, 2004); and Roy Kaushik, *The Army in British India: From Colonial Warfare to Total War 1857–1947* (New York: Bloomsbury, 2013).
42. Thomas G. Mahnken, *Technology and the American Way of War since 1945* (New York: Columbia University Press, 2010), 4.
43. Stephen Grey, *Operation Snakebite: The Explosive True Story of an Afghan Desert Siege* (New York: Penguin, 2010), 22.
44. Kevin Mervin, *Weekend Warrior: A Territorial Soldier's War in Iraq* (Edinburgh: Mainstream, 2005), 108.
45. Rigden, *British Approach to Counter-Insurgency*, 5.
46. Morris Janowitz, *The Professional Soldier: A Social and Political Portrait* (New York: Free Press, 1960), 83; Christopher Dandeker and David Mason, "Ethnic Diversity in the British Armed Forces," in *Cultural Diversity in the Armed Forces: An International Comparison*, ed. Joseph L. Soeters and Jan Van der Meulen (New York: Routledge, 2007); and Stuart Crawford, "Women in the Army," in *The British Army, Manpower, and Society into the Twenty-First Century*, ed. Hew Strachan (New York: Frank Cass, 2000).
47. Martin Beckford, "One in Ten Members of Armed Forces Was Born Abroad," *Telegraph*, October 1, 2012, http://www.telegraph.co.uk/news/uknews/defence/9577167/One-in-ten-members-of-Armed-Forces-was-born-abroad.html.
48. For some of the many examples of this, see Brendan Simms, *The Longest Afternoon: The 400 Men Who Decided the Battle of Waterloo* (New York: Penguin, 2014); Chris Bellamy, *The Gurkhas: Special Force* (London: Hachette, 2011); and Charles Esdaile, *The Peninsular War: A New History* (New York: Penguin, 2003).

49. John A. Nagl and Peter J. Schoomaker, *Learning to Eat Soup with a Knife: Counterinsurgency Lessons from Malaya and Vietnam* (Chicago: University of Chicago Press, 2002), 65.
50. Ibid., 100.
51. Jack Fairweather, *War of Choice: The British in Iraq, 2003–9* (London: Jonathan Cape, 2011); and Ledwidge, *Losing Small Wars.*
52. Christopher Elliott, *High Command: British Military Leadership in the Iraq and Afghanistan Wars* (New York: Oxford University Press, 2015), 122.
53. Nagl, *Learning to Eat Soup with a Knife*; Rogelio Alonso, *The IRA and Armed Struggle* (New York: Routledge, 2003); and Tony Geraghty, *The Irish War* (London: HarperCollins, 1998).
54. Greg Kennedy, "Introduction: The Concept of Imperial Defence," in *Imperial Defence: The Old World Order, 1856–1956,* ed. G. Kennedy (New York: Routledge, 2008); and John Newsinger, *British Counterinsurgency: From Palestine to Northern Ireland* (New York: Palgrave, 2002).
55. Ledwidge, *Losing Small Wars,* 10.
56. *Security and Stabilisation,* 3.
57. Aylwin-Foster, "Changing the Army for Counterinsurgency Operations," 6.
58. Ibid., 3.
59. Newsinger, *British Counterinsurgency,* 219.
60. Doug Beattie and Philip Gomm, *Task Force Helmand* (London: Pocket Books, 2009), 28.
61. Ibid., 29.
62. Geraghty, *Irish War,* 60–65.
63. Richard Norton-Taylor, "Bloody Sunday: Scenes from the Saville Inquiry," in *Bloody Sunday: Trauma, Pain and Politics,* ed. Patrick Hayes and Jim Campbell (London: Pluto Press, 2005).
64. Dermot Walsh, *Bloody Sunday and the Rule of Law in Northern Ireland* (London: Palgrave, 2000).
65. Huw Bennett, *Fighting the Mau Mau: The British Army and Counter-Insurgency in the Kenya Emergency* (Cambridge: Cambridge University Press, 2013), 152.
66. Rachel Kerr, "A Force for Good? War, Crime and Legitimacy: The British Army in Iraq," *Defense & Security Analysis* 24, no. 4 (2008): 401–19; Richard Norton-Taylor, Rob Evans, and Emma Graham-Harrison, "Four More UK Soldiers Disciplined after Afghan Civilians Killed or Injured," *Guardian,* March 29, 2012, http://www.theguardian.com/uk/2012/mar/29/uk-soldiers-disciplined-afghanistan; Press Association, "British Soldiers Admit Abusing Afghan Civilians," *Guardian,* June 4, 2013, http://www.theguardian.com/uk/2013/jun/04/british-soldiers-admit-abusing-afghan-civilians; and Ben Farmer, "Soldiers to Face 11 More 'Trials' over Iraq Deaths," *Telegraph,* December 7, 2013, http://www.telegraph.co.uk/news/uknews/defence/10503268/Soldiers-to-face-11-more-trials-over-Iraq-deaths.html.

67. Josh White, "Abu Ghraib Tactics Were First Used in Guantanamo," *Washington Post*, July 14, 2005.
68. Vikram Dodd, "British Soldiers Accused of Raping Iraqi Man," *Guardian*, September 14, 2009.
69. Andrew Johnson, "British Soldiers Accused of Sickening Sex Assault on Iraqi Boy, 14," *Independent*, July 13, 2008, http://www.independent.co.uk/news/uk/home-news/british-soldiers-accused-of-sickening-sex-assault-on-iraqi-boy-14-866482.html.
70. "Jailed Marine Sgt Alexander Blackman Was 'Morally Disengaged,'" *BBC News*, September 16, 2015, http://www.bbc.co.uk/news/uk-34267936.

Chapter 8: The British Military's Adaptive Struggle

1. Paul Gibson, "Chilcot Should Target the Military, Not Blair," *Times*, February 5, 2011.
2. Dan Mills, *Sniper One: The Blistering True Story of a British Battle Group under Siege* (New York: Penguin, 2008), 52.
3. Quintin Wright, "Rules of Engagement," *Guardian*, November 17, 2004, https://www.theguardian.com/uk/2004/nov/17/military.usa.
4. James Fergusson, *A Million Bullets: The Real Story of the British Army in Afghanistan* (London: Penguin Books, 2009).
5. July 13, 2011, London, United Kingdom; and June 16, 2014, London, United Kingdom.
6. Mike Rossiter, *Target Basra* (London: Transworld, 2008), 352–53.
7. Ibid., 218.
8. Emile Simpson, *War from the Ground Up* (Oxford: Oxford University Press, 2012), 3.
9. Toby Harnden, *Dead Men Risen: The Welsh Guards and the Defining Story of Britain's War in Afghanistan* (London: Quercus, 2011), 133.
10. July 16, 2011, London, United Kingdom.
11. May 15, 2014, Colchester, United Kingdom.
12. July 22, 2011, Oxford, United Kingdom.
13. July 13, 2011, London, United Kingdom.
14. Ewen Southby-Tailyour, *3 Commando Brigade: Helmand, Afghanistan* (London: Ebury Press, 2009).
15. Chiyuki Aoi, *Legitimacy and the Use of Armed Force: Stability Missions in the Post–Cold War Era* (New York: Routledge, 2011), 209–13.
16. July 16, 2011, London, United Kingdom.
17. David Wiseman, *Helmand to the Himalayas: One Soldier's Inspirational Journey* (Oxford: Osprey, 2014), 9.
18. Fergusson, *Million Bullets*, 96.
19. July 22, 2011, Oxford, United Kingdom.

20. June 12, 2014, London, United Kingdom.
21. August 27, 2014, Poole, United Kingdom.
22. September 1, 2014, Leeds, United Kingdom.
23. Ben Anderson, *No Worse Enemy: The Inside Story of the Chaotic Struggle for Afghanistan* (Oxford: Oneworld Publications, 2011).
24. June 12, 2014, London, United Kingdom.
25. Mills, *Sniper One*, 188.
26. June 12, 2014, London, United Kingdom.
27. April 18, 2014, Leeds, United Kingdom.
28. April 18, 2014, Leeds, United Kingdom.
29. Patrick Bishop, *Ground Truth: 3 Para Return to Afghanistan* (London: William Collins, 2010), 50.
30. August 1, 2011, Nottingham, United Kingdom.
31. For example, see Fergusson, *Million Bullets*.
32. Bishop, *Ground Truth*, 50.
33. "Sir John Chilcot's Public Statement," *The Iraq Inquiry*, July 6, 2016, http://www.iraqinquiry.org.uk/the-inquiry/sir-john-chilcots-public-statement/.
34. "Britain Suffered Defeat in Iraq, Says US General," *BBC News*, September 29, 2010, http://www.bbc.co.uk/news/uk-11419878.
35. Celestino Perez, "The Embedded Morality in FM 3-24 Counterinsurgency," *Military Review* (2010): 59–67.
36. Gibson, "Chilcot Should Target the Military, Not Blair."
37. June 12, 2014, London, United Kingdom.
38. Eitan Shamir, *Transforming Command: The Pursuit of Mission Command in the US, British, and Israeli Armies* (Stanford, CA: Stanford University Press, 2011), 156.
39. Jon Moran, *From Northern Ireland to Afghanistan: British Military Intelligence Operations, Ethics and Human Rights* (Burlington, VT: Ashgate, 2013), 75.
40. Frank Ledwidge, *Losing Small Wars: British Military Failure in Iraq and Afghanistan* (New Haven, CT: Yale University Press, 2011), 23.
41. Ibid., 39.
42. Ibid., 28.
43. Ibid., 41.
44. Ibid., 29.
45. Ibid., 130.
46. Fergusson, *Million Bullets*, 49.
47. Ibid., 119.
48. Ibid.
49. Harnden, *Dead Men Risen*, 130.
50. Ian Rigden, *The British Approach to Counter-Insurgency: Myths, Realities, and Strategic Challenges* (Carlisle Barracks, PA: US Army War College, 2008).

51. Christopher Elliott, *High Command: British Military Leadership in the Iraq and Afghanistan Wars* (New York: Oxford University Press, 2015), 109.
52. Rory Stewart, "The Irresistible Illusion," *London Review of Books* 31, no. 13 (2009): 3–6.
53. June 11, 2014, London, United Kingdom.
54. Elliott, *High Command*, 157.
55. Ibid.
56. Doug Beattie, *Task Force Helmand: Life, Death and Combat on the Afghan Front Line* (London: Simon and Schuster, 2009), 295.
57. Ibid., 294.
58. Ibid.

Chapter 9: The Israel Defense Forces

1. Erica Weiss, *Conscientious Objectors in Israel: Citizenship, Sacrifice, Trials of Fealty* (Philadelphia: University of Pennsylvania Press, 2014).
2. Raffaella A. Del Sarto, *Israel under Siege* (Washington, DC: Georgetown University Press, 2017).
3. See Michael Walzer, *Just and Unjust Wars: A Moral Argument with Historical Illustrations* (New York: Basic Books, 1977); and Igor Primoratz, "Civilian Immunity, Supreme Emergency, and Moral Disaster," *Journal of Ethics* 15, no. 4 (December 2011): 371–86.
4. Eitan Shamir, *Transforming Command: The Pursuit of Mission Command in the US, British, and Israeli Armies* (Stanford, CA: Stanford University Press, 2011).
5. Asa Kasher, "Military Ethics of Facing Fellow Citizens: IDF Preparations for Disengagement," in *Ethics Education for Irregular Warfare*, ed. Don Carrick, James Connelly, and Paul Robinson (Burlington, VT: Ashgate, 2009), 135.
6. Uzi Ben-Shalom and Shaul Fox, "Military Psychology in the Israel Defense Forces: A Perspective of Continuity and Change," *Armed Forces & Society* 36, no. 1 (2009): 103–19.
7. Martin van Creveld, *The Sword and the Olive: A Critical History of the Israeli Defense Force* (New York: Public Affairs, 2002), 346.
8. Ibid., 199.
9. Ron Schleifer, "Jewish and Contemporary Origins of Israeli Hasbara," *Jewish Political Studies Review* 15, nos. 1–2 (2003): 123–53; and Eytan Gilboa, "Public Diplomacy: The Missing Component in Israel's Foreign Policy," *Israel Affairs* 12, no. 4 (2006): 715–47.
10. See Paul Robinson, introduction to *Ethics Education in the Military*, ed. Paul Robinson, Nigel De Lee, and Don Carrick (Burlington, VT: Ashgate, 2008), 7.
11. April 8, 2011, Fort Bragg, North Carolina.

12. James Eastwood, *Ethics as a Weapon of War* (Cambridge: Cambridge University Press, 2017), 8.
13. Stuart A. Cohen, "The Israel Defense Forces (IDF): From a 'People's Army' to a 'Professional Military'—Causes and Implications," *Armed Forces & Society* 21, no. 2 (1995): 237–54.
14. Fred Kaplan, "Dumb and Dumber: The US Army Lowers Recruitment Standards . . . Again," *Slate*, January 24, 2008, http://www.slate.com/articles/news_and_politics/war_stories/2008/01/dumb_and_dumber.html.
15. Stuart A. Cohen, "Portrait of the New Israeli Soldier," *MERIA: Middle East Review of International Affairs* 1, no. 4 (December 3, 1997), http://www.rubincenter.org/1997/12/cohen-1997-12-03/.
16. Reuven Gal, *A Portrait of the Israeli Soldier* (Westport, CT: Greenwood Press, 1986).
17. See MHAT IV, US Army Medical Department, 2006, http://armymedicine.mil/Pages/Mental-Health-Advisory-Team-IV-Information.aspx.
18. Samuel M. Katz, *Israeli Defense Forces since 1973* (London: Osprey, 1991), 17; and Alex Mintz, "Military-Industrial Linkages in Israel," *Armed Forces & Society* 12, no. 1 (1985): 9–27.
19. Yaakov Katz, "60 Percent of Israelis Won't Serve in IDF by 2020," *Jerusalem Post*, November 18, 2011, http://www.jpost.com/Defense/60-percent-of-Israelis-wont-serve-in-IDF-by-2020.
20. For the latest numbers of military personnel for each country, see GlobalFirepower.com, http://www.globalfirepower.com.
21. Thomas Ricks, "The Widening Gap between the Military and Society," *Atlantic Monthly*, July 1997, 66–76; and David R. Segal and Mandy Wechsler Segal, "America's Military Population," *Population Bulletin* 59, no. 4 (2004): 3–25.
22. Karen Guttieri, "Professional Military Education in Democracies," in *Who Guards the Guardians and How?*, ed. Thomas C. Bruneau and Scott D. Tollefson (Austin: University of Texas Press, 2006), 240.
23. Stuart A. Cohen, *Israel and Its Army: From Cohesion to Confusion* (New York: Routledge, 2008), 1.
24. Edwin R. Micewski, "Conscription or the All-Volunteer Force: Recruitment in a Democratic Society," in *Who Guards the Guardians and How?*, ed. Thomas C. Bruneau and Scott D. Tollefson (Austin: University of Texas Press, 2006), 209.
25. Stuart A. Cohen, "Reversing the Tide of Jewish History: Culture and the Creation of Israel's 'People's Army,'" in *The New Citizen Armies: Israel's Armed Forces in Comparative Perspective*, ed. Stuart Cohen (New York: Routledge, 2010), 58.
26. Eligar Sadeh, *Militarization and State Power in the Arab-Israeli Conflict: Case Study of Israel, 1948–1982* (PhD diss., Hebrew University of Jerusalem, 1997), 74.
27. Katz, *Israeli Defense Forces since 1973*, 17.

28. Kobi Michael, "An Intellectual Journey through the Civil-Military Relationship in Israel," *Israel Studies Review* 29, no. 2 (2014): 140–45.
29. Asa Kasher, "Teaching and Training Military Ethics: An Israeli Experience," in *Ethics Training and Development in the Military*, ed. Paul Robinson, Nigel De Lee, and Donald Carrick, 133–45 (Abingdon, Oxon, UK: Ashgate, 2008), 142.
30. For example, Nefesh B'Nefesh, "Army Service Programs," n.d., http://www.nbn.org.il/aliyahpedia/army-national-service/idf-sherut-leumi/army-service-programs/; and The Jewish Agency for Israel, "Garin Tzabar: Instant Family for IDF Recruits," n.d., http://www.jewishagency.org/young-aliyah/program/1336.
31. "IDF Shaves Four Months off Men's Mandatory Service," *Times of Israel*, July 6, 2015, http://www.timesofisrael.com/idf-shaves-four-months-off-mens-mandatory-service/.
32. Yoram Hazony, *The Jewish State: The Struggle for Israel's Soul* (New York: Basic Books, 2001), 53.
33. Cohen, "Portrait of the New Israeli Soldier."
34. Asa Kasher and Amos Yadlin, "Military Ethics of Fighting Terror: An Israeli Perspective," *Journal of Military Ethics* 4, no. 1 (2005): 4.
35. Kasher, "Military Ethics of Facing Fellow Citizens," 140.
36. Ibid.
37. Tzvi Hauser, "The Spirit of the IDF," *Azure* (1997): 66.
38. Ibid.
39. "Code of Ethics and Mission," *Israel Defense Forces*, https://www.idf.il/en/minisites/code-of-ethics-and-mission/.
40. Ibid.
41. Ibid.
42. Ibid.
43. Ibid.
44. Kasher, "Teaching and Training Military Ethics," 139.
45. Quoted from Hazony, *Jewish State*, 56.
46. March 8, 2012, Albany, New York.
47. Noam Amir and Maariv Hashavua, "Israeli Combat Troops React Angrily to New Rules of Engagement in West Bank," *Jerusalem Post*, August 12, 2015, http://www.jpost.com/Arab-Israeli-Conflict/Israel-tightens-rules-of-engagement-for-combat-troops-in-West-Bank-411868.
48. Hauser, "Spirit of the IDF," 64.
49. Ibid.
50. "Main Doctrine," 2011, http://dover.idf.il/IDF/English/about/doctrine/main_doctrine.htm.
51. "Code of Ethics and Mission."
52. Michael, "Intellectual Journey," 140.

53. Weiss, *Conscientious Objectors in Israel.*
54. Alexander B. Downes, "Desperate Times, Desperate Measures: The Causes of Civilian Victimization in War," *International Security* 30, no. 4 (2006): 152–95; Alexander B. Downes, *Targeting Civilians in War* (Ithaca, NY: Cornell University Press, 2008); and Hugo Slim, *Killing Civilians: Method, Madness, and Morality in War* (New York: Columbia University Press, 2010).
55. Michael L. Gross, "The Second Lebanon War: The Question of Proportionality and the Prospect of Non-Lethal Warfare," *Journal of Military Ethics* 7, no. 1 (2008): 1–22, at 8.
56. Daniel Byman, *A High Price: The Triumphs and Failures of Israeli Counterterrorism* (New York: Oxford University Press, 2011); Gross, "Second Lebanon War," 13; and Mike Berry and Greg Philo, *Israel and Palestine: Competing Histories* (Ann Arbor, MI: Pluto Press, 2004), 77.
57. Sergio Catignani, *Israeli Counter-Insurgency and the Intifadas: Dilemmas of a Conventional Army* (New York: Routledge, 2008), 150.
58. Breaking the Silence, http://www.breakingthesilence.org.il.

Chapter 10: The Ethics of Israeli Counterinsurgency Operations

1. March 18, 2012, email correspondence.
2. Yoni Kempinski, "The IDF Is the Most Moral Army in the World," *Arutz Sheva* 7, December 21, 2015.
3. James Eastwood, *Ethics as a Weapon of War* (Cambridge: Cambridge University Press, 2017), 5.
4. "Soldiers' Testimonies from Operation Cast Lead," Breaking the Silence (website), 2009, 80. http://www.breakingthesilence.org.il/wp-content/uploads/2011/02/Operation_Cast_Lead_Gaza_2009_Eng.pdf.
5. March 14, 2012, email correspondence.
6. March 23, 2012, email correspondence.
7. "Gaza Crisis: Toll of Operations in Gaza," *BBC News*, September 1, 2014, http://www.bbc.co.uk/news/world-middle-east-28439404.
8. "Intifada Toll 2000–2005," *BBC News*, February 8, 2005, http://news.bbc.co.uk/1/hi/world/middle_east/3694350.stm.
9. May 13, 2012, Jerusalem, Israel.
10. Adam Harmon, *Lonely Soldier* (New York: Ballantine, 2006), 211.
11. March 14, 2012, email correspondence.
12. "Soldiers' Testimonies from Operation Cast Lead," 37.
13. Ibid., 46.
14. April 2, 2012, New York.
15. "Soldiers' Testimonies from Operation Cast Lead," 87.

16. "Israeli Soldier Testimonies from the South Hebron Hills," Breaking the Silence (website), 59. http://www.breakingthesilence.org.il/wp-content/uploads/2011/07/Soldiers_Testimonies_from_the_South_Hebron_Hills_2000_2008_Eng.pdf.
17. Ibid.
18. May 13, 2012, Jerusalem, Israel.
19. "Occupation of the Territories: Israeli Soldier Testimonies 2000–2010," Breaking the Silence (website), 29, http://www.breakingthesilence.org.il.
20. Ibid., 29.
21. This was a major campaign launched in 2002, during the Second Intifada. See Norman G. Finkelstein, *Image and Reality of the Israel-Palestine Conflict* (New York: Verso, 1995), xxiii.
22. May 15, 2012, Jerusalem, Israel.
23. May 13, 2012, Jerusalem, Israel.
24. "Israeli Soldier Testimonies from the South Hebron Hills," 11.
25. Douglas A. Pryer, *The Fight for the High Ground: The U.S. Army and Interrogation during Operation Iraqi Freedom May 2003–April 2004* (Fort Leavenworth, KS: CGSC Foundation Press, 2009).
26. March 11, 2012, email correspondence.
27. May 15, 2012, Jerusalem, Israel.
28. Sandra Nasr, "Israel's Other Terrorism Challenge," in *Contemporary State Terrorism: Theory and Practice*, ed. Richard Jackson, Eamon Murphy, and Scott Poynting (New York: Routledge, 2010), 73.
29. This is clear from Kant's moral theory, which is based on a universally binding categorical imperative. See Immanuel Kant, "Critique of Practical Reason," in *Practical Philosophy*, ed. Mary J. Gregor (New York: Cambridge University Press, 1996); and Immanuel Kant, "Groundwork on the Metaphysics of Morals," in *Practical Philosophy*, ed. Mary J. Gregor (New York: Cambridge University Press, 1996).
30. March 11, 2012, email correspondence.
31. May 13, 2012, Jerusalem, Israel.

Conclusion

1. Eitan Shamir, *Transforming Command: The Pursuit of Mission Command in the US, British, and Israeli Armies* (Stanford, CA: Stanford University Press, 2011), 159.
2. Don Carrick, "The Future of Ethics Education in the Military: A Comparative Analysis," in *Ethics Education in the Military*, ed. Paul Robinson, Nigel De Lee, and Don Carrick (Burlington, VT: Ashgate, 2008).
3. Jessica Wolfendale, "What Is the Point of Teaching Ethics in the Military?," in *Ethics Education in the Military*, ed. Paul Robinson, Nigel De Lee, and Don Carrick (Burlington, VT: Ashgate, 2008), 168–69.

4. For a detailed discussion of this, see David Kilcullen, *Out of the Mountains: The Coming Age of the Urban Guerrilla* (New York: Oxford University Press, 2013), 288–89.
5. David A. Koplow, *Non-Lethal Weapons: The Law and Policy of Revolutionary Technologies for the Military and Law Enforcement* (Cambridge: Cambridge University Press, 2006).

Index

About the Author

Marcus Schulzke is a former lecturer in the Department of Politics at the University of York, specializing in security studies. He is the author of *Drones and Support for the Use of Force,* with James Igoe Walsh (University of Michigan Press, 2018), *Just War Theory and Civilian Casualties* (Cambridge University Press, 2017), and *The Morality of Drone Warfare and the Politics of Regulation* (Palgrave, 2017).

www.ingramcontent.com/pod-product-compliance
Lightning Source LLC
LaVergne TN
LVHW050151080826
844660LV00002B/161

* 9 7 8 1 6 2 6 1 6 6 5 7 8 *